Beyond the Self

BEYOND THE SELF
Virtue Ethics and the Problem of Culture

Raymond Hain
Editor

BAYLOR UNIVERSITY PRESS

© 2019 by Baylor University Press
Waco, Texas 76798

This volume was made possible through the sponsorship of the de Nicola Center for Ethics and Culture. The de Nicola Center is committed to sharing the richness of the Catholic moral and intellectual tradition through teaching, research, and dialogue, at the highest level and across a range of disciplines. Through student formation, scholarly research and publications, public policy outreach, and support for the distinctive mission of the university, the de Nicola Center strengthens Notre Dame's Catholic character on campus and brings the university's voice into the public discussion of the most vital issues of our day. David Solomon was appointed the first director of the Center upon its establishment in 1999 and served in that capacity until 2012.

All Rights Reserved. No part of this publication may be reproduced, stored in a retrieval system, or transmitted, in any form or by any means, electronic, mechanical, photocopying, recording, or otherwise, without the prior permission in writing of Baylor University Press.

Unless otherwise stated, Scripture quotations are from the New Revised Standard Version Bible, copyright 1989, Division of Christian Education of the National Council of the Churches of Christ in the United States of America. Used by permission. All rights reserved.

Cover design by Savanah N. Landerholm
Book design by Scribe Inc.

The Library of Congress has cataloged this book under ISBN 978-1-4813-1041-3.

CONTENTS

Introduction   1

Part One: Historical Themes

1   Intrinsic Aptness and the Embodied Self:
The Role of External Goods in Eudaimonia   9
Christopher Toner

2   The Complexity of Justice: Thomas Aquinas'
Interpretation of the Fifth Book of Aristotle's
Nicomachean Ethics   25
Kevin L. Flannery, S.J.

3   Fearless Mercy beyond Justice: Aquinas and
Nussbaum's Pity Tradition   43
John O'Callaghan

4   The Problem of Justice: Anscombe, Solomon,
and Radical Virtue Ethics   69
Thomas Hibbs

Part Two: Normative Ethics

5   Whither Moral Philosophy?   91
John Haldane

6   Philippa Foot and Iris Murdoch on (Natural) Goodness   113
Michael D. Beaty

7   David Solomon on Egoism and Virtue   135
Irfan Khawaja

8   You Owe It to Yourself   149
Candace Vogler

Part Three: Ethics and Culture

9   Dignity and the Challenge of Agreement   173
Bryan C. Pilkington

10   Against the "Autonomy" and "Best Interest" Defenses of Medically Assisted Death   189
Raymond Hain

11   Some Thoughts on Secularization   205
Alasdair MacIntyre

12   Elizabeth Anscombe and the Late Twentieth-Century Revival of Virtue Ethics   223
W. David Solomon

Notes   245
List of Contributors   287

To David
scholar, teacher, friend

INTRODUCTION

Almost since its inception, with the publication in 1958 of G. E. M. Anscombe's "Modern Moral Philosophy,"[1] David Solomon has been at the center of the contemporary revival of Anglophone virtue ethics. A historically sensitive and persistent advocate for an Aristotelian and Thomistic alternative to Kantian and consequentialist ethics, his work has played a key role in solidifying virtue ethics as a viable approach within contemporary moral philosophy. His essays over the years helped set the agenda for the infancy and steady growth of virtue ethics. His forty-seven doctoral students, more than any other Notre Dame philosophy professor since the school's founding, remain a rich and diverse set of scholars dedicated to the retrieval and renewal of classical virtue ethics. Thousands of undergraduate students at Notre Dame attended his long-running and justly famous courses on "Morality and Modernity" and "Medical Ethics," and hundreds of graduate students participated in his "Twentieth-Century Ethics" seminars. For several decades he organized annual conferences in medical ethics inspired by the belief that a retrieval of Aristotelian and Thomistic moral philosophy could bear powerful and immediately practical fruit. And he founded the Notre Dame Center for Ethics and Culture,

1

one of the most influential champions within higher education of a classical approach to contemporary moral and cultural issues.

In May 2014, a conference in David's honor was held at Notre Dame that brought together most of his doctoral students and many of his collaborators in the revival of virtue ethics. The majority of the essays in this volume were first presented in earlier versions at this conference. Four contributions were commissioned afterward (Kevin Flannery, Michael Beaty, Thomas Hibbs, and Candace Vogler), and David's own concluding essay was added once the rest of the manuscript was complete.

The eleven essays that precede David's own contribution are organized under three themes that reflect David's long-term interests and the core interests of those who, like him, are working for a contemporary renewal of Aristotelian and Thomistic moral philosophy. The first division focuses on the careful interpretation and appropriation of Aristotle and Aquinas. The virtue ethics tradition of which this volume is a part and which traces its most immediate heritage to Anscombe's "Modern Moral Philosophy" has a special relationship to its historical roots, a relationship more crucial, in certain ways, than the relations between contemporary Kantian ethics and consequentialist ethics and their own philosophical forebears. For contemporary Anscombian moral philosophy, Aristotle and Aquinas remain the exemplary expressions of the virtue ethics tradition, and so the careful reading and defense of their texts is a deeply important feature of contemporary virtue ethics. Christopher Toner's essay on "Intrinsic Aptness and the Embodied Self" (chapter 1) considers a very old puzzle in the Aristotelian tradition about the relationship between external goods and eudaimonia, and he develops a solution to this puzzle that renders Aristotle's position coherent and plausible. Kevin Flannery's "The Complexity of Justice" (chapter 2) is a careful reading of Aquinas' appropriation of the fifth book of Aristotle's *Nicomachean Ethics* that defends Aquinas' account against those who would criticize it as both internally unpersuasive and unfaithful to Aristotle's texts. In "Fearless Mercy Beyond Justice" (chapter 3), John O'Callaghan responds to Martha Nussbaum's account of the "pity tradition" by a close reading of Aquinas on mercy that shows not only that the omission of Aquinas in Nussbaum's work is a mistake but that Aquinas' own account defends the sorts of claims in which Nussbaum is interested in an entirely different and much deeper way. And Thomas Hibb's essay on "The Problem of Justice" (chapter 4) argues that Aquinas' account of justice, sensitive to the concerns of contemporary philosophers like Charles Taylor and others, is precisely what

David Solomon is gesturing toward when he calls for a "radical virtue ethics."

The second group of essays is most immediately concerned with contemporary moral philosophy and the development and defense of a contemporary alternative to the Kantian and consequentialist traditions. Here we see another central feature of the Anscombian revival of virtue ethics. Each of these four essays places a special emphasis on critique, both of those who are outside of the virtue ethics tradition and those who are within it. In the background is the thought that whatever Anscombe was calling for in "Modern Moral Philosophy," it is larger than what we have achieved, and perhaps also larger than what we have yet imagined. In part because Aristotle and Aquinas remain our exemplars, there is an abiding uneasiness with constructive contemporary accounts of virtue ethics that fall short of the grand visions of the practical life articulated by Aristotle and Aquinas. John Haldane's "Whither Moral Philosophy" (chapter 5), for example, criticizes the field of academic ethics as such and argues that its history in the twentieth century shows how contemporary academic socialization obfuscates more often than it clarifies. He retrieves from this history, and then defends, a restatement and clarification of the normative force of natural kind terms as the bedrock of a viable virtue ethics but concludes that what moral philosophy needs now is not more theorizing (though we might need to do more remembering of past theorizing) but instead more careful reflection on lived experience. In "Philippa Foot and Iris Murdoch on (Natural) Goodness" (chapter 6), Michael Beaty compares the Platonic ethics of Iris Murdoch with the Aristotelian ethics of Philippa Foot, two of Anscombe's close friends and philosophical colleagues. Their friendly rivalry is a reminder that the relationship between the ethics of Plato and the ethics of Aristotle (resolved in one contentious way by Aquinas, for whom "Good" became "God") remains unresolved in contemporary Anscombian virtue ethics. Irfan Khawaja, in "David Solomon on Egoism and Virtue" (chapter 7), reconsiders David Solomon's 1988 paper "Intrinsic Objections to Virtue Ethics." Khawaja focuses especially on the self-centeredness objection and concludes that attempts to answer this objection, including Solomon's own attempt in "Intrinsic Objections to Virtue Ethics," are doomed to failure unless we first work on the much larger problems of metaphysics and philosophical anthropology, something it seems no one within contemporary analytic ethics is prepared to do. Finally, Candace Vogler's "You Owe It to Yourself" (chapter 8) argues against one of the pillars of contemporary neo-Kantian moral philosophy: the claim that I have a fundamental obligation to govern myself, an obligation rooted in practical reason and owed to myself as a rational being.

The final group of essays addresses larger cultural problems, and this again reminds us of David Solomon's long-term interests in modern culture and the nature of Anscombian virtue ethics more generally. Cultural issues and moral philosophy have been deeply entangled within this tradition since Anscombe's criticism of President Harry Truman's honorary Oxford degree became the inspiration for her work in ethics and the publication of "Modern Moral Philosophy" and her book *Intention*.[2] And this fact in some ways helps explain the critical and incomplete character of the attempts to develop a theoretical foundation for a revived virtue ethics; not only might moral philosophy be inextricably entangled with metaphysics and anthropology, but it might also be just as entangled with the problems of history and culture, as Alasdair MacIntyre has argued, so that a satisfying renewal of virtue ethics would engage all these problems at once and together. In keeping with this broad thought about the important connections between Anscombian virtue ethics and contemporary cultural problems, Bryan Pilkington's "Dignity and the Challenge of Agreement" (chapter 9) explores the unresolved tension between merit and equality in our contemporary use of the concept of human dignity. The secular attempt to resolve this tension developed by Jeremy Waldron and the Judeo-Christian attempt of Gilbert Meilaender are both insufficient in different ways, and Pilkington concludes that our only alternative is to think of this problem in terms of much larger intellectual traditions that might be able to give a coherent foundation for human dignity. In "Against the 'Autonomy' and 'Best Interest' Defenses of Medically Assisted Death" (chapter 10), I argue that two fundamental arguments in support of euthanasia and physician-assisted suicide are failures. Because "autonomy" and "best interest" arguments are jointly required to provide an overall defense but each vitiates the force of the other, we are left without a coherent defense of medically assisted death on its own terms, and all that remains are arguments that defend such practices by trying to show that they are morally equivalent to morally acceptable practices (such as the forgoing of "extraordinary" medical treatment). Finally, Alasdair MacIntyre's essay, "Some Thoughts on Secularization" (chapter 11), considers the relationship between secular belief and religious (especially Christian) belief. He finds the recent accounts of Charles Taylor and Philip Rieff inadequate, partly because they are so pessimistic about the potential of secular belief, and he looks to Aquinas for a more persuasive and comprehensive approach that can help us think about the contemporary problem of secularization and can likewise help us think about the relation between virtue ethics and religious belief.

David Solomon's concluding essay, "Elizabeth Anscombe and the Late Twentieth-Century Revival of Virtue Ethics," brings these three themes together by retelling the history of twentieth-century ethics and the remarkable achievements of Anscombe and her heirs as they continue to unsettle the standard academic assumptions about the role and scope of theoretical ethics. As such, it is a précis of his long-standing project on the history of twentieth-century ethics, a work that once completed will be our definitive account.

David Solomon has been and remains one of the most important figures in the revival of Aristotelian and Thomistic virtue ethics. Through his writing and teaching, he has helped generations of students and philosophers see the possibility and promise of a contemporary reappropriation of classical virtue ethics. And his engagement with contemporary cultural problems, most especially with respect to medical ethics and the fragile and vulnerable among us, has given us an example of what it means to be a philosopher who is also a courageous public champion on behalf of the difficult truths that our society so desperately needs to remember. But most of all, his friendship has shown us how to embody what most people merely talk about. His is an example we would all do well to follow, and it is with gratitude and admiration that we offer him this volume in his honor.

Raymond Hain
On the Feast of the Assumption
August 15, 2017

Bibliography

Anscombe, G. E. M. *Intention*. Oxford: Basil Blackwell, 1957.
———. "Modern Moral Philosophy." *Philosophy* 33, no. 124 (1958): 1–19.

Part One
HISTORICAL THEMES

I

INTRINSIC APTNESS AND THE EMBODIED SELF
The Role of External Goods in Eudaimonia

Christopher Toner

Much of Cicero's *De finibus* is devoted to presenting a debate—perhaps the chief debate of the Hellenistic period—between Peripatetics and Stoics concerning the nature of eudaimonia (*vita beata*). Both sides agreed, not only that virtue was necessary, but that it was the primary or controlling aspect of eudaimonia. They differed over the role of external goods: The Peripatetics maintained the intuitive view that, as Aristotle had put it, "happiness evidently also needs external goods to be added";[1] as for one who suffers such misfortunes as Priam, "no one counts him happy."[2] No one, that is, but the Stoics, who held that virtue was sufficient for eudaimonia (in fact, there are no external goods, only preferred indifferents).

Aristotle's view strikes many as obviously more plausible (if anything, people may be more inclined to doubt the necessity of virtue for a good life than to affirm its sufficiency). I nevertheless will undertake to defend it here, for it has been, and continues to be, the object of acute criticisms, from the Stoics down to current thinkers such as Julia Annas. Cicero's own view seems to be that while the Peripatetics have intuitive plausibility on their side, the Stoic view possesses another theoretical virtue, one that he worries the Peripatetic view lacks, that of consistency[3]—we could call this

Cicero's dilemma: one who accepts the idea, shared by Stoics and Peripatetics, that virtue controls eudaimonia must choose either consistency or intuitiveness, but not both.

But why think the Aristotelian view lacks consistency? We will see that, once we have chosen the intuitive horn of Cicero's dilemma, we seem to confront a succession of further dilemmas. In what follows, I will seek to defend the Aristotelian view by showing how one can navigate safely through them.

The First Two Dilemmas

In *Ethics* 1.10, Aristotle asserts what Daniel Russell calls the *control thesis* ("it is upon virtuous activity above all else that human happiness depends") and the *dependency thesis* ("there are bodily and external goods that are necessary for and parts of happiness";[4] hereafter I shall refer to both types of goods simply as "external goods"). Aristotle asserts the former because of his understanding of human beings as practical reasoners and thus primarily as rational agents (consider the function argument of 1.7) and the latter because of his common-sense reaction to what Russell calls "the Priam problem"—Priam was a good man who "lost everything—his kingdom, his family, and then his own life in an impious murder.... No one could take seriously the suggestion that Priam's life was a happy one."[5] Despite the commonsensicality of this reaction, Russell thinks that it, together with the acceptance of a third thesis, leads Aristotle into an inconsistent triad:

1. Happiness is controlled by virtuous activity [control thesis];
2. There are ... external goods that are parts of happiness [dependency thesis]; and
3. These ... external goods are not themselves activity or parts of activity [formalized thesis].[6]

Russell holds that there are two ways out of this inconsistency (assuming the control thesis is nonnegotiable as it was for Stoics and Peripatetics alike): reject the dependency thesis (the Stoic option) or reject the formalized thesis in favor of an "embodied" conception of activity and of the self (Russell's own option). Before turning to this, however, we should get clear on why Russell thinks this triad is inconsistent.

The crux of the problem is that, at least if we hold fixed the formalized thesis (as Russell thinks both Stoics and Peripatetics did), "either the commitment to the dependency thesis will attenuate the commitment to the control thesis, or the latter will attenuate the former" (call this Russell's Dilemma).[7] Why? Russell seeks to justify this claim by pointing to the failure of a succession of Peripatetic attempts to articulate a consistent Aristotelian view.

Consider first the position that seems to have been held by Theophrastus, that "happiness depends simply on a plurality of goods,"[8] the lack of any of which would render a life unhappy. This would embrace dependency but, by putting external goods on a par with virtue, reject control.

Consider next the view of Critolaus, according to which virtue is a dominant good, so that "if in one scale he puts the good that belongs to the soul [virtue], and in the other the good that belongs to the body and good things which come from outside the man [external goods], the first scale sinks so far as to outweigh the second with land and seas thrown in as well."[9] Such a view seems to accept control at the expense of dependency—in what sense can eudaimonia really be said to depend on external goods when they matter so little?

Then there is the view of Antiochus, who distinguishes between the happy life and the most happy life (in *De finibus* 5, Cicero uses the terms *vita beata* and *vita beatissima*; Russell suggests that Antiochus was drawing on Aristotle's use of the terms *eudaimon* and *makarios*, blessed). Antiochus held that virtue sufficed for happiness but that external goods were needed for blessedness. But as Russell points out, this does not offer a way out of the dilemma; in fact, Antiochus impales himself, successively, on each horn: virtue controls happiness, but at this level dependency is rejected; as for blessedness, this does depend on external goods, but virtue no longer controls it, since, as was the case with Theophrastus, virtue and external goods seem to be on a par.[10] For neither level of happiness can both theses be affirmed.

Finally, we should consider Arius Didymus' summary of Peripatetic ethics, in which happiness is defined as virtuous activity in favorable circumstances. Since, for example, one can "be generous in a complete way" only if one commands at least modest resources, external goods are "necessary for happiness . . . [because they] are necessary for virtuous activity itself."[11] One of the problems Russell raised for this view is that "it gives many goods the wrong place in happiness"; for example, Arius' view denies the difference between lack and loss (e.g., never having had children and having lost the ones one had): "In each case, the circle of opportunities is just smaller or less appealing than otherwise. That is not only deeply implausible but also at odds with our reaction to Priam: it is a strike against his happiness to lose his kingdom, even though it is no strike against another's happiness never to have had a kingdom at all."[12] Now Russell has effectively pointed out a problem for the Peripatetic view, but I am not certain that he has shown that there is no way out of the dilemma other than the one he will offer (and to which we will turn shortly). For example, might one not accept dependency (on the grounds that eudaimonia is supposed to be complete and self-sufficient and that being stretched on the rack or seeing one's children die would leave something further to be wished for) and yet still intelligibly assert control (perhaps by defending an asymmetry between virtue and external goods such that external evils can deprive one of happiness but only vice can render one actually unhappy[13])? Yet even if so, Russell's idea is, I think, an elegant way out and is persuasive on other grounds as well. In any event, even if one finds a way out of Russell's dilemma (Russell's own way or another), one would immediately confront another, which I will call Annas' dilemma: if we accept dependency, we must go on to say *how* eudaimonia depends on external goods and in doing so must choose between what she calls an "internal-use" and an "external-use" view—both of which turn out to have unacceptable implications.

On the internal-use view, the value of external goods is "instrumental" and "never independent of their contribution to the agent's virtuous activity."[14] External goods may contribute in two ways: First, they may be necessary means, as money or some form of plenitude of resources is needed to exercise generosity. Second, they may be necessary for the "wide and varied range of activities" in which a good person would wish to exercise her virtue.[15] Plausible as these claims seem, the initial claim that external goods are not independently valuable and that these are the only ways in which they contribute to eudaimonia leads quickly to trouble. For on this view, "the loss of external goods [e.g., losing one's children] will affect one's happiness only because of the way it prevents one from exercising the virtues." "Intuitively," however, "this is outrageous.... Losing children is a terrible thing in itself, and not just because it deprives us of the chance to help our children on their careers and to look after grandchildren."[16] But it is supposed to be one of the chief merits of an Aristotelian approach as opposed to a Stoic, that it saves our intuitions.

Perhaps, then, we should opt for the external-use view, according to which external goods not only serve virtuous activity but also are (or some at least of them are) such as to make an independent contribution to eudaimonia: "While health enables us to exercise the virtue of temperance, it is also just a good thing to be healthy"; good children too, we may say, just on their own make a parent's life better, in addition to affording all sorts of opportunity for the exercise of parental virtue. Intuitively pleasing as this alternative may seem, choosing this horn of the dilemma leads to two problems, which we might call the problems of the floor and of the ceiling. The first concerns the question What makes an adequate supply of external goods adequate? For example, how much wealth, how many friends, does one need? Perhaps there is a good answer, but, Annas says, Aristotle does not supply it.[17]

The problem of the ceiling takes the form of a further dilemma. As Annas writes, "Having some of these things is needed to make me happy; so surely having more of them will make me happier? . . . The more external goods I have, the more I can expand the range and scope of my virtuous activity. This, however, runs into the claim that happiness is complete and self-sufficient. Something which meets these conditions precisely cannot be made better by the addition of any other good."[18] So here is the dilemma—either one accepting the external-use view must say that, although external goods contribute to one's eudaimonia, they "cannot make him happier by being increased. But this is deeply mysterious." Or one must say that "happiness is not complete, since it can be increased by the addition of further goods. But this would be to go back on a fundamental point of his [Aristotle's] ethical structure."[19]

One way out of Annas' dilemma, the Stoic way with which she has considerable sympathy, is simply to deny that externals are goods at all, to reject, that is, the dependency thesis. But it may be that Russell's rejection of the formalized thesis provides another way out. It is to his view that I now turn.

The Embodied Self: Russell's Construal of Eudaimonia as Embodied Virtuous Activity

Russell outlines the conception of eudaimonia he will advocate as follows: it is active, centered on engagement with relationships and projects; it must be, and be experienced as, fulfilling; it must be lived virtuously (with practical wisdom and emotional soundness); and it is inextricably invested in and bound up with the particular ends the agent lives for. As he sums up the conception, eudaimonia is "*a life of embodied virtuous activity.*"[20] Our focus is on the final condition, the idea that the activity constituting eudaimonia is inextricable from—embodied in—particular ends, for it is this claim that puts Russell in position to agree with the Stoics that eudaimonia just is virtuous activity and yet also agree with the Peripatetics that it depends on the presence of external goods.

Recall that according to the formalized thesis, "external goods are not themselves activity or parts of activity." On this view, to be a father, and to engage in parenting activity, is for a man to exercise his faculty of choice in ways that have his child as an object, and it is in his "patterns of exercising his will" that the man "experiences his life as his own." But we might think of things differently: we might hold that the man's parenting activity "just is his relationship with this particular child" and that that relationship and the activities partly constituting it "are part of who he takes himself to be."[21] This line of thought rejects the formalized thesis—external goods are now seen as part of activity—and points to what Russell calls the "embodied conception of the self," where "self" is to be understood as referring not to a metaphysical entity but to "a person's own sense of what person he or she is." One's self or "psychological identity" includes "the totality of those central relationships, commitments, attachments, and projects that give one's life its unique shape as being one's own."[22] My self, then, is strictly speaking not what I am but something I have, my comportment toward the world. And having a self is something I do and about which I can make choices—for example, whether to consider my self as, and thereby whether to have, a formalized or embodied self. (Of course we can still talk, as Russell does, about this as determining what "self to be."[23])

Now given an embodied conception of the self, one's activity, including one's virtuous activity (which is simply activity that is "adopted and pursued within one's life with practical wisdom and emotional balance"), is "always a multitude of *activities,* in the plural—*this* relationship with *this* child, . . . *this* participation in *this* community."[24] And since one's activity "has as its very substance one's particular attachments and relationships . . . [that] are vulnerable to fortune [e.g., one's child could die]" and since happiness consists in virtuous activity, "happiness itself must be vulnerable to fortune."[25] Significant losses, then, are "*threats to our activity, our happiness, and our very selves,*" and "*particular bodily and external goods are necessary for and even parts of happiness,* insofar as such goods constitute the possibility of continuing in embodied virtuous activities—that is, in activities that are embodied within one's particular attachments and ends."[26]

We can now return to control and dependency. Given a formalized conception of the self, on which virtuous activity "just is the practically wise and emotionally sound exercise of will, and it takes no particular object in order to do that,"[27] "the control and dependency theses are zero-sum."[28] Thus the Stoics, who accepted the control thesis and, Russell argues at length,[29] the formalized thesis, consistently rejected dependency. But if we reject the formalized thesis and accept an embodied conception of the self, the tension between the control and dependency theses disappears. In fact, "if the control thesis is true and it is upon virtuous activity above all that happiness depends, *and if* such activity is embodied activity, then the dependency thesis *must also* be true, . . . not true in spite of the control thesis, but *precisely because of it.*"[30]

Thus one attracted to both the control and dependency theses (as were the Peripatetics) should also find the embodied conception attractive, as it not only renders the theses consistent but actually makes the latter follow from the former. Russell suggests that Aristotle actually developed a view along the lines of the embodied conception in his writings on friendship but finds that neither he nor his followers applied it to treatments of the relation of external goods to eudaimonia, thus leaving the Peripatetics with the inconsistent triad of the control, dependency, and formalized theses.[31] But an Aristotelian today can so apply it.

So the embodied conception of the self resolves what I called Russell's dilemma; does it help with Annas'? First, it helps at least in this way: Annas has pointed out that Aristotelians often adopt either an internal-use or external-use view of the role of external goods vis-à-vis eudaimonia and that both have problematic implications. But the embodied conception of the self allows for an Aristotelian view that implies neither internal use nor external use (let me dub it a "median-use" view, as it, so to speak, slides in between the other two views), and so its view of the role of external goods is not immediately subject to her criticisms.

To explain: on the internal-use view, external goods are of merely instrumental value, as aiding virtuous activity.[32] On the median-use view implied by the embodied conception of the self, while of course some external goods are of merely instrumental value (e.g., the few bank notes in my wallet), others (my family) are not—they are actually partly constitutive of eudaimonia (or would be if I had it). On the external-use view, external goods, just as such, when present make life better. This is not true on the median-use view—present external goods contribute to eudaimonia only insofar as they are embraced by virtuous activity.

So the embodied conception implies a third, distinct Aristotelian view of the role of external goods in eudaimonia. Still, Annas is raising problems for the dependency thesis, and it may be that some of her criticisms apply to the median-use view despite her not explicitly considering it. Does Russell's view successfully address them? I think that it does. As we saw, Annas holds that it is "intuitively outrageous" to say, as a proponent of the internal-use view must, that the loss of a child is a loss only because it reduces the parents' opportunity for virtuous activity (helping the child in her career and so forth), and she also points out that such a loss would actually present an "opportunity" for heroically virtuous activity in dealing well with tragedy. The embodied conception is not vulnerable in these ways: the loss of a child is a loss because the parents' eudaimonia is embodied in "*this* relationship with *this* child"; it is not just that the loss curtails certain good activities (which might be replaced, even to advantage, by other virtuous activities such as mourning well, generously comforting each other, etc.)—these particular activities, this relationship, this child herself were parts of their eudaimonia, indeed parts of their selves (Russell discusses how the loss of a loved one is often experienced, and correctly experienced, as similar to the loss of a limb, part of oneself[33]), and they are gone. So the proponent of this view can agree that "losing children is a terrible thing in itself."[34]

What about the worry, addressed to the external-use view, that since the presence of external goods helps make life good, the presence of more would seem always to make life better—either, says Annas, we must admit (as we cannot if we are Aristotelians) that eudaimonia is not complete and self-sufficient, or we must deny that an increase of external goods must increase eudaimonia, which would be "deeply mysterious."[35] We must choose the second option, and the median-use view can help dispel the mystery: since eudaimonia does not consist in virtuous activity *plus* external goods but in embodied virtuous activity (which includes external goods within itself), it is not mysterious that the mere presence of more external goods need not make life better. For the formerly rich man whose magnificence is now stymied, a windfall may be a godsend; for others, it may mean nothing or simply be a hassle—consider here Thomas Merton's comment on the rustic French couple he stayed with as a child: "Their farm, their family, and their Church were all that occupied these good souls; and their lives were full."[36]

Dilemmas for Russell's View

At the end of his book, Russell poses a dilemma for himself: "Whether or not we take virtue to be sufficient for happiness depends on our choice between two conceptions of the self, what I have called the formalized and the embodied conceptions. But I have also argued that either way, the stakes are very high."[37] The stakes are high because on the embodied conception, one's eudaimonia is vulnerable, hostage to fortune, but on the formalized conception, externals do not matter a whit for one's eudaimonia—paraphrasing Epictetus, Russell tells us that on this view, one comes to see everything as "easily untied" and "to regard one's property, spouse, or children as mere pieces in a child's game." He sees this not as a theoretical choice (he does not think a theorist can decisively justify one option or the other) but as a practical one, a decision about who to be, what sort of self to have. He tells us that he opts for the embodied conception because "I have chosen to accept the risks on this side of the dilemma over those on the Stoics' side";[38] despite Stoic concerns there is "also a point to thinking" that we find happiness in relationships and meaningful projects so that it is "rational for the sake of our happiness to include such things within the boundaries of the self."[39]

Russell's solution to his self-posed dilemma consists in a personal, quasi-existentialist choice. The decision to include relationships and projects within the boundaries of the self is not exactly arbitrary—it is guided by a conception of eudaimonia. But that conception itself is just a best guess—"No *proof* as to what happiness is, on either side, will ever be in the offing.... The best we can hope for is to make a choice we can live with."[40] This element of quasi-existentialist choice shows up in numerous places in Russell's work: human life is something "to construct, by finding ends to live for and then living for them";[41] he later speaks of a man *choosing* to make being a father to his daughter an end to live for and a source of reasons.[42] It is as if, casting about for rewarding ends to live for, he thinks, "Why not her?" Why must we make this sort of theoretically unguided and unguidable choice? Russell sees us as weighing an invulnerable but somewhat desiccated happiness against a richer but vulnerable happiness and being somewhat perplexed. Why does not Russell instead say that the embodied conception is correct and that vulnerability is simply to be accepted, even if regretted? Part of the answer lies in the fact that he sees the self as constructed—we choose whether to allow others "in," whether to live in embodied or formalized fashion. But this choice is guided by practical reason—why is it not one that practical reason can get right or wrong?

I think the most important part of the answer can be found in something he says at the beginning of the book. Before defining eudaimonia as a life of embodied virtuous activity, he makes a formal claim about what sort of thing eudaimonia must be: "When I ask how I might live so as to give myself the gift of happiness, the gift of a good life, I am asking about something that will be good for me; I'm not asking how I might give a gift to my species, or to history, or to the universe.... It is clear that giving myself that gift means finding things to live for.... I need to find things that I find fulfilling to devote myself to and that make my life identifiable as uniquely mine."[43] He immediately assures us, "The things I live for don't have to be selfish aims—in fact, making those aims selfish, I think, would be a particularly ineffective way of trying to give myself a good life,"[44] and it is clear throughout the book that he thinks caring for others, for their own sake, is crucial to living well. Russell's view, then, is a version of formal egoism. For reasons I set out elsewhere, I think it is, therefore and just as such, wrong.[45] Here I will focus on particular problems this egoistic understanding of the pursuit of eudaimonia raises for the embodied conception and its potential for helping us navigate the dilemmas that arise for one accepting the dependency thesis.

The first problem is the perplexity just mentioned. The corollary of "Live for things (projects, people) when and because doing so is good *for you*, when and because you find doing so fulfilling" is "Do not live for them when doing so is not fulfilling." The perplexity arises from wondering if in general living for others in the way recommended by the embodied conception does promise to be fulfilling. It seems as though differently situated people might reasonably come to different resolutions of Russell's self-posed dilemma, and one wonders if he would recommend Stoicism in times of plague or zombie apocalypse. Investing oneself in family and friends likely to be eaten in the near future does not promise to be very fulfilling or to hold out much hope for maintaining the integrity of one's self.[46]

A second problem takes the form of a final dilemma, arising from the fact (as I take it to be) that one should so invest oneself even in such circumstances. As we saw, Russell speaks of a man choosing to make his daughter and their relationship part of his life. Russell is right that he has to *choose* to do this (after all, he might choose not to), but it is also the case that the man *has to* choose to do so, on pain of viciousness. His daughter, as his daughter, has a claim on him to be included in his life. She is his child, not a piece in a child's game, and for her father to see her in the latter way, even if he takes good care of the game piece, is already to do her wrong.[47] Here we should recall Julia Annas' point that in eudaimonism, "the good of others is introduced in ways which make it formally part of the agent's own good; but we fail to grasp its place in ancient theories if we think of it as derived from or justified in terms of the agent's own good—for if that were the case, we would be misconceiving what the good of others is."[48] Giving myself a gift is not the sole point of my life; I *should* ask about how I might give a gift to the world (no doubt a very small one). If in asking how to live a good life, I were not asking that but asking *only* about how to give myself a gift, then I would need to ask that as a separate question—I would need to embrace a dualism of final ends, as do Kantians or Scotists.[49]

We can, then, pose one final dilemma that confronts one drawn to Russell's view: one must accept either Russell's egoism (rejecting what I claimed to be a fact, that others may have a claim on us to be included in our lives, whether we find that inclusion rewarding or not) or a version of dualism alien to a eudaimonist approach.

Intrinsic Aptness: An Amendment of Russell's View

The egoism and perplexity are bookends of Russell's argument for an embodied conception of eudaimonia; neither is essential to it. In the remainder of this chapter, I will outline a view of external goods—what I will call the intrinsic aptness view—that will allow us to resolve our two remaining dilemmas (Russell's self-posed dilemma and the egoism/dualism dilemma) while preserving the gains made (in terms of resolving the previous dilemmas) by embracing an embodied conception.

To begin to describe this view, let me note a comment Annas makes in setting out the internal-use view: according to this view, "external goods do not just in themselves have any intrinsic value, or add anything to the good life."[50] Notice that these two phrases are not equivalent: something could have intrinsic value without adding anything to the goodness of a person's life. An excellent child may add nothing to the goodness of a parent's life (perhaps he is indifferent to her) or even take away from it (perhaps the child becomes a constant temptation to vanity or to resentment). This much follows from the "median-use" view implied by an embodied conception of eudaimonia. The view I am advocating adds to this the claim that intrinsically valuable external goods may be intrinsically apt to become parts of an agent's eudaimonia and that they may be so in either of two senses we may assign to "apt": first, such a good may be well suited to become part of one's embodied virtuous activity so that investing oneself in that good would constitute one way to make an agent's life better, all else equal; second, it may be uniquely suited to become part of one's embodied virtuous activity in such a way that investing oneself in that good is actually required by virtue.[51]

To elaborate, consider some possible intrinsically apt external goods: careers that employ and extend human physical or cognitive powers and that tend to contribute in some way to the common good (sports medicine, neuroscience, military service, civil engineering, nursing, teaching, etc.), friends or family members, vulnerable people, or an ecosystem. Different as these are, all are, plausibly, intrinsically valuable things, apt in some way to become part of a good life; they are so apt in that they "call for" virtuous activity in relation to themselves—the first type of good, careers, are paths along which such activity is to be pursued; the others are "things" or systems of things that can be objects of, or partners in, virtuous activity. Now the form the calling takes can differ. It may be an invitation that can be inculpably refused (absent some special story, a promising student may pursue neuroscience, or sports medicine, or any of dozens of other career paths with equal rectitude; a friendly person who has not yet formed friendships with members of a certain social circle may pursue closer relationships with some of its members or none; a generous person may opt to work with orphaned children or do something else). Or it may be a requirement that emerges from a relationship or peculiar history (absent some *very* special story, the mere existence of a daughter makes a powerful moral demand upon her father to be part of his life; likewise for children orphaned through the agent's own driving accident). Call these, respectively, intrinsically inviting and intrinsically demanding external goods.

Let me note that the acceptance of intrinsically demanding goods is compatible with all the following: We can still hold that many external goods are of merely instrumental value (those few bank notes in my wallet). We can still hold that many externals are not goods for us at all, even though they may be intrinsically good (a career in sports medicine, as-yet-undiscovered intelligent Martians). We can still embrace Russell's embodied conception of virtuous activity and eudaimonia, with its median-use view of external goods. And the acceptance of intrinsically demanding goods is of course compatible with thinking that there are external goods that are merely intrinsically inviting. The acceptance of intrinsically demanding goods carries only the cost of renouncing the claim that we have complete freedom in our choices regarding which external goods we are to invest ourselves in; it brings the benefit of putting us in position to resolve our last two dilemmas.

Again, the first was Russell's self-posed dilemma: Should a given agent choose a formalized self with an invulnerable but somewhat desiccated happiness or an embodied self with a richer but vulnerable happiness? If we admit intrinsically demanding external goods and assume that at least some are present in a given agent's life, then the first horn of the dilemma is not so much as a coherent option. To try to take it would be a vicious course of action (refusing a just demand from the world) and so could not lead to eudaimonia, desiccated or otherwise. Of course in many circumstances, it may be wise to limit one's investments of oneself in externals (perhaps keeping intrinsically inviting goods to the periphery), but intrinsically demanding goods are simply to be admitted into one's life, and the attendant vulnerability is simply to be accepted. Here the acceptance of such goods resolves the dilemma, not by finding an attractive third way, but only by eliminating the perplexity by indicating on which horn one is rationally required to impale oneself—doing so will still hurt.

As for the final dilemma—that one must accept either Russell's egoism or a version of dualism of final ends alien to a eudaimonist approach—the acceptance of intrinsically demanding external goods can help us to find a third way, one neither egoistic nor dualist.

When the reflective eudaimonist agent asks, "How should I live, what is it best for me to do and pursue?" she should not be asking just about what is best *for her* (or how best to give herself a gift). She should be asking the question in the same spirit in which a reflective pitcher might ask, "What is the best pitching strategy for me (to adopt for this game)?" He is not asking, let us hope, whether a certain mix of fastballs, breaking balls, and off-speed pitches will feel best or win him the best scouting report; he is asking which approach best fits the situation, given his abilities and the opposing team's, which approach promises to help him help his team win. Likewise, the eudaimonist agent should be asking which way of life, which present course of action, best enables her to achieve a proper fit between herself and the world. This will certainly have much to do with her abilities, goals, and so forth; it will also have much to do with the goods at stake; in particular, it will have to do with any relevant intrinsically demanding goods. Acknowledging the existence of such goods requires us not to see the world as a bed of oysters, from which we may select the choicest pearls. We must now understand differently Russell's dictum—"Find ends to live for, and then live for them"—"find" must be read not as we read it in "find something to do" but as we read it in "find out what is to be done." We must understand the dictum to mean, at least in part, "Recognize the ends that are given to us by intrinsically demanding goods in our lives, and give of ourselves to and for them." There is one final end, and it is eudaimonia, but its pursuit is not egoistic. Eudaimonia consists in relating rightly, virtuously, to the good (to things in accordance with their degrees and kinds of goodness). Part of the good life may involve giving *to oneself* a gift; much of it will involve giving *of oneself as a gift*.[52]

Conclusion

As noted at the outset, the acceptance of the dependency thesis, however intuitive, leads to a series of dilemmas. I have argued that Russell's embodied conception of virtuous activity (and thus of eudaimonia) enables us to navigate some of them successfully: it elegantly harmonizes dependency with the control thesis central to much ancient eudaimonism and charts a course between the commonly held but problematic internal- and external-use views of the place of external goods in eudaimonia. But in Russell's hands, eudaimonia is conceived as a life good *for the agent* (who seeks to give himself the gift of a good life, as Russell puts it). This leads to two further dilemmas: a perplexing choice between accepting the embodied conception of the self along with its vulnerability and accepting a formalized conception of the self and a choice between Russell's formal egoism and a Scotistic dualism. I have argued that the acceptance of intrinsically demanding goods can eliminate the perplexity in favor of the embodied conception and indicate a third way between egoism and dualism. This acceptance entails rejection of the problematic claims that bookend Russell's main argument but leaves the core of his view, and its capacity to resolve the initial pair of dilemmas, intact. So finally, Cicero's dilemma too is resolved: the Peripatetic horn of his dilemma, once adjusted to embrace the embodied conception of the self, turns out to be consistent as well as intuitive.[53]

Bibliography

Annas, Julia. *The Morality of Happiness.* Oxford: Oxford University Press, 1993.

Aristotle. *Nicomachean Ethics.* 2nd ed. Translated by Terence Irwin. Indianapolis: Hackett, 1999.

Baril, Anne. "The Role of Welfare in Eudaimonism." *Southern Journal of Philosophy* 51 (2013): 511–35.

Cicero, *Cicero: Tusculan Disputations.* Translated by J. E. King. Cambridge, Mass.: Harvard University Press, 1927.

Cicero. *On Ends* [*De finibus bonorum et malorum*]. 2nd ed. Translated by H. Rackham. Cambridge, Mass.: Harvard University Press, 1931.

Heinaman, Robert. "Eudaimonia and Self-Sufficiency in the *Nicomachean Ethics*." *Phronesis* 33 (1988): 31–53.

Merton, Thomas. *The Seven Storey Mountain*. San Diego: Harcourt Brace Jovanovich, 1948.
Russell, Daniel. *Happiness for Humans*. Oxford: Oxford University Press, 2012.
Solomon, W. David. "Internal Objections to Virtue Ethics." In *Midwest Studies in Philosophy XIII: Ethical Theory: Character and Virtue*, edited by P. French, T. Uehling, and H. Wettstein, 428–41. Notre Dame: University of Notre Dame Press, 1988.
Toner, Christopher. "Virtue Ethics and Egoism." In *The Routledge Companion to Virtue Ethics*, edited by Lorraine Besser-Jones and Michael Slote, 345–57. New York: Routledge, 2015.

THE COMPLEXITY OF JUSTICE
Thomas Aquinas' Interpretation of the
Fifth Book of Aristotle's *Nicomachean Ethics*

Kevin L. Flannery, S.J.

In his lectures on twentieth-century ethics for the International Catholic University, David Solomon calls attention to the change that occurred in the English-speaking philosophical world in the early 1970s from a concern with more metaethical issues such as the objective (or nonobjective) nature of moral judgments to an interest in "more traditional" issues, such as the role of the virtues in ethics. The work that was most decisive for this change, he says, was John Rawls' *A Theory of Justice* (1971), but he also acknowledges that Alasdair MacIntyre and Elizabeth Anscombe influenced the channeling of philosophical research in this direction both before and after Rawls' book. The present chapter draws inspiration and substance from this tributary of moral theory, for it was a series of MacIntyre's lectures (which eventually became the book *Whose Justice? Which Rationality?*) I attended as a neophyte student of philosophy that pulled my interests definitively in the direction of the history of ethics, where they have remained ever since. No less importantly, it was David—whose current work will establish him as *the* historian of twentieth-century ethics—who, through his friendship and by his generosity as director of the Notre Dame Center for Ethics and Culture, provided me at one point with an environment in which to deepen my knowledge of the river upstream of the tributary that he understands like few others.

Our earliest treatise on the virtue of justice—unless, rather implausibly, one considers Plato's *Republic* a treatise—is to be found in the fifth book of Aristotle's *Nicomachean Ethics* (*NE* 5). That book, the intent of which is clearly to bring order to the various and interrelated significations of the terms *justice, the just, just* (δικαιοσύνη, τὸ δίκαιον, δίκαιος), and so on, has had an enormous influence upon Western ethical and legal thought and, in particular, upon those who associate themselves with the intellectual legacy of Thomas Aquinas, and yet what that order intended by Aristotle *is*—or would be—is by no means apparent. John Finnis, for instance, in his book *Aquinas: Moral, Political, and Legal Theory*, says that "Aquinas' efforts to follow Aristotle in classifying types of justice—its species, parts, and associated forms—yield no really clear and stable analytical pattern."[1] He attributes this instability to Thomas' "adherence to Aristotle's framework" for discussing justice in *NE* 5 and to "the structure of the *Summa Theologiae*" itself, which, as he says, looks to the virtues rather than to "what reason requires, what acts are consistent with pursuing human goods and avoiding evil."[2]

The present chapter makes no attempt to refute this general claim, which involves many and disparate texts in the Thomistic corpus. It attempts rather simply to show that Aristotle's theory of justice makes good sense and captures fundamental truths regarding justice and that Thomas' reading of *NE* 5 helps to bring these truths into relief.[3] If it is true that Thomas' interpretation—found in his commentary on the *Ethics* and in questions 57 to 61 of the *Secunda secundae* of his *Summa Theologiae*—smooths out some of the rough spots in Aristotle's presentation of the theory, it does so in a way that identifies the deeper principles of the theory.[4] This leaves us with a stable theoretical basis for interpreting Aristotle's complex theory of justice.

This chapter considers primarily the distinctions set out in the first five chapters of *NE* 5: the division of justice itself into general and particular justice and the further division of particular justice into distributive justice and what Aristotle appears to call "corrective justice" but what Thomas calls "commutative justice." It does not consider—or considers only briefly—some philosophically important distinctions Aristotle makes in the remaining six chapters, such as the distinction between political justice and other "analogous" forms of justice such as domestic and paternal justice and the distinction between political and natural justice.

The chapter argues that general justice, for both Aristotle and Thomas, is primarily a virtue of the lawmaker and that, therefore, general justice's scope is limited by its object: the establishment of laws. It argues similarly that the analysis of distributive justice (in certain regards) looks primarily not to the civil authority that normally makes the distribution but to those to whom the distribution is made. Finally, it sets out some reasons we should—or at least could—follow Thomas in reading chapters 4 and 5 of NE 5 as a unit in which Aristotle sets out his understanding of a single type of justice: what Thomas calls commutative justice.

General or Legal Justice

The first distinction that Aristotle makes in NE 5 is between general and particular justice. Actually, Aristotle speaks of the former justice more often as legal justice (τὸ δίκαιον νόμιμον), but since later in book five he draws an entirely different distinction between legal justice (τὸ δίκαιον νομικὸν) and natural justice,[5] some confusion can be avoided by calling legal justice (for the most part) general justice.[6]

It is important, however, to bear in mind that Aristotle has good philosophical reasons for calling general justice also legal justice. Although the term itself would suggest otherwise, general justice pertains in a *particular*—that is, nongeneral—way to the political man or lawmaker. Aristotle says that general justice is "perfect virtue"—although it is not perfect simply speaking but "towards the other."[7] A couple of lines later, he says, "It is also perfect in a special way because it is the actual use of perfect virtue, and it is perfect because he who possesses it can use the virtue also towards another and not merely with respect to himself—for many can exercise virtue in their own affairs but in their relations with others are quite incapable. This is why the saying of Bias is well regarded, that 'rule will show the man,' for a ruler is necessarily in relation with the other and in community."[8] Thomas confirms this understanding of general justice both in his commentary on the *Nicomachean Ethics* and in the *Summa Theologiae*.[9]

As we learn near the beginning of NE 1, the task of politics—that is to say, of lawmaking—is to determine which of the other disciplines shall be learned in the city, up to what point, and by whom and to determine by legislation "what one must do and what refrain from doing."[10] This certainly sounds to us as if Aristotle advocates government of the most obtrusive sort—and there would certainly be aspects of an Aristotelian-sanctioned regime that we would find unduly interfering with personal freedom. He maintains, for instance, that legislation might encourage not only abortion but even infanticide.[11] But however intrusive such legislation might be, it is certainly not "big government" intrusiveness. Aristotle's remarks have to do with the city—the πόλις—the population of which, he says, cannot reach a hundred thousand without ceasing to be a city,[12] and he was strongly in favor of allowing these smaller political entities to determine their own laws, as is apparent throughout his *Politics*.

So general justice is the virtue proper to the lawmaker. Particular justice, on the other hand, is the virtue proper to the individual citizen in such dealings with other individuals as potentially involve loss or gain (construed quite broadly).[13] Calling legal justice general and contrasting it with particular justice gives the impression that the latter is a species within the genus of general justice—and, indeed, Aristotle himself makes a number of remarks that seem to confirm this conception. He asserts, for instance, that general justice is not a part of virtue but the whole[14] and, in the second clause of the same sentence, calls the other "the justice that is the part of virtue" (τὴν ἐν μέρει ἀρετῆς δικαιοσύνην).[15]

But Aristotle also asserts the following: "It is clear, therefore, that besides injustice in the wide sense there is another, particular, injustice which has the same name, since its definition is within the same genus."[16] By implication, therefore, general (or legal) justice and particular justice are two species within the same genus. Aristotle goes on then immediately to explain that both general and particular injustice are concerned with "the other" but that particular injustice concerns *gaining* something at the expense of the other (honor or money or whatever), general injustice with all the things that concern also the good man (ὁ σπουδαῖος).[17] Thomas expands upon this remark, saying that particular injustice concerns an individual's dealings with other individuals, general injustice with offenses against the common good.[18]

What this approach in effect does is to preserve the independent intelligibility of what the lawmaker does—his "vocation," so to speak—as distinct from the intelligibility of what the individual citizen does when he deals with his neighbor in matters where he could get the upper hand but will not if he is just. If it were true that particular justice is a species of general justice, when you pay a just price for your neighbor's old wheelbarrow, you would somehow be participating in what the lawmaker does in the legislature as he brings into effect a law regulating commerce. And not only would dealing justly with your neighbor become participation in a legislative act but so also would standing strong in battle[19] or telling the truth to others about your own abilities[20]—for general justice would be the genus not only for particular justice but for all the other species of virtue that this supposedly generic virtue comprises.[21] But then—if one is an Aristotelian—there would be a problem in saying what exactly characterizes as good what the lawmaker does. If generic justice includes under a species paying a just price for a wheelbarrow, standing strong in battle, and telling the truth, what is the justice that pertains to lawmaking? It cannot be a species of itself, so it cannot take its place among these ways of being just. Nor is it a compendium of these specific ways of being just. Nor is it present in paying a just price, standing strong, or telling the truth.

This is not a merely logical point about genera and species but one that has practical significance. In setting out these ideas, Aristotle certainly has in mind the ideal city of Plato's *Republic*, which he regards as inadequate precisely because it conceives of the city's macrostructure, overseen by the lawmaker (or lawmakers), as identical qua structure to the microstructures within it (households and marriages, for instance—and even the individual soul), the only difference being that the macrostructure comprises more individuals than the microstructures.[22] Such an approach lends itself to totalitarianism because for a lawmaker to reach down into the lower levels of the macrostructure would simply be for him to reach down into a smaller sector of the very structure for which he is responsible: he would be doing his proper task.

Although Aristotle clearly recognizes a connection between the city as a whole and the institutions within it, he recognizes too that the vocation of the lawmaker is quite different even structurally from the vocation, for instance, of the master of a household (ὁ οἰκονομικός)—that is, of a husband, father, and slave owner.[23] The proper object of the lawmaker's activity is laws and has nothing *directly* to do with (for instance) families. In the *Republic*, Plato's Socrates would abolish the family (at least for the guardians of the city) and the institution of marriage (women would be shared) on the grounds that this will make the city more unified. In reaction, Aristotle says, "Is it not obvious that a state may at length attain such a degree of unity as to be no longer a state?"[24]

Aristotle never really explains the nature of the relationship between general justice and the other virtues, but Thomas Aquinas does—indeed, he is quite concerned to show that general justice is not the same in essence (*per essentiam*) with any other virtue and that particular justice has its own "special matter" (or object).[25] The reason legal justice is called general justice is not that it is a genus in which is contained the other special virtues ("species virtues") but rather because it *orders* all the other virtues to the common good. In this way temperance, courage, truthfulness, and so on remain what they are, even while connected to the larger political entity insofar as a lawmaker might enact laws punishing intemperance, cowardice (especially in battle), and false testimony. In fact, says Thomas, even general justice remains "a special virtue according to its essence, according to which it looks to the common good as its proper object."[26] In speaking of the common good, Thomas clearly has in mind Aristotle's remark in the first chapter of *NE* 5: "The laws make proclamations about all things, aiming at the common advantage [κοινῇ συμφέροντος] either of all or of the best or of those with authority either due to virtue or some such thing."[27]

Obviously, the fact that general justice is a special virtue does not make it "special justice" (or particular justice). Each of these has its own object and therefore its own species: for general justice, it is, as we have just seen, the common good (understood as the object of its ordering activity); for particular justice, it is the good of the other person with whom one is dealing by way of particular exterior acts.[28] Thomas considers the objection that this does not sufficiently diversify the respective objects of general and particular justice, for they are both concerned with the good of the other: it is only that, with the former, the good is multiplied many times over. Thomas' blunt response paraphrases Aristotle: "Those err who say that the city and the household and other such things differ only in terms of more and less and not in species."[29]

Very significant also is Thomas' mention in *ST* 2-2.58.8 of exterior acts. Exterior acts issue from one's limbs[30] and go toward specific objects. The lawmaker pushes a pen and signs *a law*; the individual pushes a pen and buys *a house* or an insurance policy or whatever. These different objects determine that the corresponding exterior acts are different. Justice, we are beginning to see, is complex virtue: it crops up everywhere and in very particular, concrete ways.[31]

Particular Justice and Its Various Relations, Internal and External

To add to the complexity, Aristotle identifies within particular justice two other types of justice: distributive justice (τὸ διανεμητικὸν δίκαιον) and what he calls—at least sometimes—corrective justice (τὸ διορθωτικὸν δίκαιον). There is some controversy about the latter denomination especially for Thomists, since Thomas speaks rather of distributive and commutative justice ("iustitia commutativa"), but this is an issue we can put off, for the most part, until the next section, which is devoted exclusively to the latter (i.e., to commutative justice).

The special mark of distributive justice is the involvement of what Aristotle calls geometrical proportion (ἀναλογία γεωμετρική). Geometrical proportion is not a matter of simply "counting things up": it uses numbers but is not directly about quantities; rather, it is about proportions themselves. Distributive justice has to do with both persons and things. Since the relative qualities of persons are not commensurable in a straightforward (or arithmetical) way—either among themselves or with commensurable things—geometrical proportion is ideally suited to the task of determining what is a just distribution. The just distributor, exercising general justice (since his object is the common good), determines, for reasons that correspond to distributive justice, that Mr. A deserves a smaller share of the common goods than Mr. B. Let us say that he determines that to Mr. A's desert can be assigned the number six and to Mr. B's desert the number twelve. In assigning these numbers, he is not "counting anything up" but simply ordering the relevant factors. And let us say too that the common goods in question are twelve in number; these by contrast are commensurate, at least among themselves, as in twelve coins.[32] The distributor acts justly if he gives four of these things to Mr. A and eight to Mr. B, since the two proportions—four to six and eight to twelve—are equal. As four is to six, so is eight to twelve: the proportions (two to three in each case) are equal; the distribution is geometrically proportional.[33]

Recognizing that general and distributive are distinct types of justice is to recognize, in another way, that there are limits upon general justice. It is just, by way of general justice, that persons put in charge of the common good issue decrees in order to promote the common good. To a certain extent, they *create* justice: what a decree specifies is (in certain cases) just, simply because someone with the proper authority has issued the decree. But when a law has to do with the distribution of goods, the persons entrusted with general justice must respect distributive justice. If they do not—if, for instance, their ordering of individuals in the city is not according to genuine merit but according to monies received—they have abused the authority they have in general justice by failing to respect distributive justice. Since merit is not subject to strict commensuration, persons holding office in general justice enjoy the benefit of the doubt in distribution, but that benefit itself has limits. At a certain point, it will become obvious that a particular distribution is not just.

Arithmetical proportion (ἀναλογία ἀριθμητική), which is characteristic of corrective justice, has *solely* to do with things that are commensurable. Aristotle gives the example of a judge applying corrective justice: "The judge restores equality. It is as if there were a line divided into unequal parts and he should take away that by which the greater segment exceeds the half of the line and add it to the smaller segment."[34] Suppose, for instance, that at the starting position both Mr. A and Mr. B have three things and that this is just. If Mr. A takes one thing from Mr. B, he will have four and Mr. B will have two. In order to restore justice (or equality), the judge takes the one thing and gives it back to Mr. B: they both once again have three things. As we shall see, arithmetical proportion can be more complicated than this, at least for Thomas, but this example serves well the purpose of showing that arithmetical proportion is more straightforward than geometrical proportion. We noted previously that geometrical proportion is not about commensurable objects but about proportions; arithmetical proportion *is* about commensurable objects—although sometimes they are only commensurable given a previous application of distributive justice.

It is important to understand correctly not only the relationship between distributive and corrective (or commutative) justice—to which we shall return in the next section—but also the relationship (or relationships) between these two types of particular justice and general justice. By juxtaposing two articles in the *Summa Theologiae*—2-2.58.5 and 2-2.61.1—we can put together a schematic account, in terms of parts and whole, of all the distinctions we have seen thus far.

In the first of these two articles, having acknowledged that justice always has to do with "the other" (is always "ad alium"), Thomas says that the other may be considered either individually or in common. Particular justice looks to the first (individuals as such), general justice to the second (individuals in common). He says, "It is clear that all individuals who are contained within some community are compared to the community as are parts to a whole. By definition, however, a part is *of* a whole—so, any good of a part is orderable toward the good of the whole."[35]

Thomas goes on to associate the relationship of part to whole with general justice. What is most interesting here is that this account of general justice looks first to the individual—to the part. The whole comes in only insofar as speaking of a part presupposes a whole. Moreover, in explaining the meaning of "the other in common," Thomas says that "he who *serves* some community *serves* all the men who are contained within that community."[36] General justice has to do with the relationship between *all* moral acts and the concerns of the authority whose *proper* acts look to the common good. This connection with all acts is what makes general justice, according to both Thomas and Aristotle, in some sense coterminous with morality itself, even while it remains the responsibility of a particular authority performing particular acts. But even these particular acts are for the sake of—at the service of—individuals (in common). Once again we see in this Aristotelian theory limits placed upon general justice.

We find the continuation of the part-whole schema in Thomas' *ST* 2-2.61.1c, about the suitability of distinguishing two species of justice, commutative and distributive.

> Particular justice is ordered toward some private person, who is compared to the community as a part to the whole. But a twofold order may be considered in relation to a part. One is the order of one part to another, which is similar to the order of one private person to another. This order is directed by commutative justice, which consists in the mutual dealings that come about between two persons. Another order is that of the whole towards the parts, and to this order is assimilated the order of that which is common to individual persons. This order is directed by distributive justice, which distributes things held in common in a proportionate manner. And so there are two species of justice: distributive and commutative.

The question that immediately arises when reading this is, How then is distributive justice different from the general justice that an authority ought to have as he oversees the common good? An initial answer to this question is attained by noticing that, although distributive justice is described here as proceeding from the whole to the parts, it still falls under particular justice—which is about the parts. We learn more, however, in Thomas' answer, in the same article, to the third objection.[37] The objection argues that the notion of distributive justice places justice only in the hands of the sovereign (the "princeps"), whereas it has already been shown (in *ST* 2-2.58.6) that even general justice pertains to the sovereign's subordinates. Thomas responds, "The *act* of distributing, which is of common goods, belongs solely to the person who has charge of the common goods; but distributive *justice* is in the subordinates, to whom the distribution is made, in as much, that is, as they are contented with a just distribution."[38] As we have already seen under the heading of general justice, that virtue pertains primarily to the person who has responsibility for the common good. Under the present heading—of particular justice—attention turns to those whom this authority serves: the parts. Granted that the designated authority is obliged to perform his task with general (or legal) justice, it is a further question, Thomas is saying, whether it is right (or just) for you or me to *have* the things we have. This is determined with *respect* to the larger whole (the common good) but has to do with *us*, the parts.

In the strictest Aristotelian sense, the distributive justice qua present at the level of the parts is not a moral habit (or "having" [ἕξις]), since a moral habit (or virtue) is associated with the actions of the person who acts with it, but in this case the action is performed by another. Aristotle confronts this problem later in *NE* 5, when he considers distributive injustice:

> It is plain too that the distributor acts unjustly, but not always the man who has the excessive share; for it is not he to whom what is unjust appertains that acts unjustly, but he to whom it appertains to do the unjust act voluntarily, i.e. the person in whom lies the origin of the action, and this lies in the distributor not in the receiver. Again, since things are said to do things in different senses, and there is a sense in which lifeless things, or a hand, or a servant who obeys an order, may be said to slay, he who gets an excessive share does not act unjustly; though he does what is unjust.[39]

That justice exists at the level of parts in this objective sense is what leads Aristotle, in *NE* 5.8, to distinguish unjust *things* from injustices: "so that something will be unjust but not yet an injustice if voluntariness is not present."[40] It is perfectly intelligible to say, "There is injustice here," pointing to the holdings and/or the privileges of individuals, without yet saying that one of *them* has been unjust. Of course, it may be the case that one (or more) of the individuals has been unjust—but that is another issue and another sense of injustice. In any case, however, we see here that the *burden* of distributive justice is upon the distributor: he cannot in justice simply do what he wants to do.

To return though to Thomas' *ST* 2-2.61.1, the response already partially quoted (ad 3) adds the further point that "it can also be the case that a distribution of common goods is not to a city but to a single family, the distribution of which [goods] can be effected by the authority of some private person."[41] There are a number of things worthy of note here. First of all, and obviously, Thomas says that distributive justice might be affected not just by a sovereign—a central government—but also by an individual whose responsibility it is to determine in some way who gets what. Aristotle too appears to recognize as a distributor any individual who is somehow in charge of a distribution.[42] Thomas speaks here of distribution within a family—which is important, since a household, also according to Aristotle, is ordered by a different species of justice.[43] This means, along the same lines previously suggested, that the central government (of whatever sort it might be) cannot assume that distributive justice as applied at a lower (less general) level is *its* distributive justice, incarnated at the level of particulars.[44] It cannot—without further ado—substitute itself for distributive justice at a lower level.

Second, and not so obviously, even the whole is said to be not in the distributor but in the parts, for the distribution is made *to* the city and *to* the family ("civitati"/"familiae"). As we have seen, the distributor is simply the one who performs the act of distribution. Indeed, in the immediately preceding response,[45] Thomas says that "part and whole are in a certain sense the same thing, so that that which is of the whole is in a certain sense of the part."[46]

John Finnis faults Cajetan (Thomas de Vio) for having introduced into the interpretation of Thomas' theory of justice talk of parts and wholes. The key idea of Cajetan's comment is contained in the following remark: "For legal justice orients the parts to the whole, distributive the whole to the parts, while commutative orients the parts one to another."[47] I find nothing in Cajetan's remarks that is not found also in Thomas, but Finnis' more general point is well taken—and that is that certain later interpreters of Thomas (he mentions Dominic Soto and B.-H. Merkelbach), attending only superficially to what Cajetan says about the "part-whole" relationships among the various types of justice, came away with the idea that "the duties of distributive justice belong only to the state or the personified 'whole' (community)."[48] This is certainly not Thomas' position—nor was it Aristotle's. For both, as we have seen, a distributor might not be involved in government in any way.

Finnis presses this point against the libertarian philosopher Robert Nozick, who argues, in a chapter of *Anarchy, State, and Utopia* titled "Distributive Justice," that once someone has by his own efforts acquired property or capacities, "it is unjust for anyone, including the State, to deprive him of any of those holdings, or to conscript any of his capacities, for the purpose of aiding other persons."⁴⁹ Once it is acknowledged that there is such a thing as distributive justice and that responsibility for it falls not just upon an oppressive (and distant) state but upon anyone who is in a position to decide what is a fair opportunity or holding, Nozick's articulate indignation loses much of its persuasive force.

Aristotle and Thomas are not inventing distributive justice but rather describing something that corresponds to our moral intuitions (and so to natural law). We may not accept the idea that a moral aristocracy deserves a greater share of the common goods, but neither did Aristotle insist upon that being the sole criterion of merit.⁵⁰ There are very few of us who would not acknowledge that persons in certain types of work or positions deserve higher pay or, at the least, greater honor.⁵¹ Working out the details is the task of distributive justice—or, more practically, of the servant of the common good.⁵²

The Legitimacy of Commutative Justice

We come finally to the issue of whether it is legitimate to speak of commutative justice, as does Thomas Aquinas. There are actually three interconnected issues here: the first having to do with the very term *commutative*; the second with conceiving of chapters 4 and 5 of *NE* 5 as a unit—that is, as a unit about commutative justice; and the third with the type of proportionality to be associated with commutative justice. This latter is an issue since Aristotle associates types of justice so closely with types of proportionality. Since the types of proportionality employed in chapters 4 and 5 appear to be quite different, it would seem that the two chapters could not be about the same type of justice.

Regarding the first issue, therefore, as mentioned earlier, Aristotle does not employ the expression "commutative justice"; he speaks rather of corrective justice (τὸ διορθωτικόν δίκαιον). The former, besides not being Aristotelian, is a more inclusive expression, referring quite generally to what we might call "common dealings": direct contacts between individuals in which loss or gain is possible. Aristotle himself argues in *NE* 5.4.1132a10–14 that the terms *gain* (κέρδος) and *loss* (ζημία) must be interpreted very loosely so that even adultery or battery might be understood as a loss for one person and a gain (an unjust gain) for another. It is partially due to the inclusivity of the expression "commutative justice" that Thomas is able to understand both chapters 4 and 5 as treating the same thing. More recent authors tend to understand chapter 4 as treating corrective justice, chapter 5 "commercial justice" (or the justice of exchanges).⁵³

In speaking of commutative justice, Thomas is not, however, recasting Aristotle to his own liking: he is simply following his translators.[54] In none of the translations of the *Nicomachean Ethics* available in Thomas' day was the word διορθωτικόν translated "corrective" (or "correctivum" as in "iustum correctivum"); it was always translated "directive" (or "directivum" as in "iustum directivum").[55] At the first appearance in *NE* of the word διορθωτικόν, the Latin Thomas was reading speaks of "una [iustitia] ... in commutationibus directiva": "a type of justice ... directive of commutations"—or to use more standard English, "directive of common dealings."[56] Thomas himself on one occasion refers to commutative justice as "iustitia directiva commutationum,"[57] so it is clear that he does not reject the word "directiva" in the expression "iustitia in commutationibus directiva"; he just thinks it important to emphasize the "commutationes" of which this type of justice is directive. It was not Thomas, therefore, but rather his translators who were initially convinced that Aristotle, in using the term διορθωτικόν, must have had a broader concept in mind. They conveyed this broader conception by means of the translation "directiva" (and cognates); Thomas, without rejecting the idea that the type of justice at issue was "directiva," preferred the expression "iustitia commutativa." They all—Thomas, but more immediately his translators—took this approach because they thought that the term had to include not just the material of *NE* 5.4, which is clearly "corrective" in character, but also the material of *NE* 5.5, which has to do more generally with common dealings.

We are already, therefore, into the substance of the second issue, whether chapters 4 and 5 ought to be read as a unit. In rendering διορθωτικόν as "directivum," the Latin translators pull the term's meaning away from correction and toward that which correction is meant to achieve: a "setting to rights."[58] Following the same approach, we might even render διορθωτικόν δίκαιον into English as "righting justice"—which contains the idea of correcting but also brings to the fore what is more fundamental to any type of justice: right as opposed to wrong.[59] It also more easily comprehends the contents not only of chapter 4, which (as we have said) is about correcting, but also of chapter 5, which is about *correct* common dealings. So although the translation "directivum" is a bit of a stretch, it is not wholly without justification, both linguistically and philosophically.

There is also good reason to say that, although chapter 5 does not concern itself with correction, Aristotle does conceive of it as concerning the same type of justice as chapter 4. In the first line of chapter 5, Aristotle introduces a way of conceiving justice with which—if understood simplistically—he does not agree: "Some think that reciprocity is, simply speaking, justice." He immediately adds, "But reciprocity corresponds to neither distributive nor διορθωτικόν justice."[60] Aristotle goes on then to explain how the concept of reciprocity needs to be understood if it is to represent either distributive justice or διορθωτικόν δίκαιον—although his emphasis in chapter 5 is clearly not on distribution but on common dealings. So these introductory remarks of *NE* 5.5 themselves suggest that διορθωτικόν δίκαιον should be given a broader sense than that conveyed by the translation "corrective justice." They suggest also that Aristotle's own attention has shifted to the broader idea.

That brings us to the third and final issue associated with the legitimacy of commutative justice: Aristotle's apparent use of a different type of proportionality in chapters 4 and 5 of *NE* 5. As we have already seen, in chapter 4, in the course of explaining what is usually identified as corrective justice, he speaks of a very simple procedure of restoring to one person that which was taken from him. Initially (as we supposed) Mr. A and Mr. B both have three things. If Mr. A takes one thing from Mr. B, he will have four and Mr. B will have two. The judge corrects this situation—establishes justice—by taking the one thing and giving it back to Mr. B so that both once again have two things. Aristotle says that the judge in such cases employs arithmetical proportion.

But in chapter 5, the establishment of justice appears to involve a version of geometrical proportion. As we have seen, Aristotle rejects at the beginning of chapter 5 reciprocity (τὸ ἀντιπεπονθὸς) as an adequate account of justice. But he almost immediately acknowledges that, correctly understood, reciprocity does give an adequate account of what Thomas would call commutative justice. "But in common dealings," he says, "such justice does hold men together; this is reciprocal justice—according to proportion, however, and not according to equality. For it is in requiting proportionately that the city holds together."[61]

Suppose that there is in the city a builder (A) and the house he has built (C), a shoemaker (B) and a pair of shoes he has made (D). If we suppose that the house and the pair of shoes are of equal value, and even if we suppose that building and shoemaking are not equal activities, these elements are geometrically proportionate to one another:

$$A + D : B + C :: A : B$$

and so

$$A : B :: D : C^{62}$$

If the individuals simply exchange products, all will be well: in this small regard, the city holds together.[63] But if (as is more plausible) the house and the shoes are not of equal value, maintaining community requires equalizing the things that are exchanged, for (as we have just heard) "it is in requiting *proportionately* that the city holds together."[64] The pair of shoes must be multiplied in some way (i.e., by x) so as to maintain geometrical proportionality:

$$A + xD : B + C :: A : B$$

and so

$$A : B :: xD : C$$

Is it not obvious then that such commercial transactions involve not arithmetical but rather geometrical proportionality? And since they involve different types of proportion, how can Thomas say that chapters 4 and 5 are about one and the same type of justice—that is to say, commutative justice, which is defined in terms of arithmetical proportion?

It is not as if Thomas is unaware of the problem. He confronts it directly in his commentary on the relevant passage in chapter 5:

> It seems that this is contrary to what was said above [*in EN* §950] that in commutative justice the mean is taken not according to geometrical proportionality, which consists in an equality of proportion, but according to arithmetic proportionality, which consists in an equality of quantity. It needs to be said, however, that, with respect to commutative justice, what is required is always an equality of thing to thing—not, however, of action and passion, which implies reciprocity. But in this matter, proportionality must be employed in order that there might be an equality of things in so far as the action of one craftsman is greater than the action of the other—as, for instance, building is greater than the manufacture of a knife. Thus, if the builder should commute his action to the action of the knife-maker, there would not be equality of thing given and taken, that is, of the house and the knife.[65]

In other words, what Aristotle is describing in NE 5.5 is the way in which differences taken into consideration in distributive justice are reduced to simple quantities of things that—if the exchange has proceeded according to commutative justice—leaves both parties with equal portions. Supposing, for instance, that a house is worth 100 knives, both before and after the transaction, either individual will have the equivalent of one house or 100 knives. If, for instance, it turns out that the builder ends up with 80 knives, so that the knife maker has in effect 120 (i.e., the house plus the 20 knives he did not give to the builder), a judge can step in and give the 20 knives to the builder. We are back in the realm of arithmetical proportionality.

Is this a plausible understanding of what Aristotle is doing in chapter 5? It certainly is. It is true that in that chapter, Aristotle speaks about geometrical proportion, but his point is that such situations can be reduced to something similar to reciprocity (τὸ ἀντιπεπονθὸς): to "this for that." Indeed, this is the whole thrust of the chapter, in which, besides the ideas we have just expounded, Aristotle explains how money and demand (χρεία)[66] render commensurate—and so ultimately equalize (ἰσασθῆναι)[67]—disparate activities and products, thus holding the city together as "one something."[68] Thomas does not ignore the fact that NE 5.5 also alludes to distributive justice—that, indeed, would be to ignore the chapter's introduction, which, as we have seen, speaks about both distributive justice and διορθωτικόν δίκαιον[69]—but he maintains that, insofar as it speaks about the "equality of thing to thing [aequalitatem rei ad rem]," it is speaking about commutative justice.

Conclusion

I conclude, therefore, that Thomas Aquinas' interpretation of NE 5 (especially its first five chapters) is by no means an implausible one. He has a very precise understanding of the nature of general (or legal) justice, an understanding that attends closely to Aristotle's own words. The corresponding theory constitutes in many ways Aristotle's rejection of Plato's more monolithic model of the just city (the just πόλις) in the *Republic*. Thomas also gives a reasonable account of the distinction between distributive justice and whatever we choose to call the justice discussed in NE 5.4–5: corrective, directive, commercial, or commutative justice. Since the details of Thomas' account make up a coherent interpretation of Aristotle's words, it is not, as John Finnis suggests, unstable. It holds together as an account of the complexity of justice.

Bibliography

Albert the Great. *Commentarii in octo libros Politicorum Aristotelis.* Vol. 8, *Opera Omnia.* Paris: Vivés, 1891.

Barnes, Jonathan, ed. *The Complete Works of Aristotle: The Revised Oxford Translation.* Princeton: Princeton University Press, 1984.

Bywater, Ingram, ed. *Aristotelis Ethica Nicomachea.* Oxford Classical Texts. Oxford: Clarendon, 1894.

Dognin, Paul-Dominique. "Justice particulière comporte-t-elle deux espèces?," *Revue Thomiste* 65 (1965): 398–425.

Finnis, John. *Aquinas: Moral, Political and Legal Theory.* Oxford: Oxford University Press, 1998.

———. *Natural Law and Natural Rights.* Oxford: Oxford University Press, 2011.

Flannery, Kevin L. *Acts amid Precepts: The Aristotelian Logical Structure of Thomas Aquinas' Moral Theory.* Washington, D.C.: Catholic University of America Press, 2001.

Gauthier, René-Antoine. *Aristoteles Latinus.* 26, 1–3, *Ethica Nicomachea. Fasc. 5, Indices verborum.* Corpus Philosophorum Medii Aevi. Leiden: Brill, 1973.

Gauthier, René-Antoine, and Jean Yves Jolif. *L'Éthique a Nicomaque: Introduction, traduction et commentaire.* Louvain-la-neuve, Belgium: Éditions Peeters, 2002.

Grant, Alexander. *The Ethics of Aristotle: Illustrated with Notes and Essays.* London: Longmans, Green, 1885.

Jackson, Henry, ed. *The Fifth Book of the* Nicomachean Ethics *of Aristotle.* Cambridge: Cambridge University Press, 1879.

Nozick, Robert. *Anarchy, State, and Utopia.* New York: Basic Books, 1974.

Susemihl, Franciscus, and Otto Apelt, eds. *Aristotelis Ethica Nicomachea.* Teubner: Leipzig, 1912.

Thomas Aquinas. *In decem ethicorum Aristotelis ad Nicomachum expositio.* Edited by A. M. Pirotta. Turin: Marietti, 1964.

———. *Sententia libri ethicorum.* Vol. 47, *Opera Omnia.* Rome: Commissio Leonina, 1969.

———. *Summa Theologiae, cura et studio Instituti Studiorum Medievalium Ottaviensis.* Ottawa: Garden City, 1941.

Thomas Aquinas and Thomas de Vio Cajetan. *Summa Theologiae cum commentariis Thomae de Vio Caietani Ordinis Praedicatorum.* Vols. 4–12, *Opera Omnia.* Rome: Typographia polyglotta S. C. de Propaganda Fide (Commissio Leonina), 1888–1906.

3

FEARLESS MERCY BEYOND JUSTICE
Aquinas and Nussbaum's Pity Tradition

John O'Callaghan

Introduction

Over the course of a number of papers and book chapters, Martha Nussbaum has argued for the existence of what she calls a "pity tradition" in Western philosophy.[1] It begins in ancient Greece with the poets and tragic drama portraying pity in various settings. She translates the Greek ἔλεος into contemporary English as "pity."[2] According to Nussbaum, the pity tradition finds its original theoretical philosophical analysis and justification in Aristotle's reflections on ἔλεος in his works *The Poetics* and *The Rhetoric*. It then essentially disappears under pressure from Socratically inspired notions of self-sufficiency, Plato's denigration of poetry, and Greek and Roman Stoicism, to reappear in the eighteenth century in the work of Jean Jacques Rousseau and Adam Smith on the passions and sentiments, but now universalized to all of humanity by the latter.[3]

Despite the inherent interest of the particular figures Nussbaum considers in this tradition, what stands out by its absence in her account is the twenty-century-long gap within it. The pity tradition began roughly twenty-six centuries ago in Greek tragedy but has only been significantly manifest in six of those centuries. The vast majority of the gap in

Nussbaum's tradition spans what could be called the Christian era up to the eighteenth century. Going even further than Nietzsche's criticism of Christianity, Nussbaum claims that it was a stoic otherworldliness of Christianity that forced it to denigrate and downplay the importance of the love of this world with its contingencies. "[Nietzsche] fails . . . to see what the Stoicism he endorses has in common with the Christianity he criticizes, what 'hardness' has in common with otherworldliness: both are forms of self-protection, both express a fear of this world and its contingencies, both are incompatible with the deepest sort of love." Christianity is guilty of "alienating us from our love of the world and all its chanciness," as if the sufferings of this world were immaterial to the salvation that awaits the blessed.[4] In that respect, Christianity is part of what Nussbaum calls elsewhere the "anti-compassion tradition."[5]

I will address this theorizing of pity through philosophical history by discussing Aquinas' account of the virtue of *misericordia*, or as commonly translated into English, mercy.[6] It provides one single case within the theological and philosophical tradition of Christianity that directly addresses the claims Nussbaum makes about the pity tradition. If we may take Aquinas as a representative Christian figure in the tradition of reflection upon deserved or undeserved human suffering, he provides an alternative account or better accounts of mercy as more than just a passion but rather a virtue, accounts that both embody the positives of Nussbaum's pity tradition but are also arguably philosophically more rich than that tradition. Still, the richness of Aquinas' discussion, however philosophically cogent on its own, cannot be separated as a matter of history from its sources in theological reflection upon divine revelation and the figure of Christ. Indeed, one specific feature of Nussbaum's account of pity, its universal scope, is most plausibly seen not as a modern innovation of Rousseau and Smith but rather as arising specifically out of the Christian tradition of which Aquinas is used here as an exemplar. Nussbaum's pity tradition then looks like a nostalgic return to the pre-Christian Greek tradition while trying to hold on to the universalizing moral inertia of Christianity. The thesis of this chapter is that the greater richness of Aquinas' account consists in the role played by universal human friendship as the setting for a distinct virtue of mercy without fear that goes beyond justice, indeed a mercy in which justice finds its completion.[7]

Nussbaum's Pity Tradition

The contemporary relevance for Nussbaum of the pity tradition is that it can be put to service in developing a richer, more adequate theory of justice than one finds in typical neo-Kantians like John Rawls. Rawls developed a theory of justice reflecting upon what rationality ideally demands of one, if one posits an "original position" involving a "veil of ignorance" about one's own social status and resources in relation to the social status and resources of all other members of a community. If representative persons were behind this veil of ignorance, what principles would they adopt in order best to act rationally to promote their self-interest? The principles of an impartial rational order of justice would arise out of such reflection, if all were to posit this veil of ignorance for themselves and rationally act upon it in the ordering of society. The order of justice is the ideally rational construction of impartial social relations that results from reasoning and acting in a self-interested way having posited as a hypothesis broad ignorance about the condition of oneself and others.[8]

While acknowledging the similarity to Rawls, Nussbaum points out that by integrating pity for the sufferings of others to establish human solidarity with an eye toward justice, she does not assume ignorance of any particular conception of the good life as is required by Rawls. On the contrary, while conceptions of the good life may change over time, the one who experiences pity and attempts to act upon it "operates with a general conception of human flourishing that is the best one she can find. . . . She does stake herself to a single general conception, when asking whether and to what extent disease, hunger, losses of children, losses of freedom, and so forth, are really bad things."[9] Acknowledging the role of the passions in life, particularly the passion of pity or human sympathy for others, enriches the acknowledgment of the contingency of suffering that a theory of justice ought to address. Thus Nussbaum suggests that while pity or compassion is not sufficient for justice, it is necessary and "is an essential bridge to justice."[10]

So first, pity is a passion involving a feeling of pain that one experiences upon seeing another suffering. Second, pity is a passion embodying cognitive judgment, as opposed to assumptions about the nonrational or even normatively irrational character of the emotions and pity in particular, assumptions made in many quarters of contemporary economic, political, and legal thought.[11] Because of their cognitive content, the Aristotelian passions, particularly pity, are rather part and parcel of rational deliberation itself. So third, among other things, the rational content of pity involves the judgment that the one suffering is very much like oneself. Fourth, it further involves the cognitive judgment that the present suffering involves a significant reversal of fortune that is undeserved in the one suffering. Fifth, because of the recognition of the likeness to oneself, it prompts a *fear* in oneself for one's own future, φόβος in Aristotle's Greek, a fear that a similar fate may befall one in the future. So pity (ἔλεος) for another is always accompanied by fear (φόβος) for oneself; without the accompanying fear for oneself, there is no pity.[12]

However, what ἔλεος does not do in Aristotle is prompt one to act to alleviate the suffering that one has observed. After all, Aristotle mostly theorizes about ἔλεος in *The Poetics*, the discussion of tragic drama in which it would be impossible to act to alleviate the sufferings of those one sees being played out on the stage, and *The Rhetoric* where he is diagnosing appeals to pity in forensic settings and how to avoid being affected by them. While he lists it among the passions in the *Nicomachean Ethics* (NE), he does not discuss it at all beyond mentioning it. So for understanding the pity tradition, it is important that while Aristotle mentions ἔλεος in NE, he nowhere discusses a virtue associated with action that accompanies it;[13] certainly he does not associate it with his discussion of justice in that work. So in Nussbaum's account, Aristotelian pity is a passion and not a virtue.

Nussbaum, however, wants to develop an ethical framework that does concern itself with pity, and that framework, it turns out, is justice. In order to develop this line of the tradition, she turns to Rousseau and Adam Smith. What they provide is a way to universalize pity as a condition for the development of the principles of a theory of justice. In Aristotle, the passion of ἔλεος is tied to those one recognizes as very similar to oneself; indeed, they are those who are portrayed as generally well off enough to suffer an undeserved and significant reversal of fortune—the high who are like oneself are brought low undeservedly, and one fears such degradation for oneself seeing that such can happen to someone so like oneself. If this thought about ἔλεος is extended beyond the boundaries of poetry and rhetoric into a broader consideration of ethics and politics, then manifestly these conditions of likeness and significant loss limit in many ways the scope of ἔλεος in Aristotle to the higher echelons of society who have significant goods to lose.

Rousseau and Smith, however, universalize pity or sympathy, extending it to all human beings, whatever their state in life and without concern for a reversal of fortune. Given its rational content, once pity is universalized, it can be deployed within the realm of reason to enrich our understanding of what justice universally demands for all. Rather than operating from within a strict veil of ignorance, one can consider the fact that the kinds of significant suffering any human being may undergo are kinds of sufferings that might happen to oneself; motivated by the passion of pity and then fear for oneself, one will act to alleviate and even more prevent such suffering in a just social order. Thus Nussbaum emphasizes the importance for justice of good education in classical literature and modern fiction that stress the contingencies and tragedies of human suffering, an education that will serve to enhance in the reader the cognitively rich passion of pity in its capacity to see human suffering as universal.[14]

The Aristotelian presence of fear and self-interest remains as psychologically motivating, but rational reflection upon that fear and self-interest suggests that one should act in such a way to build a society that lessens the odds of the suffering that one fears may befall oneself.[15] So if there is a virtue associated with pity, it is not Aristotle's justice but a more sympathetic and less abstract liberal justice, an account of justice that remains rationally self-interested but motivated by a kind of rational fear for oneself universalized by pity for others.

The Tradition of *Misericordia* in Aquinas

Aquinas recognizes a *misericordia* that involves fear for oneself. But there are two salient points of contrast with Nussbaum's treatment of the pity tradition. First, he does not subordinate this *misericordia* to justice. He argues that *misericordia* is more than a passion; it is a virtue in its own right distinct from justice. Second, he argues for a second higher form of the virtue of *misericordia* that does not involve fear for oneself, indeed in which such fear is absent; it is rather grounded in universal friendship for all human beings. He describes this higher form of the virtue as both the highest of all virtues considered in itself and as godlike in its character. However, while remaining generally philosophical in its analysis, his account of the virtue of *misericordia* is informed and universalized by his biblical and theological understanding of all human beings as natural friends of one another.[16]

The two specific aspects of this godlike *misericordia* analyzed by Aquinas that are not found in Aristotle's discussion of ἔλεος have biblical precedents—the feature of universal and natural friendship and the impetus to act to alleviate the suffering prompted by compassion, which involves genuine suffering with another. Although Aquinas wrote no direct commentary on the Gospel of Luke, the parable of the Good Samaritan in Luke and the raising of Lazarus reported in John provide the impetus for his transformation of Aristotelian ἔλεος away from fear for oneself toward friendship for those who suffer.

Aquinas addresses the virtue of *misericordia* in *Summa Theologiae* question 30 of the second part of the second part (*ST* 2.2.30) as one of the three effects of the theological virtue *caritas*. A person characterized by *misericordia* is moved to alleviate suffering if possible by a passion of misery or pain experienced upon the observation of the suffering of another. Because of the element of alleviating suffering, an action, there can be an "operative habit," a virtue of so acting—the habit of acting well to alleviate suffering. Subject to the comprehension of intellect apprehending the good of alleviating the suffering of others, the will itself is moved by its own intellectually informed passion, and so the virtue is an operative habit of the will. Because it pertains to a passion of the will informed by reason in particular, it is cognitively rich, as Nussbaum has argued about pity.

Despite being one of the effects of *caritas*, *misericordia* is a moral virtue, distinct from the theological virtues.[17] The evidence that Aquinas thinks that there is a moral virtue of *misericordia* that can be acquired and is subject to philosophical analysis is straightforward.[18] Within the *Summa* discussion itself, despite the theological setting, to develop his discussion of *misericordia*, he employs what he takes to be Aristotle's analysis of it, drawing upon many of the same sources as Nussbaum but suggesting beyond her that there is an acquired habit of *misericordia* that belongs with the other moral virtues that he believes Aristotle gave broadly adequate accounts of in *NE*. However, to attribute to Aristotle an account of a distinct virtue of ἔλεος is in fact highly problematic. From the perspective of the pity tradition, it is problematic because Nussbaum treats it exclusively as a passion in Aristotle's account. On its own, it is problematic because Aristotle mentions it only once in *NE* as a passion and never analyzes it; he never discusses a virtue associated with it there or elsewhere. But it cannot be denied that Aquinas himself credits Aristotle with having given an account of the moral virtue.[19]

The two forms of *misericordia* Aquinas analyzes differ in very marked respects to the point that *misericordia* is applied only analogously to them. The first form he argues is related to the passion of ἔλεος that Aristotle discusses at length in *Poetics* and *Rhetoric*. Aquinas would not have read the Greek version of those texts, but the Latin translation of Aristotle's ἔλεος was "*misericordia*."[20]

As we have seen, in Aristotle, someone who experiences ἔλεος is someone in good fortune who observes someone else sufficiently like himself in that good fortune suffer the loss of it and recognizes the possibility that a similar fate could befall him. For instance, a poor man will not experience ἔλεος upon observing a rich man undeservedly lose his fortune and be brought to the state of the poor man.[21] Nor will a rich man experience ἔλεος if he is certain that he has the strength to avoid such a fate; the rich man may be foolish in this certitude, but then his foolishness is the reason he does not experience ἔλεος.

These features of ἔλεος explain why the Aristotelian field of application of ἔλεος is by and large the powerful and well-off of society who have significant goods but who are not so powerful that those goods cannot be lost through a turn of bad fortune or luck; it does not have application among the wretched of society. If in one's wretchedness one is not similarly placed and significantly well off in the way the sufferer was before his bad fortune and loss, one has no reason to fear the loss. So one will not experience ἔλεος when one sees the mighty brought low. Even more so, those who have always been among the wretched will not occasion ἔλεος in others who observe their plight, since there is no loss due to a change of fortune among them.

In addition, ἔλεος does not require that one be a friend to the sufferer. The likeness involved is not constituted by or on the basis of friendship among equals that Aristotle analyzes in NE. The sufferer could be a competitor and enemy in the pursuit of political power like Willie Stark in Robert Penn Warren's *All the King's Men*. He could even be an enemy in war—ἔλεος is attributed to Achilles in the *Iliad* when Priam begs for Hector's body.[22] Or he could simply be someone else in one's society who is like one in his wealth but with whom one has no particular acquaintance, like the stockbroker reduced to begging after the great crash of 1929. Indeed, if we think of the experience of an audience watching or reading a tragedy, it is impossible that the audience be friends with those whose sufferings they observe, insofar as they are mere works of fiction, figments of the imagination or myth,[23] figures with whom one can have no friendship even as one recognizes protagonists like oneself in various respects—Fitzgerald's Jay Gatsby or Okonkwo of Achebe's *Things Fall Apart*, for instance. I can fear that what happens to the fictional character Gatsby may happen to me, but I cannot be his friend; his friends are as unreal as he is.

So as Aristotle analyzes ἔλεος, particularly in *Poetics*, while it is occasioned by observing the suffering of another, and one even identifies in some sense with the other by a likenesses of power, wealth, and social standing, it is fundamentally self-directed; the raison d'être of ἔλεος seems to be the φόβος about one's own future that it occasions, and ἔλεος is thus directed upon one's own good. In other words, the ethical key to understanding Aristotle's account of the suffering of others like oneself is not so much ἔλεος but rather the φόβος it prompts.

However, despite attributing an account of the virtue to Aristotle, Aquinas departs from him in significant respects. Aquinas thinks that as a virtue, *misericordia*'s specific defining act is to alleviate suffering.[24] Aristotle says precious little about that act, except perhaps indirectly in *Rhetoric*, which suggests a jury or judge might act prompted by ἔλεος and φόβος to prevent the suffering of the accused that will come with a guilty verdict. But of course it is the task of the prosecution to recognize the effort to appeal to ἔλεος and block it from having that effect. In *Poetics* it is not generally suggested that the one who experiences ἔλεος will act to alleviate suffering, even within the confines of the tragedy. Achilles in the *Iliad* does.[25] But his ἔλεος is hardly presented there as an expression of a virtue Achilles possesses, given what he has just done to Priam's son Hector. If anything, Achilles only acts to release Priam from the suffering he himself has caused. In terms of later Roman stoicism, Achilles' act seems more akin to the *clementia* that Seneca urges upon Nero or Cicero urges upon Caesar.[26]

If we are to think that it is the audience of a tragedy that is supposed to experience ἔλεος upon watching the portrayal of suffering in the characters, it is quite impossible for members of the audience to exercise a virtue in acting to alleviate the suffering of those who are observed to suffer, the characters of the drama, as if a theatergoer could act to alleviate Shylock's suffering in Shakespeare's *The Merchant of Venice*, as opposed to the Venetians within the play so acting had Shakespeare chosen to portray them that way. Indeed, with regard to the audience, insofar as ἔλεος prompts φόβος, fear for oneself, if there were a virtue associated with it in Aristotle, one would think that it ought to be courage, which, unlike justice, bears upon one's own good by governing the passion of fear, a courage that would not imply acting to alleviate the suffering one observes but rather facing well one's own fears of it.

In addition, ἔλεος should not be thought of as compassion; it does not involve suffering with another, which is the heart of the meaning of compassion. ἔλεος is, rather, suffering upon the occasion of another's suffering. Indeed, if we give as much weight to *Poetics* for understanding ἔλεος as Nussbaum does, the occasion of another's suffering need not even be real.[27] Yet Aquinas is explicit in redescribing the passion experienced upon the sight of suffering as compassion; he uses the Latin term *compassio*,[28] suffering with, to describe how it is specifically directed toward alleviating that suffering by action, action for which it is necessary that its object exist and for whom the suffering is real.

So in some measure it is extraordinary for Aquinas to read these Aristotelian texts and attribute to Aristotle more than just an account of the passion of ἔλεος. In that specific respect, it is arguable that Nussbaum's reading of Aristotle is more faithful to the letter of Aristotle's text in restricting ἔλεος merely to a passion.

It is also difficult to attribute ἔλεος to a god,[29] either the gods of the Greek pantheon or the philosophically sophisticated account of a god as pure act that one finds in Aristotle. The gods of the pantheon, while in many ways conceived of in anthropomorphic fashion, were not thought to be particularly like enough to human beings such that the sufferings of human beings might prompt fears of a similar fate in the gods or such that the sufferings of the gods such as they were might prompt fears of a similar fate in human beings. Gods might be concerned with the affairs of human beings, but not because prompted by fear for themselves. It is important that Achilles is not a god but semidivine when he feels ἔλεος in the presence of Priam. It is not the thought of his divine mother but, rather, the thought of his human father Peleus, king of the Myrmidons, that prompts his anguish at the vision of Priam weeping.[30] Of course a god philosophically conceived of as pure act and thus impassible, such as Aristotle gives us, cannot have a passion for any reason, much less experience a fear—φόβος—for the loss of some significant good.

Aquinas displays concern for this problem about *misericordia* and divinity. Given the Christian context of his belief in the incarnation of Christ, he could not help but do so. Consider the prayer *Salve mater Misericordiae*, which Aquinas would have regularly sung at Compline.[31] In it Mary, the mother of God, is described as *mater Misericordiae*, mother of Mercy, while Christ himself is identified with *Misericordia* itself—it is not so much that Christ has the attribute of *misericordia* but that Christ is identified as *misericordia* itself.[32] In addition, Aquinas argues that considered in itself, *misericordia* is the most godlike virtue.[33] But we cannot be like God in our *misericordia* if *misericordia* cannot be said of God Himself.

Much earlier in the *Summa* in question 21 of the first part discussing God's justice and *misericordia*, Aquinas explicitly considers the objection that *misericordia* cannot be attributed to God because it involves and is prompted by a passion that God cannot have as pure act. Aquinas grants the objection in part but rejects the conclusion. *Misericordia* is not attributed to God according to the passion suffered by human beings but is attributed to God as through divine action achieving the object of the virtue—namely, the alleviation of suffering. Aquinas will further argue that both justice and *misericordia* are found in all the works of God, including the act of creation itself, but considered on the part of the effect rather more *misericordia* than justice.[34] So if the only form of *misericordia* was the form associated with Aristotle's discussion of the passion of ἔλεος, Aquinas would find it impossible to sustain central biblically inspired theological claims and religious practices of prayer that he makes about and directs to God—that God is a god of *misericordia*.

However, this objection about divinity only pertains to the form of *misericordia* involving ἔλεος, because ἔλεος involves a passion, a passive being affected by. The other form of *misericordia* that Aquinas identifies is, on the contrary, much more suited to being attributed to God. It involves and is prompted by friendship for one who is suffering. As we have seen, Aristotle's discussion of ἔλεος is at best neutral with regard to friendship between the sufferer and the one who observes it and experiences ἔλεος. However, Aquinas grounds this second form of *misericordia* in the discussion of friendship in *NE*, where Aristotle writes that a mark of friendship is found in "one who grieves and rejoices with his friend."[35] Aristotle himself says this mark of friendship is particularly distinctive of friendship among mothers, although Aquinas ignores that claim in his use of the notion.

However, in this context Aristotle is not discussing ἔλεος but συναλγεῖν. In *NE* the simple mention without discussion of the passion ἔλεος is in book 2. The discussion of grieving with a friend is in the extensive discussion of friendship in book 9. Where ἔλεος refers to a passion, συναλγεῖν refers to an act—the act of grieving with a friend. And where ἔλεος is translated *misericordia*, συναλγεῖν is translated with the verb *condolere* in the Latin text of *NE* that Aquinas read, which when etymologically distinguished into *con* and *dolere*, specifically captures the sense of grieving with another.

The fact that the Latin text of Aristotle that Aquinas read has "*condolere,*" is significant. Had it had "*miserere,*" a broader term, one could readily understand why Aquinas would attribute to Aristotle an account of the virtue of *misericordia* in that text given the etymological similarity of the words *miserere* and *misericordia*. But the Latin text has "*condolere*," which means to grieve with. So reading the text as referring to *misericordia* represents a clear decision or choice on the part of Aquinas; it suggests more than a plain reading of Aristotle's text would suggest.

The words *condolere* and *miserere* may seem alike in meaning. So Aquinas might seem justified in treating the text as if it had "*miserere*." But *miserere* actually involves the notion of responding to a plea for assistance—acting, that is, to assist or alleviate. It is not obvious, however, that grieving with another requires that one act to alleviate the suffering of the one with whom one grieves. Think of the loss of a friend's child. One's friend is grieving for that loss. If one is childless, one will not fear the future loss of one's own children, so ἔλεος, which prompts φόβος, has no place here. And yet Aristotle recognizes one may grieve with a friend in the absence of a fear for oneself. Still, there is no suggestion in him of alleviating the misery of one's friend or that the grieving with the friend will itself alleviate that suffering.[36]

Indeed, Aristotle suggests that the possibility of this συναλγεῖν, this grieving with friends, is a reason to limit the scope of one's friendships. If one has many friends, one is more likely to be prompted to this grief with them. Conversely, he suggests that manliness requires of one that one not be the occasion of συναλγεῖν for one's friends. One should not be the cause of or welcome his or her weeping with one; after all, Aristotle suggests, it is particularly characteristic of the friendship of mothers, not men, and writes, "People of a manly nature guard against making their friends grieve with them. . . . In general such a man does not admit fellow-mourners because he is not himself given to mourning: but women and womanly men enjoy sympathizers in their grief, and love them as friends and companions in sorrow. But in all things one obviously ought to imitate the better type of person."[37] In both instances—one's own suffering or the suffering of a friend—one ought to limit one's friends to a small number, since it seems συναλγεῖν is to be avoided. So again, in Aristotle, it does not look to be an act associated with a virtue any more than ἔλεος was a passion associated with a virtue, a virtue the object of which is to alleviate the suffering of others.

However, Aquinas takes both ἔλεος and συναλγεῖν to be at the heart of *misericordia*, although in two very different ways. He distinguishes these two forms of *misericordia* by distinguishing two ways in which one might be related to the suffering of another. In the second article of question 30, he had written that in general, *misericordia* looks upon the suffering of another as one's own. This identification with the other in his or her pain already goes beyond Aristotle's description of ἔλεος, since in Aristotle, while one feels pain upon the occasion of the suffering of another, what it immediately prompts is not an identification with the other and a treatment of his suffering as one's own but fear for oneself and one's own future; in effect, in Aristotle's transition from ἔλεος to φόβος, one turns away from observing the present suffering of another to look to one's own future.

Aquinas, on the other hand, immediately distinguishes two ways in which one might look upon the distress of the other as one's own—two ways, that is, in which one might identify with the other's suffering. It may happen through what he describes as a "real union, for instance as when the injury of others is near to us so as to pass from them to us."[38] And here he explicitly relates this to the discussion in Aristotle of ἔλεος, citing *Rhetoric* that "human beings are distressed about those who are like them, because they judge that a similar thing may happen to them."[39] For Aquinas, that one fears a similar fate is the condition for this form of *misericordia*, just as it had been for ἔλεος in Aristotle.

The other way of being united to the suffering of another is "according to the union of affections which happens through love. Because the lover counts a friend as himself, he counts his [friend's] injury as his own injury, and so grieves (*dolet*) about his friend's injury as if it were his own."[40] The presence of grief stands out here as the key for associating this form of *misericordia* with συναλγεῖν. Aquinas concludes of both forms of *misericordia* that "therefore an injury is always the reason of being distressed, either because one looks upon the injury of another as one's own according to the union of love or because of the possibility of suffering in the same way."[41]

In the *misericordia* that springs from friendship, precisely because it involves friendship, there is no fear for oneself of future suffering; there is no fear for oneself precisely because one already treats the suffering of one's friend as one's own. His or her suffering just is my own—not that I may suffer someday but rather that I am suffering now. In addition, it is not confined to the powerful and well-off of society, for one can be friends with those who are not as well-off as one is, and there are friendships among those who are not well-off at all. Presumably it need not involve the actual undeserved loss of some good due to a turn of fortune, as a suffering may be suffering in grief for what one's friend never had but perhaps should have. It might even involve suffering in grief at a friend being justly punished, even as one acknowledges the justice of the punishment.[42] This last possibility is striking, since in Nussbaum's account of pity, it cannot be extended to those who are being justly punished. So there is no pity for a wretched offender against justice, but for Aquinas there can be *misericordia*.

Because the friendship that prompts this *misericordia* has a different scope of application from fear for oneself, it is appropriate to distinguish these two forms of *misericordia*, one associated with Aristotle's notion of ἔλεος and the other associated by Aquinas with Aristotle's notion of συναλγεῖν.

However, God qua divine cannot suffer a passion as human beings suffer passions. So the form of *misericordia* that involves fear for oneself cannot be attributed to God. On the other hand, while one may at first assume that the *misericordia* prompted by love and friendship involves an injury within oneself caused by observing the injury in one's friend, just as the other form of *misericordia* does, one can nevertheless at least ask the question whether such suffering within oneself is necessary in the specific sense of undergoing a passion. Can a friend treat an injury to a friend as his or her own without suffering an injury within himself or herself—without, that is, suffering what amounts to an additional injury, a doubling of the suffering as Nietzsche would later argue?[43] Or is the suffering of the friend itself sufficient to prompt *misericordia*?

Consider the inverse. A friend makes the good of the other his or her own. What does this mean? Does it mean that in the friend's achieving some good, there is a second instance or token of good within oneself that is also achieved? Or is it that in fact it is just the good of the other that is identically one's own good by one's friendly act of love identifying with the other? Aquinas thinks the latter is the case.[44] In friendship there need not be two instances of good, your good and my good that are related somehow; if I must have a second good within myself that I possess apart from you, even if caused by your good, your good is not truly my own through the identification of love. So there is but one instance of good that is your good and identically my good.[45] I will call this view the externality of the good in friendship to contrast it with the internal goods an individual achieves or acquires for himself or herself. There are goods external to one but internal to one's friends, the achievement of which by one's friends are one's own goods through identification precisely because they are external to one.

The case is similar with the *misericordia* that involves love and friendship. The harm that occurs to you is the harm that occurs to me, to which I respond with sorrow, not because there are two injuries—one in you and one in me—that are related, but because there is but the one injury in you that is yours and that is mine as well by an act of identification through love.[46] I will call this view the externality of suffering in friendship. The harm suffered by a friend cannot in friendship be one's own injury if it requires of necessity that another numerically distinct injury be caused within one. For it to be truly a friend suffering with a friend, it has to be the latter's very suffering, the friend's individual instance of suffering, that is the former's.

The externality of injury in friendship appears to be the only way to make sense of Aquinas' response to the first objection that concerned God. The objection argued that it is proper to God to be merciful. It tacitly relied upon the thesis that God as pure act cannot suffer an injury or harm, from which it concluded that an injury is not required in the one who acts from *misericordia*. Aquinas does not reject the conclusion of the objection but grants it, only to add in response that "it is only through love alone that God is distressed by our suffering, insofar as He loves us as belonging to him."[47] Because we belong to Him by love, our injuries belong to Him as His own. So love is sufficient for the injury of a friend to be one's own injury by identification without another second injury being done to one.

For Aquinas it is a contingent fact about *misericordia* that human beings very often do suffer an additional injury within themselves when their friends suffer, an injury that prompts the act of relieving suffering in one's friend. And yet for it to be *misericordia*, properly it must be the harm suffered by one's friend that one make's one's own and that prompts one to assist one's friend if one can. At least in the case of the divine, love suffices for the injuries done to those whom God loves to be His own. So when Aquinas claims that *misericordia* considered in itself is the highest of all virtues because it is the most godlike, it is clear that he has in mind this form of *misericordia* prompted by the love of friendship, not the self-interested *misericordia* associated with ἔλεος and fear for oneself. One is most like God not when one fears for oneself but when through love one is "distressed" by—that is, one sorrows with—one's friends at their injuries and hardships, through love adopting those injuries as one's own; one is not distressed by, does not sorrow at, one's own injuries conceived of as internal to oneself.

This difference between the two forms of *misericordia* provides two different contexts for the acts that one performs to alleviate the suffering of others. Consider the ἔλεος that prompts φόβος. Even though not discussed by Aristotle, why would acting for another to alleviate his or her suffering prompted by ἔλεος exhibit the sort of rationality characteristic of a virtue? It would seem that one acts to alleviate the suffering of the other out of a fear for oneself, out of a fear that one may suffer a similar fate in the future. But how would alleviating someone else's suffering in the here and now rationally and virtuously address one's fear for oneself in the future? Well, one might argue that by cultivating such a virtue in oneself and by example in others, if a similar fate did in fact befall one in the future, it too would be addressed by those others whose virtue of alleviating ἔλεος was learned from and inculcated by one's own.

Recall here the biblical injunction "Do unto others as you would have them do unto you." To coin a barbarous phrase, I will call this form of *misericordia* "eleotic *misericordia*." The virtue of *eleotic misericordia* is fundamentally self-directed. Its purpose is to alleviate one's own suffering and fear about the future by building a society in which others address the tragedies that befall one another. However, this virtue prompted by and appropriate to ἔλεος is not justice, the terminus of Nussbaum's pity tradition, because its scope is wider in addressing all sorts of suffering, not simply undeserved suffering.[48] While its aim is self-directed and self-interested, it has the good effect of alleviating the sufferings of others.

As the reference to the biblical injunction "Do unto others as you would have them do unto you" suggests, there is a place for such *eleotic misericordia* in understanding Scripture. Indeed, many of the contexts within which ἔλεος appears in Holy Scripture and its Hebrew equivalent of צדקה (*tsedaqa*)[49] display just that concern for the future for oneself that characterizes *eleotic misericordia*. Acts of charity associated with it in Scripture are often portrayed as instances of laying up treasure for oneself in Heaven. It is a kind of investment.[50] One provides for the needy in this life in the hope of a greater return on one's investment in Heaven, where God will justly reward those who have made that investment.[51] In effect, in this way of understanding the economy of salvation, God justly owes a debt in return to those who have displayed *eleotic misericordia* in this life.[52]

To the extent that classical Greek ἔλεος did not prompt action to alleviate the suffering observed, we see in Aquinas' discussion a filling out and thus partial transformation of its role from a merely passive emotional response toward agency prompted by compassion. On the other hand, Aquinas' discussion of *eleotic misericordia* does not fundamentally transform the classical source insofar as it suggests a kind of self-interested fearful looking to secure one's own future. Φόβος is still the operative passion doing the heavy moral lifting.

It is the other form of *misericordia* associated with συναλγεῖν that is fundamentally transformed by Aquinas against the background of Scripture. I can do no more than gesture at how it does so. Coining another and perhaps even more barbarous phrase, I will call this form of *misericordia* "synalgic *misericordia*." I have already placed a great deal of emphasis upon the importance in Aquinas of being able to say that God is merciful, indeed *misericordia* itself, and that the appropriate form for being able to do so is *synalgic misericordia*, not *eleotic misericordia*. What is important in the discussion of God is the emphasis that Aquinas places upon *misericordia* as giving rise to acts that alleviate suffering. It is in virtue of God being able to achieve the object of *misericordia*, the alleviation of suffering, that *misericordia* is attributed to God. This emphasis upon action to alleviate suffering was absent from Aristotle's discussion of ἔλεος and even his discussion of συναλγεῖν.

There is a difficulty here in Aquinas' account. Although attributing an analysis of the virtue to Aristotle, he actually employs Augustine to define it, quoting the latter writing in *The City of God* that "*misericordia* is compassion in our hearts for the suffering of another, by which of course we are compelled to assist if we can."[53] So Aquinas' authority for the emphasis upon action in *misericordia* turns out to be the theological authority of Augustine, not the philosophical authority of Aristotle.

Still, there is a problem with the appeal to Augustine in looking for a biblical origin for the emphasis upon action—namely, that Augustine himself appeals not to Scripture in forming this definition but rather to the philosophical context of Cicero praising Caesar for his clemency or forgiveness.[54] However, Augustine is at worst misreading or at best charitably reading Cicero because the actual discussion in Cicero is about judicial clemency, which in Cicero is quite different from *misericordia*. Cicero, in some ways reflecting the forensic techniques of Aristotle's *Rhetoric*, is trying to get Caesar to lessen the punishment he has imposed upon the traitorous general Liguria, and he is using the term *misericordia* for what Seneca will later define as *clementia*. Indeed, in pleading on behalf of Liguria, Cicero appeals to Caesar's sense of his own greatness to show his power by granting pardon,[55] just as Seneca will urge Nero to grant *clementia*. On the other hand, in the *Tusculan Disputations*, Cicero abuses the *misericordia* that suffers with others, describing it as a mental illness in a way that sets the stage for Seneca's abuse of it a century later.[56]

More than the influence of Aristotle or Augustine, the key to understanding Aquinas' transformation of *misericordia* is the biblical notion of friendship that he relies on. The heart of *synalgic misericordia*, distinguishing it from *eleotic misericordia*, concerns the role of friendship in the former and its absence in the latter. With *eleotic misericordia* I suggested the importance of its relationship to the biblical injunction "Do unto others as you would have them do unto you." That injunction occurs twice in the Gospels, once at Matthew 7:9-12 and the other at Luke 6:31-36. On its surface it has a self-directed character. If you would like to be treated in such and such fashion, then treat others in that same fashion. In his scriptural commentary on the text of Matthew, Aquinas says very little about this injunction except to paraphrase it as concerning the forgiveness one would like to receive.[57] If you would like to be forgiven, forgive others. You are storing up God's debt to you by forgiving others.[58] Friendship for the one who suffers or is in need of forgiveness appears to play no role in the text from Matthew. Luke, however, is different, for there the injunction is associated with *misericordia*[59] and specified as involving, among other things, the love of enemies.

With *synalgic misericordia* the relevant biblical injunction is "Love your neighbor as yourself." That injunction occurs in Matthew 22:39, Mark 12:31, and Luke 10:25-37. In both Matthew and Mark, it is described as the greatest commandment after loving God, summarizing with the love of God the whole of the law and the prophets. It is particularly significant, however, that it is not restricted to or concerned specifically with forgiveness as the previous injunction more clearly seems to be but is much more general. In his commentary on Matthew, Aquinas points out that the statement raises the question of who counts as a neighbor when it says "love your neighbor." The answer Aquinas writes is to be found in Luke 10:27 with the parable of the Good Samaritan. He says "neighbor" means all those to whom we ought to show *misericordia* and who ought to show us the same.[60] And yet who are they?

In the story of the Good Samaritan, Aquinas' point is confirmed and given greater specification. Both the priest and the Levite pass by the man set upon by thieves, each perhaps moved by fear to avoid ritual impurity by coming into contact with what might turn out to be a dead body[61] and thus taking the "other side." But the Samaritan "is moved by a distressed heart"[62] and thus moves toward the man to come to his aid. So in response to Christ's question "Who was neighbor to the man?" the "man of the law," who had initially asked Christ the question "Who is my neighbor?" responds in Luke's Greek, "Ὁ ποιήσας τὸ ἔλεος," which is translated in the Latin Aquinas read as "qui fecit misericordiam"—that is, "the one who accomplished *misericordia*." Notice the transition in the text from being first moved by *misericordia* as a passion to achieving *misericordia* as an act.

There is a striking reversal here when Christ does not answer the man of the law with an assertion but a question—"Who was neighbor to the man?" The man of the law is looking for a characteristic in the other to determine whom he should love as his neighbor—that is, whom he should love as himself and presumably whom, by the absence of that characteristic, he should not. Christ's reversal of the question ignores the man of the law's question, or better, inverts it, as if to take it for granted that the other, the ανθρωπός, the human being, is simply to be loved as oneself—not because of some characteristic he does or does not have, but simply because he is human. Thus Christ, taking it for granted that an ανθρωπός who suffers is one's neighbor, inverts the original question to ask instead, "Are you neighbor to him?"

What Christ's reversal of the question accomplishes is that it focuses upon the man of the law to ask him what characteristic he, the man of the law, must have to be a neighbor to those whom he meets—what characteristic must he have to be one who loves others as himself? What must I be like to love others as I should? And the answer to Christ's question, as given by the man of the law, is straightforward—I must be a man of *misericordia*. So the virtue of *misericordia* is fundamental for understanding the second great commandment. This Aquinas captures in his commentary when he writes that "neighbor" means all those to whom we ought to show *misericordia* and who ought to show us the same.

It is clear from the story that despite the Greek word ἔλεος in Luke, this *misericordia* is not what I have identified as *eleotic misericordia*. The Samaritan does not show fear for himself and his future in approaching the man. He is not characterized as a man of courage who persists in a difficult task despite his fear. It is the priest and the Levite who appear to experience fear, and their fear drives them away from the man to the other side, while the Samaritan is simply described as "moved by a distressed heart" toward the man. The heart of the story focuses upon the point that *misericordia* is directed to any human being who suffers, involves being distressed by that suffering, and is expressed in acts that alleviate that suffering.

In this respect it is important that the man set upon by thieves is not described in any actual detail except as "a human being." He is an "ανθρωπός" in Greek and "*homo*" in Latin. The only characteristic attributed to the human being is that he is suffering. For the purpose of the great commandment, one's neighbor is anyone who suffers. So Christ gives specification to the commandment—love as yourself those who suffer; one is not a neighbor to fellow human beings if one lacks *misericordia*.

In the commentary on Matthew 22:39, Aquinas continues referring to this text of Luke, specifying that it does not mean that one should love the sufferer as much as one loves oneself, which he thinks is contrary to the order of charity. The point of the text is that answering the question "Who is my neighbor?" specifies one's end or *telos* as that which one is to desire, love, and act on behalf of. Because God as beloved friend is one's end, one loves also that which belongs to God. Other humans belong to God, not as possessions and not as instrumental means to achieve the love of God, but as standing in the relation of friendship with Him, the sense of belonging we have in mind when saying something like, "He belongs to their fellowship." So in particular, the parable of the Good Samaritan specifies that those who suffer are to be loved as one's own end for their sake as among the friends of God. As one's end, one is to love the sufferer for God's sake, just as one is to love God for God's sake; by loving them, one loves God and achieves one's end. So your neighbor, your friend, is the human being who suffers; achieving your end then consists in addressing that suffering "moved by a distressed heart."

Two contexts for the discussion of friendship in the *Summa* help shed light on the parable and Aquinas' understanding of it. One is a response to an objection in the discussion of the virtue of friendship. The objector suggests that to treat a stranger as a friend involves a kind of deception, since the point of characterizing him as a stranger is that he is not a friend. Aquinas responds that there is a kind of natural friendship among all human beings that precedes questions of who is and who is not in fact a stranger to one. Even if someone is unknown to one, he or she is nonetheless a friend by nature. Here Aquinas does not appeal to Aristotle's philosophical authority, even though perhaps he could have.[63] On the contrary, he appeals to biblical authority, quoting Sirach 13:15 that "every animal loves its kind; and this love is represented by exterior signs of love which one shows in words and deeds even to strangers and those unknown to us."[64] The human being fallen along the road that one just happens upon is of course a paradigmatic instance of a stranger unknown to one.

Thus however much modern and secularizing philosophical reflection upon pity may be understood to depart from medieval religious thought, the claim that the universalizing of compassionate concern for others, extending it to all human beings, is a distinct and original contribution of figures like Rousseau and Smith apart from the Christian tradition that precedes them simply cannot be sustained, unless perhaps one restricts the nature of such concern to the narrow sense of pity or *eleotic misericordia* that is motivated by fear for oneself.

The other setting is in the question devoted to the precepts of *caritas*, question 44 of the second part of the second part of the *Summa*. There are two precepts of *caritas*, and they are expressed by the two great commandments. Article 7 asks whether the precept to love one's neighbor as oneself is suitably given; the first objection says it is unsuitably given because while "the love of *caritas* is extended to all human beings even to our enemies,"[65] the term *neighbor* signifies a closeness that does not similarly extend to all.

However, Aquinas argues in response that the precept is suitably given. Echoing his commentary on Matthew, he writes, "The manner of love is touched upon when [the precept] says 'as oneself.' Which ought not to be understood as 'as much as oneself' as if one loves a neighbor equally to oneself, but [rather] in a manner similar to oneself . . . on the part of the end, as one loves a neighbor according to God [as end], just as one ought to love oneself according to God [as end]—this is a holy love of neighbor."[66] Again, the love of neighbor is one's end or *telos* as part of the love of God to whom one's neighbor belongs through the bond of divine and human friendship.

Aquinas had first written in response, "The reason for loving is touched upon when he is called 'neighbor,' for according to charity we ought to love others because they are our neighbors both with regard to the natural image of God and according to the capacity for glory." From question 93 of the first part of the *Summa*, we know that all human beings are images of God in the first place according to their rational nature,[67] which as we have seen is the basis also of their natural friendship for one another. So the affection of neighborly love is universalized by human nature because of the image of God to be found in all as well as the common destiny of all for glory in beatitude and felicity.[68] Aquinas immediately adds in 44.7, "And it does not matter whether he is called 'neighbor' or 'brother' according to 1 John IV or 'friend' according to Leviticus 19, because all of these express the same affinity." Leviticus 19 is the Old Testament source for the discussion in the Gospels of the second great commandment. So in response to the objection about loving enemies, Aquinas simply says, "This response suffices for the objection." One is to love one's enemy as one's neighbor, friend, or brother.

This passage from 44.7 is very significant for understanding the difference between *eleotic misericordia* and *synalgic misericordia*. In the former, one is moved and motivated by seeing in the other a likeness of oneself. In the latter, one is moved and motivated by seeing in the other a likeness of God, a participation in the divine. This shift from the likeness of oneself to the likeness of God then is a genuine development departing from Greek ἔλεος to *synalgic misericordia*. Greek ἔλεος was not associated with friendship but with fear for oneself, as is the *eleotic misericordia* that Aquinas recognizes. And Aristotle's συναλγεῖν, while associated with friendship, was of narrow extent, not extending to all human beings but rather, a reason for limiting one's friendship to a very small group. Neither involved acting to alleviate suffering.

Aquinas' *synalgic misericordia* is like Nussbaum's pity in this respect: it is of universal extent taking all human beings within its scope. But it is unlike Nussbaum's pity in at least three respects. *Synalgic misericordia* involves no fear for oneself, it involves friendship, and it is intrinsically ordered toward alleviating the suffering of those friends motivated by suffering with them through the union of love. Thus Aquinas is giving a deeper specification of the nature of friendship as of universal extent and intrinsically specified by the virtue of *misericordia*.

Here is the last point. Aquinas acknowledges and welcomes the association of *misericordia* with weeping. The fact that weeping was associated with *misericordia* was a reason for the ancient Stoics to reject it as a virtue, since they thought weeping a sign of weakness, a mental illness or vice, where a virtue is precisely a strength. Seneca went so far as to associate it with the tears of "wretched and old women," and he mocked a friend for weeping over the death of a son.[69] Yet Aquinas, describing the "union of affections" in question IaIIae.30 and its bearing upon the suffering of others, cites Romans 12:15: "Rejoice with those who rejoice; we weep with those who weep."[70]

According to Scripture, Christ wept just before he raised Lazarus from the dead. In the story of Lazarus from the gospel of John, Christ refers to Lazarus as "our friend." Furthermore, Christ is presented as the friend of Mary and Martha as well. So Christ weeps over the death of his friend and for his friends who have lost their brother; he sorrows over Lazarus and grieves with Mary and Martha. In the commentary on John, Aquinas cites Romans 12:15 again and argues explicitly that Christ by his tears teaches against the Stoics in particular that weeping for a friend is indeed rational and an expression of virtue, although excessive weeping is not.[71] And yet Christ's *misericordia* for his friends is not exhausted by his sorrow for Lazarus and grieving with Mary and Martha, as one would have in simple Aristotelian συναλγεῖν. Christ acts with *synalgic misericordia* to alleviate the suffering of his friends by raising Lazarus from the dead. What the story of Lazarus presents is the nature of *synalgic misericordia* as involving action to alleviate suffering to the extent that one can, motivated by friendship for those who suffer. Where the theatergoer contemplates human suffering out of fear for himself, the *misericors* sees in the face of the other, another human being, a friend who suffers and acts to alleviate that suffering out of love.

According to the metaphysics of divinity that Aquinas argues for, Christ cannot weep according to the impassible divine nature that he has.[72] He can only weep according to the human nature he possesses that is the result of His incarnation. Where divinity as such does not allow for the experience of compassion, Christ who is divine experiences it through his humanity.[73] What is significant about this metaphysical point is that the incarnation and what follows from it are the expression of the act of divine *misericordia* by which God acts to alleviate the suffering of the human beings whose suffering belongs to Him through the union of love, which is friendship. It is because God has made us, indeed created us as His friends, because He is and acts as our neighbor, that our suffering belongs to Him as his own through the union of love, and He acts to alleviate that suffering.[74] The "man of the law" is commanded to go and do likewise, to love those who suffer and alleviate that suffering to the extent possible.

So in the case of Christ, the passion signified by His weeping does not precede and prompt the divine act of alleviating suffering, as in human *eleotic misericordia*.[75] On the contrary, His compassion follows from the divine act of alleviating suffering, which springs from the prior divine act of friendship, *synalgic misericordia*, for all human beings. In *synalgic misericordia*, one does not suffer first and then act to alleviate suffering;[76] one has already begun the act of *misericordia* simply by the original act of love by which one identifies with others in friendship and then adopts both their good and their suffering as one's own.

Aquinas writes in his commentary on John that in almost every act of Christ, something of his humanity is made manifest and something of his divinity.[77] From Christ's humanity He expresses compassion and weeps with them that weep. But from His divinity, he acts to alleviate the suffering of those for whom He weeps. In *eleotic misericordia* we suffer and fear for ourselves upon observing the suffering of another, and perhaps to eliminate that fear, we act to alleviate the suffering. However, in *synalgic misericordia* we suffer in compassion for our friends and even weep for them, but we do not experience fear. On the contrary, in our love, in our friendship for our neighbor—every human being who suffers—we are an image of Christ's humanity; we are men and women of *misericordia*. Even more so, when in the friendship of *synalgic misericordia*, we act to alleviate the suffering of our neighbor; we are an image of Christ's divinity.

This is *mercy* beyond fear; as Aquinas describes it, it is the fulfillment and superabundance of justice,[78] but it is not a justice among abstract or imagined likenesses of oneself; it is a justice among all human beings as friends in the image and likeness of God, particularly the images of God in the world who suffer.

Conclusion

The point here is not to "give credit where credit is due," as if to give the responsibility for positing the universal scope of compassionate concern for one's fellow human beings to Aquinas as opposed to Rousseau or Smith. Nussbaum emphasizes the existence of a "pity tradition" in which universalization is a rather late stage. However, Aquinas himself was operating within the context of a tradition, what I will call the tradition of *misericordia*, a tradition within which the universal scope of *synalgic misericordia* was a foundational principle.

Unfortunately, Aquinas does not give us a direct commentary on Luke. But in the *Catena Aurea* section on the Good Samaritan, it is clear from his choice of texts that like the authors he quotes, he thinks the Samaritan is a figure of Christ.[79] So the command with which the parable ends—the command to the "man of the law" to go and do likewise—is a command to be Christlike. And to be Christlike is to recognize that your neighbor, your brother, your friend, is any ανθρωπός, any *homo*, any human being one encounters and who may suffer.

Against the background of this tradition of *misericordia*, in which Aquinas plays a significant part between Sirach, Luke, and Rousseau, Nussbaum's pity tradition cannot help but look like a move away from that tradition; now those who suffer are no longer seen as one's friends, thus falling back to an older Greek tradition of a self-interested ἔλεος animated by fear while at the same time attempting not to lose the universal scope of the newer tradition of *synalgic misericordia* even as it turns away from it.[80] Perhaps Nussbaum tacitly acknowledges this nostalgic aspect of the pity tradition, as she argues that the Greek vision of fear, and similar possibilities that animate it but also limit its scope, is not essential to it but merely a causal and motivating psychological factor that can presumably be done away with, and yet the lack of friendship remains.

"When men are friends they have no need of justice, while when they are just they need friendship as well, and the truest form of justice is thought to be a friendly quality."[81] Aquinas' reflection from within the tradition of *misericordia* upon the phenomenon of solidarity in suffering, employing in a particularly clear and systematic way both philosophical and biblical sources, provides an argument for a distinct virtue of *misericordia* that goes beyond justice, is not reducible to it, and springs from universal human friendship. If philosophical reasoning is deepened and enriched by operating within and from a tradition, as Nussbaum's reflections upon the pity tradition both suggest and exemplify, it is important that such a tradition not artificially cut itself off from its many real sources.

Bibliography

Anderson, Gary A. *Charity*. New Haven: Yale University Press, 2013.

Augustine of Hippo. *Concerning the City of God against the Pagans*. Translated by Henry Bettenson. London: Penguin Books, 2003.

Bauckham, Richard. "The Scrupulous Priest and the Good Samaritan: Jesus' Parabolic Interpretation of the Law of Moses." *New Testament Studies* 44 (1998): 475–89.

Cicero. "On Behalf of Ligarius." In *The Speeches with an English Translation*, translated by N. H. Watts, 458–93. London: William Heinemann, 1931.

———. *Tusculan Disputations*. Translated by J. E. King. London: William Heinemann, 1927.

Curley, Augustine. "Cicero, Marcus Tullius." In *Augustine through the Ages: An Encyclopedia*, edited by Allan D. Fitzgerald, O.S.A., 190–93. Grand Rapids: Eerdmans, 1999.

Gallagher, David. "Thomas Aquinas on Self-Love as the Basis for Love of Others." *Acta Philosophica* 8 (1999): 31.

Jones, W. H. S. *Pausanias Description of Greece with an English Translation*. 6 vols. London: William Heinemann, 1931.

Konstan, David. *Pity Transformed*. London: Gerald Duckworth, 2001.

Nietzsche, Friedrich. *Daybreak: Thoughts on the Prejudices of Morality*. Edited by Maudemarie Clark and Brian Leiter. Translated by R. J. Hollingdale. Cambridge: Cambridge University Press, 1997.

Nussbaum, Martha. "Compassion: Human and Animal." In *Ethics and Humanity: Themes from the Philosophy of Jonathan Glover*, edited by N. Ann David, Richard Keshen, and Jeff McMahan, 202–26. Oxford: Oxford University Press, 2010.

———. "Compassion: The Basic Social Emotion." *Social Philosophy and Policy* 13, no. 1 (1996): 27–58.

———. "Equity and Mercy." *Philosophy and Public Affairs* 22 (1993): 83–125.

———. "Pity and Mercy: Nietzsche's Stoicism." In *Nietzsche, Genealogy, Morality: Essays on Nietzsche's Genealogy of Morals*, edited by Richard Schacht, 139–67. Berkeley: University of California Press, 1994.

———. "Tragedy and Self-Sufficiency: Plato and Aristotle on Fear and Pity." *Oxford Studies in Ancient Philosophy* 10 (1992): 108–59.

———. *Upheavals of Thought*. Cambridge: Cambridge University Press, 2001.

O'Callaghan, John. "Imago Dei: A Test Case for St. Thomas' Augustinianism." In *Aquinas the Augustinian*, edited by Michael Dauphninais, Barry David, and Matthew Levering, 100–144. Washington, D.C.: Catholic University of America Press, 2007.

———. "*Misericordia* in Aquinas: A Test Case for Theological and Natural Virtues." In *Jaarboek Thomas Instituut te Utrecht: 2013*, edited by Henk J. M. Schoot, 9–54. Utrecht: Thomas Institute te Utrecht, 2014.

———. "The Quality of Mercy: *Misericordia* and Three Forms of Forgiveness in Aquinas." In *The Virtuous Life: Thomas Aquinas on the Theological Nature of Moral Virtues*, edited by Henk Schoot and Harm Goris, 201–20. Louvain, Belgium: Peeters, 2015.

Oele, Marjolein. "Suffering, Pity and Friendship: An Aristotelian Reading of Book 24 of Homer's *Iliad*." *Electronic Antiquity* 14, no. 1 (2010): 63.

Rawls, John. "Justice as Fairness." *Philosophical Review* 67, no. 2 (1958): 164–94.

———. *A Theory of Justice*. Cambridge, Mass.: Harvard University Press, 1971.

Seneca. "De Clementia." In *Seneca: Moral Essays with an English Translation*, translated by John W. Basore, 356–447. London: William Heinemann, 1985.

———. *Seneca Ad Lucilium Epistulae Morales*. Translated by Richard M. Gummere. London: William Heinemann, 1925.

Statius. *Thebaid with an English Translation by J. H. Mozley*. 2 vols. Cambridge, Mass.: Harvard University Press, 1989.

Thomas Aquinas. *Sententia libri ethicorum*. Rome: Leonine, 1969.
———. *Super Evangelium S. Ioannis: Lectura*. Turin: Marietti, 1952.
Torrell, Jean-Pierre. *Saint Thomas Aquinas*. Vol. 1, *The Person and His Work*, rev. ed., translated by Robert Royal. Washington, D.C.: Catholic University of America Press, 2005.
Vessey, Mark, ed. *A Companion to Augustine*. West Sussex: John Wiley, 2012.

4

THE PROBLEM OF JUSTICE
Anscombe, Solomon, and Radical Virtue Ethics

Thomas Hibbs

Some years ago, Charles Taylor raised questions about the ability of the dominant Kantian and utilitarian schools of ethics to account for the "diversity of goods."[1] Similar criticisms of what might be called decision-procedure models of ethics can be found in the writings of a number of mid- to late twentieth-century moral philosophers and date back at least to the concluding paragraphs of Elizabeth Anscombe's "Modern Moral Philosophy."[2] Virtue ethics arose in part as a way of offering a better account of the diversity of goods. Yet how precisely to read Anscombe's essay is not entirely clear. Should we read it as the introductory foray in a battle between utilitarians and Kantians, on the one hand, and virtue ethicists, on the other, over who has the most compelling normative theory of ethics? Or should we read it as a more thoroughgoing repudiation of all modern moral philosophy? In an essay titled "Virtue Ethics: Radical or Routine?" David Solomon asserts, "There is no doubt that Elizabeth Anscombe thought that the return to virtue she advocated in 'Modern Moral Philosophy' would be anything but routine. Her thundering indictment of twentieth-century analytic ethics as well as her claim that there was no substantial differences among all of the 'main' moral philosophers following Sidgwick should assure her of a place among the revolutionaries."[3] In a series of essays, some of which respond to criticisms of virtue ethics, Solomon has attempted to clarify what is at stake in the revival of virtue. That is, he has tried to clarify the very idea of a virtue ethics.[4]

According to Solomon, an ethics of virtue stands in opposition to an ethics of rules or principles. Yet as Candace Vogler points out, one of Anscombe's strongest objections against utilitarianism is that it cannot make sense of moral prohibitions.[5] Vogler argues that the development of a defensible case for moral prohibitions is precisely what Anscombe's famous essay calls for.

Now throughout the essay, Anscombe focuses on questions of justice, a topic that is often seen as a source of vulnerability for virtue ethics. As is commonly known, virtue ethics has been accused of focusing exclusively on goods of the agent and downplaying or completely ignoring the goods of others; it has also been faulted for not having what Larry Louden calls an account of "intolerable acts." Yet the tradition of virtue is not without resources. For Thomas Aquinas, who has accounts both of the virtues and of the duties of the natural law, justice ranks as a preeminent virtue, whose peculiar focus is on the good of others. Moreover, diversity of types of obligation and complexity in the standards of the appraisal of human action enter into the very heart of Aquinas' account of justice; in contrast to the modern tendency toward a homogeneous account of justice, Aquinas recognizes a diversity of goods falling under the virtue of justice itself.

What follows is a "quick and dirty" examination of Aquinas on justice with an eye to situating his project in relation to Anscombe's and to determining whether Thomas meets the Solomonic criteria for a radical rather than a merely routine ethics of virtue.

Taylor in Defense of the Diversity of Goods

Focusing primarily on the rise of utilitarianism and secondarily on that of Kantianism, Charles Taylor's essay "The Diversity of Goods" begins by probing the appeal of the two dominant ethical theories in the modern period. In addition to its this-worldly humanist focus and its concern with suffering, Taylor highlights utilitarianism's epistemological appeal—a theory apparently grounded in hard evidence with a conceptually unproblematic understanding of what counts as human happiness and a lucid calculus for determining what ought to be done. Similarly, Kantian formalism offers a clear "underlying model of validation." Both "allow us to ignore the problematic distinctions between different qualities of action or modes of life, which play such a large part in our actual moral decisions." They offer the "hope of deciding ethical questions without having to determine which of a number of rival languages of moral virtue and vice, of the admirable and the contemptible, of unconditional versus conditional obligation, are valid." Taylor calls these "rival languages" the "languages of qualitative contrast."[6] With Kantianism and utilitarianism, the supposition, he goes on to explain, is that "you could finesse all this, if you could determine the cases where a maxim of action would be unrealizable if everyone adopted it, or where its universal realization was something you could not possibly desire; or if you could determine what actions you could approve no matter whose standpoint you adopted of those persons affected; or if you could circumscribe the principles that would be adopted by free rational agents in certain paradigm circumstances."[7]

Decision-procedure models of ethics, of which Kantianism and utilitarianism are examples, promise a way of eliminating or bypassing contention over rival versions of the good. In place of heterogeneity, there would be uniformity; in place of diversity, unity. As Taylor notes, the attraction of these theories is not just their apparent mimicking of scientific models of rationality but also their articulation of "substantive moral insights." Kantian formalism rests on the "universal attribution of moral personality," just as utilitarianism embraces the modern claim that there is "no defensible distinction between different classes of human beings" or that "each should count for one and only one."[8]

But this is not the only substantive moral insight on which we draw in our daily lives. We invoke, at least implicitly, a host of principles or ideals that inform our thinking about what is "morally higher or lower, noble or base, admirable or contemptible."[9] Taylor's use of the adverb "morally" is significant. The point is that the insights undergirding utilitarian and Kantian theories do not have an exclusive purchase on the notion of the moral. Only by stipulation can we relegate other insights to the category of the nonmoral. The languages of qualitative contrast can generate not just different conceptions of what it means to lead a noble or admirable human life but divergent and incompatible accounts of obligation. Indeed, "rational" as used by utilitarians is a term of a qualitative contrast: "It is the basis of moral admiration and contempt; it is a goal worthy of respect. The fact that it finds no place in their own meta-theory says a lot about the value of this theory."[10]

On the basis of these reflections, Taylor concludes, "the ethical is not a homogeneous domain, with a single kind of good, based on a single kind of consideration." Instead, there are at least three such domains. The first is that of utility, which accentuates what is productive of human happiness, while the second is that of moral personality in Kantianism.[11] Interestingly, these two theories often reach incompatible conclusions about what is morally obligatory for human agents. The fact that there are competing decision procedures, with incommensurable methods and incompatible conclusions, should give us pause. Might it be the case that the appeal in the realm of human action to scientific rationality is not as self-evident as it initially seems? If it delivers incompatible models and conclusions, it leaves us no better off than we were before the modern project got off the ground.

Taylor adds a third source, the languages of qualitative contrast, the languages we deploy to describe the noble and the base, the admirable and the contemptible. Now Taylor is somewhat ambiguous on the relationship of Kantianism and utilitarianism to the languages of qualitative contrast. Sometimes he speaks as if Kantianism and utilitarianism were on one side of a divide and the languages of qualitative contrast were on the other. Insofar as the former group attempts to escape the messiness of the languages of qualitative contrast, there is a divide. But sometimes he speaks as if they were all just different languages of qualitative contrast. One of Taylor's insights is that the languages of qualitative contrast underlie and sometimes inform utilitarianism and Kantianism. So if we step back from the theories and ask what would motivate us to embrace one or the other, we might say that it is the promise of quasi-scientific rationality combined with some element, say happiness or dignity, derived from our ordinary experience and initially embedded with the languages of qualitative contrast. There is a sense in which what we are in fact dealing with is a large set of contrasting qualitative discourses, two of which claim to offer an exit from the fuzzy and endlessly contentious realm of qualitative discourse.

Taylor includes virtue and vice within the languages of qualitative contrast; the recovery of virtue helps rescue the languages of qualitative contrast from oblivion. But how does the language of virtue and vice, rescued by contemporary ethicists, stand in relation to the decision-procedure models? Solomon spells out the basic alternative this way. On one view, the alternative account, say a virtue account, would be "structurally similar to the revival of neo-Kantian and consequentialist normative theories in that it is a return to the kinds of questions to which the comprehensive nineteenth-century normative theories were responding. It would then be operating on the same theoretical stage, as it were, with these other normative theories—asking the same questions, but giving different answers.... It would be, relative to other normative theorizing, merely routine." Alternatively, "one could see the turn to virtue as harking back to the kind of classical approach to moral philosophy that characterized the aims of that enterprise in a quite different way from the way in which they are characterized typically within modern moral philosophy. This would make the turn to virtue radical indeed."[12]

Taylor does not in this essay develop any alternative. Having punctured the modern claims to have escaped heterogeneity or to have eliminated the moral relevance of the diversity of goods, Taylor pauses to note that the "habit of treating the moral as a single domain is not just gratuitous or based on a mere mistake. The domain of ultimately important goods has a sort of prescriptive unity. Each of us has to answer all these demands in the course of a single life, and this means that we have to find some way of assessing their relative validity, or putting them in an order of priority."[13] But there are at least two ways of understanding "putting" in order. Taylor describes one way thus: the "really important question may turn out to be how we combine in our lives at least two or three different goals, or virtues, or standards, which we feel we cannot repudiate but which seem to demand incompatible things of us."[14] This, I would suggest, is not so much ordering as it is navigating or juggling conflicting claims.

Taylor's essay could, however, be seen as setting a task for ethical theory—namely, to discern so far as possible a unified account of the human good that embraces rather than denies, and includes rather than excludes, the diversity of goods. A principle articulated by Jacques Maritain, the famous French Catholic philosopher from the last century, is pertinent here: distinguish in order to unite. In Aristotelian terms, what we need is an account that saves the phenomena rather than erases them, an account that reflects and clarifies practice; thus it would have to encompass both the diversity of goods and the natural, practical task of discerning some sort of unity within the diversity. Now Taylor seems at least mildly skeptical of this, in part because he thinks this leads quite naturally to the sort of arbitrary, absolutist distinctions between the moral and the nonmoral that it is the burden of his essay to undermine. But it should be said that such a project is built into the languages of qualitative contrast as Taylor describes them, for these languages make demands upon us—whether we construe these demands as moral or not—and they frequently demand, as Taylor also notes, that we sacrifice lower goods for higher ones, partial goods for more complete goods. Furthermore, these languages, as Taylor points out specifically in the case of Marxism, often see unity not as a given of human life but as a promised result of "radical change."[15]

What Taylor does not mention here (although it is, I think, implicit in what he says) is that the emergence of utilitarianism and Kantianism presupposes a shift within the languages of qualitative contrast, an accentuation of one of the virtues—namely, justice—at the expense of the other virtues. Justice has always been a contender for supremacy among the virtues; the very fact that it brings order not just to the internal state of the soul but also to our external relations to others and that it is constitutive of the common good of the political realm has bestowed upon it an elevated status. In the modern period, the demand for justice, the desire for a justification of the political order accessible across the divisions over the languages of qualitative contrast, comes to override the demands of the goods articulated within the languages of qualitative contrast, hence the appeal of the decision-procedure models of ethics.

The Rise of Virtue Ethics

Well before Taylor's essay, Elizabeth Anscombe had already mounted a scathing attack on these models of ethics. In "Modern Moral Philosophy," Anscombe offers a critique of the midcentury focus in moral philosophy on the moral ought. Having argued that the notion of the "moral ought" has "no reasonable sense outside a law conception of ethics," Anscombe proposes that "it would be a great improvement if, instead of 'morally wrong,' one always named a genus such as 'untruthful,' 'unchaste,' 'unjust.' We should no longer ask whether doing something was 'wrong,' passing directly from some description of an action to this notion; we should ask whether, e.g., it was unjust; and the answer would sometimes be clear at once."[16] Virtue ethics can in part be traced to this passage in Anscombe's short essay. Its appeal has something to do with the diversity of assessments the virtues afford as well as their greater proximity to concrete instances of human action. The virtues are thus seen to be superior in the arena in which they appeared most vulnerable at the outset of modernity: epistemology. They aid in the identification of the precise, concrete, and complex sources of good and bad action. To suggest that an ethics of virtue should be judged by the standards of modern ethical theory would be to render it merely routine. While she is certainly addressing modern ethics, Anscombe's critique cuts quite deeply. As Solomon puts it, "the suggestion," prevalent in Anscombe's essay, "that deontological theories and consequentialist theories are simply minor variations on a style of modern moral theorizing to which an ethics of virtue is radically opposed is a common feature of those virtue theories" we should "regard as radical."[17]

It is now common to locate an array of premodern ethicists, including Thomas Aquinas, in the virtue camp. But Thomas is also famous for his development of an account of natural law. Some, including some scholars of Thomas Aquinas, have supposed that an account of rules could provide all that is needed. John Finnis, for example, speaks of the "principles which prudence uses to transform the first principles of the natural law."[18] By contrast to Finnis, consider the words of another scholar of Thomas Aquinas, Yves Simon:

> If law is a premise rather than a conclusion, if, universally, law admits of no immediate contact with the world of action, the ideal of a social science which would, in each particular case, procure a rational solution and render governmental prudence unnecessary is thoroughly deceptive. Whatever the science of man and of society has to say remains at an indeterminate distance from the world of action, and this distance can be traversed only by the most obscure methods of prudence which involve ... the power of sound inclinations. In a judgment marked by singularity and contingency we recognize features opposite to those of law. Between law and action there always is space to be filled by decisions which cannot be written into law.[19]

On this reading of Thomas, he would seem to embrace the principal "themes," as Solomon calls them, of radical virtue ethics: a suspicion of rules and principles as adequate to guiding human action; a turn for an understanding of the ethical life to concrete terms like the virtues; a focus on the importance of the whole life as the primary object of ethical evaluation in contrast to the tendency of Kantian and consequentialist theorists to give primacy to the evaluation of actions or more fragmented features of human lives; an emphasis on the narrative structure of human life as opposed to the more episodic picture of human life found in neo-Kantian and consequentialist approaches to ethics; an emphasis on the centrality of contingently based special relationships, especially with friends and family, for the ethical life in contrast to the tendency within neo-Kantian and consequentialist theories to downplay such relationships in favor of alienating ideals of universality; and a special emphasis on thick moral education understood as involving training in the virtues as opposed to models of moral education frequently associated with neo-Kantian and consequentialist moral theories that tend to emphasize growth in autonomy or in detached instrumental rationality.[20]

Thomas' affirmation of Solomon's virtue themes follows from his insistence on the primacy of prudence. For Thomas, it is prudence that commands what is to be done in concrete circumstances. The precepts of the law are universals; they do not apply themselves to specific acts, as Simon intimates. Prudence determines that an act is done in the right way, for the right reason, and at the right time. Prudence requires experience, memory, and practice in perception.[21] Moreover, a virtuous act arises from a character that has been formed in accord with virtue; it is not sufficient merely to perform the external act of virtue. The act must flow from a proper intention and from a fixed character. That in turn requires the reformation of the passions, so that the passions incline toward virtue rather than resisting the judgment of prudence. The famous mean of virtuous action is not so much an abstract proportion as it is a metaphor for an action that is done properly in every respect. Apprehending the mean involves an attunement to "diverse circumstances."[22] In actions we must consider who acted; by what aids or instruments the act was done; what was done; and where, why, how, and when the act was performed.[23] That Thomas is committed to an account of the moral life in terms of the practice of virtue is clear from his statement that the "entire structure of good works originates from the four cardinal virtues."[24] Thomas would thus resist what Solomon calls "the subordinating strategies" of the Kantians and utilitarians; his writings on ethics allow virtue "to take ethical center stage."

A Critique of Virtue Ethics: Its Silence on Justice

One common objection to virtue ethics is that it lacks an account of perfect duties, which are needed in complex, diverse political settings in which disagreement is common and there is no shared ethos regarding the virtues. As Jerome Schneewind puts it, in modern society, "the central difficulties of life" come from "disagreement—disagreement involving nations, religious sects, parties to legal disputes, and ordinary people trying to make a living in busy commercial societies." In such a political and social context, "classical virtue theory is of little or no use."[25] Justice specifies perfect duties whose performance is not optional, but obligatory. Their fulfillment is necessary for the preservation of a society of free individuals.[26] Schneewind's modern justice is indifferent even to the intentions or character of the agent: "To be just is simply to have the habit of following right reason with respect to the rights of others."[27] He goes so far as to say, "The man who regularly carries out all his perfect duties is a just man even if he dislikes acting justly."[28]

There is merit to Schneewind's critique of virtue ethics, which has had little to say about the political order or at least little to say that could not be considered routine.[29] It has little to say about the sort of duties we have toward all human beings or even toward all citizens in a democratic regime. Schneewind also touches upon a more traditional objection to virtue ethics, which surfaces in two forms: (1) it is hedonistic, focused on the happiness and pleasure of the one performing virtuous acts, and (2) its accent on the agent makes it morally suspect, since the attention of a good person should be on others and their good. A related objection is voiced by Larry Louden, who argues that virtue ethics, with its emphasis on the character of the agent and the prudential discernment of concrete circumstances, has no place for what he calls "intolerable acts,"[30] acts that ought in all cases to be avoided because they do great damage to others. There are, he insists, "certain types of act which produce harms of such magnitude that they destroy the bonds of community and render (at least temporarily) the achievement of moral goods impossible."[31] With its emphasis on moral particularism, on the variability of circumstances, virtue ethics occludes from view intolerable acts.[32]

Louden's specific critique of virtue ethics has to do with its strong agent orientation, which leads to an exclusive focus on character over acts. The prioritizing of the question "What sort of person should I become?" ignores the question "What should I do or not do, what harm to others must be avoided?" Louden makes a nice point about all contemporary ethical theories—namely, that they tend to be "mononomic," capturing and elevating to an exclusive principle only part of what is needed in an account of ethics.[33] But Louden's plea for greater inclusiveness or capaciousness in ethical theories has, according to Solomon, had the ill effect of treating virtue ethics as just one routine theory alongside the others. This in turn has generated a series of subordinating strategies, condescending stances adopted by the proponents of rival theories whose goal is to keep virtue in its place.

Solomon addresses the sorts of objections posed by Schneewind and Louden in his "Internal Objections to Virtue Ethics."[34] He distinguishes external objections, such as the accusation that it relies on an outmoded natural teleology, and internal objections, three of which he identifies: the agent-centered objection, the action-guiding objection, and the contingency objection. Versions of the first two are prominent in the essays of Schneewind and Louden. In response to the agent-centered objection, Solomon concedes that a conception of virtue does involve the moral agent keeping "his or her own character at the center of attention," but that is only one dimension or one level of the life of virtue. In another dimension or at another level, there is the "set of virtues the agent aims to embody"; here the virtues and the attention they require of the agent can be as "other regarding as one might wish."[35] In response to the action-guiding objection, Solomon worries that what contemporary ethicists especially want in this regard is guidance in the face of moral quandaries, but he insists it is part of a serious virtue ethics, a radical virtue ethics, that it resists the notion that the moral life can or should be understood in terms of isolated, bizarre episodes. Finally, he counters with the "so's your old man" argument that the algorithms provided by Kantians and utilitarians have not exactly delivered on the goods of action guidance. Solomon does not supply a response to the "intolerable acts" objection except insofar as this can be construed as a particular case of the action-guidance objection. We will return to this later.

Aquinas on Justice and the Diversity of Goods

In his account of justice, Aquinas captures what Louden thinks is needed in a virtue theory if it's to be more than mononomic and not unduly agent centered; it also captures the core of what Schneewind is after in his accent on justice as having to do with its impact on others. Unlike the due or mean of the virtues of courage and temperance, which have to do with a right ordering in the subjective passions of the agent, the mean of justice consists in "operations or things" in relation to what is due to another.[36] Justice is defined as the "good of another." Indeed, Aquinas embraces Cicero's claim that "men are chiefly called good from justice" and that "the splendor of virtue is greatest in justice."[37] The virtue of justice has a common or unifying formality that has to do with giving what is due to another, but Thomas insists that what is due varies widely: "Something is due to an equal in one way, to a superior in another, to an inferior, in yet another, and a debt varies as it arises from a contract, a promise, or a benefit received."[38] He agrees with Schneewind that the core of just acts has to do with the good of others rather than with the perfection and flourishing of the agent, even if he would not go so far as to say that the intention of the agent is irrelevant to whether we identify someone as just. Aquinas defines justice as the "perpetual and constant will to give another what is due."[39] To be called just, it is necessary but not sufficient to fulfill what is externally required. Schneewind would collapse entirely a set of distinctions we commonly make in the ordinary appraisal of the actions of ourselves and others. For example, we distinguish between someone who does what is right because of a concern for others or because of a commitment to rectitude and someone who does what is right because she calculates its long-term profitability or because of a craven desire to please others and so forth. Thus Thomas' account of justice is more differentiated and more capacious than the accounts prominent in modernity; to put this in Taylor's terms, Thomas recognizes the presence of the language of qualitative contrast *within* the realm of justice.

In contrast to the modern tendency to construe the demands of justice in terms of a contractual model, which imagines a kind of clean slate onto which we can enter debits and credits, Thomas presupposes that we are born indebted, that some of our debts arise independently of, and prior to, our conscious consent and that some of them can never be fully repaid. Such is the case with our duties to God, country, parents, and virtuous individuals who have exercised virtue on our behalf. Aquinas has a conception of justice as the virtue concerned with the goods of other persons, and his conception of justice contains rather than excludes the diversity of goods associated with justice.

Aquinas associates justice with a host of other virtues: gratitude, liberality, affability, and mercy. Liberality, which is a mean between covetousness and prodigality, concerns the virtuous use of excess riches.[40] Covetousness, the inordinate desire to possess, has a host of daughters: treachery, fraud, falsehood, perjury, violence, restlessness, and insensibility to mercy (*misericordia*), the last of which erodes our capacity to respond to, or even appropriately sympathize with, others in need.

Moral Prohibitions: Aquinas, Anscombe, and Radical Virtue Ethics

Having discussed the virtue of justice itself and its related virtues and vices, Thomas turns at the end of the treatise on justice in the *Summa Theologiae* to the question of the precepts of justice, a pattern he follows with each of the virtues, enumerating the precepts that fall under the virtue. This is an indication of the rather fluid way in which Thomas moves back and forth between precepts and virtues. If it is correct to say, with Ralph McInerny, that "it is virtuous activity that natural law precepts command," it is also correct to talk about the precepts of the virtues.[41] Thomas identifies the precepts of justice with the precepts of the Decalogue;[42] both govern behavior toward another. He devotes most of the question to the fittingness of the order of the precepts of the Decalogue (with precepts 1–3 falling under religion, 4 under piety, and 5–10 under justice commonly so called as it exists among equals[43]). Stressing the link between law and virtue, he notes that "law forms in virtue by instructing in the precepts of the Decalogue" and that the initial and most important role of law with respect to virtue is to remove obstacles to the practice of virtue.[44] Hence nearly all the precepts are negative. He claims that all other injuries against others are reducible to those prohibited in the second table of the Decalogue, those that concern murder, lust, property, and speech.[45]

Thomas' commitment to a set of precepts of the law might seem to locate him in the camp hostile to virtue, or at least in a camp opposed to Solomonic radical virtue ethics. There are large questions here. An initial test would consider to what extent Thomas deploys the sort of strategies of subordination that Solomon detects among moral theorists who would render virtue routine. One such strategy is that of master subordination, which results in an "emphasis on [a single] virtue as opposed to the virtues."[46] Moreover, the selection of the single, master virtue has to do with its ability to bring the agent into alignment with principles. Thomas certainly elevates some virtues over others, but he is happy, sometimes frustratingly so, to multiply the number and types of the virtues. The candidates for master virtue status organize the virtues in relation to the telos of human life. Prudence is inherently differentiating as it determines in concrete circumstances precisely which virtues are needed and in what way. Similarly, charity is a matter of friendship with God, but it recognizes a natural order of obligations and is connected to the gift of wisdom, which is a cognitive capacity of discernment, judgment, and ordering. Another strategy is what Solomon calls "distributive subordination," in which virtue plays a role distinct from, and subordinate to, the capacity to recognize principles. Virtue performs a motivational role. This view regards "virtues as relatively determinate states of character that embody motivation to act in accord with certain principles." Solomon is suspicious of the split between cognitive and motivational elements that this form of subordination takes, in which virtue is said to be ill suited to the first but capable of providing the second. Indeed, as he notes, it is unclear how virtue could be informed by the appropriate principles without having some capacity of recognizing them. Such a capacity would have to be in some manner cognitive. He goes on to suggest, "If we can train the virtues to move us in such a way that our motivation is structured by subtle differences among principles, why couldn't our motivation be structured by subtle differences among our situations or among the properties of the actions open to one?"[47] We could thus bypass principles entirely and rely solely on the virtues. As Solomon puts it in his response to the action-guiding objection in "Internal Objections to Virtue Ethics," it is not virtue theory that guides action but the virtues themselves: "An agent who embodies the virtue of justice may discern the justice of particular actions, projects, or institutions as specifically and decisively as some impersonally formulated rule or principles." It is precisely "because they embody a more complex capacity for discernment than do rules and principles that" the virtues "defy formulation in rules or principles."[48]

On, say, a Kantian view, "right action" is determined by principle in such a way that "the virtuousness of the state of character must depend on the content of the principle by which it is guided."[49] Now it seems to me that for Aquinas, this could not be right. Since virtue is a matter of action that is rightly ordered in multiple respects and in relation to an array of concrete and varying circumstances, the idea that what counts as a virtue could be determined by measuring it against a principle or even a set of principles seems wrongheaded. Virtue is uncodifiable.

Further difficulties afflict the "distributive subordination" model. As Solomon puts it, since virtue is irrelevant to the cognitive apprehension of principles, "an agent with no motivation to act honestly could nevertheless grasp the relevant principle determining honest behavior and understand its implications for his practice as well as any honest person. Becoming honest and becoming able to discern the honesty of a particular piece of behavior will be distinct in the important sense that the discerning ability can be learned independently of and prior to acquiring any motivational tilt toward honest behavior."[50] Where would Aquinas stand on this? My initial thought is that he would stand with Aristotle, who insists that as one is—that is, as one's character is formed—so does the good appear. Thus one who lacks virtue could not determine "honest behavior and grasp its implication for practice as well as any honest person." But he wouldn't go so far—nor I think would Solomon go so far—as to collapse the distinction between one's state of character and what one can grasp in the way of what virtue requires. Otherwise, there could be no cognitively informed development of virtue. But might there be a role for principles here? Just as an example of virtue might prod me to begin reforming my ways further in the direction of virtue, so too might the acknowledgment of a precept, say against calumny or embezzlement.

It is not accidental that I just cited precepts against—that is, negative precepts. Those associated with virtue ethics are impressed with the fact that virtue is uncodifiable.[51] It is not so clear that vice or at least that certain vice act types, as Candace Vogler calls them, are always uncodifiable. Vogler argues that "reaching a point where analytic philosophy can cope with moral prohibitions was crucial for Anscombe." Vogler sees this already evident in "Modern Moral Philosophy," which was preoccupied with the rejection of consequentialism, a rejection "bound up with recognition of moral prohibitions." Given this, Vogler expresses surprise that "analytic virtue ethics inspired by her call has devoted so little attention to the topic."[52] Now it seems to me that Vogler has hit upon a neglected theme in "Modern Moral Philosophy," but part of the problem is that Anscombe is not entirely forthcoming on precisely what she is calling for. She does indeed investigate possible bases for moral prohibitions, apart from a divine legislator, a "search," she says, that "has some interest in it."[53] She even looks to "the human virtues" as possible grounds. Yet the search for grounds apart from God is at best inconclusive. Interestingly, her example of an obvious moral prohibition falls under the virtue of justice. "Judicially punishing a man for what he is known not to have done," she writes, is "intrinsically unjust"—a "paradigm case of injustice."[54]

What *is* clear is that Anscombe recoils from the inability of her "colleagues to comprehend prohibited kinds of act as such." She writes, "It is noticeable that none of these philosophers displays any consciousness that there is such an ethic, which he is contradicting: it is pretty well taken for obvious among them all that a prohibition such as that on murder does not operate in face of some consequences. But of course the strictness of the prohibition has as its point that *you are not to be tempted by fear or hope of consequences*."[55] Vogler comments, "That is the doctrine. It comes into play whenever we are inclined to calculate the likelihood that doing something specifically bad (bad in its kind, bad because of the kind of action that it is) will result in getting something good, or in preventing something worse."[56] Vogler thinks it important to incorporate such prohibitions—what Louden calls intolerable acts—for three reasons. First, "these are among the moral act descriptions that are part and parcel of ordinary ethical life and conduct." Second, "it is very hard to see how anyone could receive a moral education without acquiring a rough and ready understanding that some kinds of acts are specifically bad." Third, "it is very hard to see how there could be such a thing as an ethically alert practical orientation without an understanding that some acts are specifically wrong. Framing someone for a capital criminal offense, rape, vivisecting the children in the local daycare center—none of these are ruled out in advance if there are no moral prohibitions. It is one thing to argue that some acts that have been regarded as specifically wrong are not, actually, specifically wrong. It is quite another to hold that there are no such things as specifically wrong acts."[57]

Vogler does not say how we are to understand the relationship of moral prohibitions to the life of virtue, although one has the sense that she sees prohibitions as circumscribing the parameters of the life of virtue, within which the virtues flourish. Aquinas would certainly concur with that. But there is a deeper connection between the two and between both and the account of the goods that rules protect and virtues nourish and embody. As Alasdair MacIntyre has argued, for Aquinas, goods, virtues, and rules are indispensable and interconnected.[58] What I have said about Aquinas indicates that he is comfortable moving from law to virtue and from virtue to law. The inherent limits, stressed by Yves Simon in a passage already quoted, to any rule-based account of ethics opens up the possibility of recovering virtue; conversely, detailed examination of the virtues reveals that one of the most prominent virtues, justice, requires serious reflection on the types of acts that do significant harm to others. It thus invites reflection on the need for moral prohibitions. To defend prohibitions does not entail the irrelevance of prudence even in cases governed by universal negative prohibitions. Prudence will be required, sometimes readily and sometimes with arduous deliberation and the taking of counsel, to discern whether this or that act falls under the prohibition. It will also be needed to determine that an act or even the avoidance of an act is correct in every respect, not just in its character of avoiding the specific prohibition. But prudence is not here weighing consequences to determine whether a universal negative prohibition should be followed or not.

It is striking that Alasdair MacIntyre, whom Solomon locates in the radical virtue ethics camp, has consistently argued for the indispensable role of rules and virtues. Dating at least back to *After Virtue* and thus predating his turn to Thomas Aquinas, MacIntyre has proposed that communities in which individuals pursue goods in common would need two types of "evaluative practice." The first would concern the excellences, the virtues, necessary for the realization and flourishing of the goods. The second would concern "certain types of action" whose performance would "destroy the bonds of community in such a way as to render the doing or achieving of good impossible in some respect at least for some time."[59] Put negatively, there are two distinct ways to fail in the ethical sphere. One can fail with regard to the standards of the virtues—that is, one can "fail to be good enough." Or one can do "positive wrong" and thus "destroy those relationships that make common pursuit of the good possible."[60]

After his embrace of Thomas Aquinas, MacIntyre developed such an account of prohibitions as a way of articulating Thomas' teaching on natural law. To violate the exceptionless precepts of the natural law is to "deprive one of their cooperation in the achievement of a good about which one still has much to learn from them. In the search for the good, everyone is a potential teacher and has therefore to be treated as one from whom I still may have to learn." In this way, the precepts are presuppositions, rather than conclusions or inferences, of moral reasoning. We shall have to obey them if we are to make any progress whatsoever in the quest for the good. He puts the point somewhat differently in terms of moral education: "We can only learn what it is to be courageous or temperate or truthful by first learning that certain types of action are always and exceptionlessly such as we must refrain from them if we are to exemplify those virtues."[61]

Now while there is obviously much further work that would have to be done to defend this account of the relationships of moral rules to the life of virtue, it should be clear that there is nothing in this account of rules that undermines the radicality of the commitment to virtue. Still, from Solomon's perspective, a reading of Anscombe that focuses on acts rather than on habits or states of character risks leading us in the wrong direction, away from the primacy of virtue. But habits themselves in Aristotle and Thomas are ordered to actualization in specific acts of the human agent. Acts are important not just because they form character in one way or another but also because they are the manifestations, indeed the realization, of the habits once possessed. Moreover, an account of intolerable acts or moral prohibitions requires not just that virtues be other regarding but that we have some account of what and who human persons are such that harming them in the ways ruled out by the precepts of justice are seen to be so grievous. More than moral psychology, what is needed is a philosophical anthropology. As Taylor puts it, the languages of qualitative contrast reflect different pictures of man and of the human condition. Given Anscombe's skepticism about whether an account of rules can be established without reference to God, would this mean that we need not just a philosophical but a theological anthropology? Perhaps.

Interestingly, while Solomon has not engaged religious or theological accounts of the virtues in his work on virtue ethics, he has attended to the religious context of ethics in his work on medical ethics. In the essay "Filling the Void: Secular Bioethics and Academic Moral Philosophy," Solomon argues, "While it is generally assumed that a secular bioethics rooted in moral philosophy will be more culturally authoritative than an approach to bioethics grounded in the contingent particularities of a religious tradition," there are good reasons to reject this assumption. An examination of "the history of the recent revival of academic bioethics as well as the state of the contemporary moral philosophy on which it is based" reveals "that secular bioethics suffers from many of the same liabilities as a carefully articulated Christian bioethics."[62] Even more forcefully, in an essay titled "Can We Do without Dignity? Disability, Bioethics, and the War between Autonomy and Dignity," Solomon draws on the writings of John Paul II, particularly the encyclical *Evangelium Vitae*. He notes the surprising turn in recent years toward a critique of the notion of dignity as the foundation of autonomy and rights and wonders how, without such a foundation, medical ethics will keep from sliding into what John Paul II identifies as the tyranny of the strong over the weak. The gist of Solomon's argument runs thus:

> John Paul II presents a picture of the development and threats to contemporary democratic culture that can be summarized as follows: Contemporary democratic culture grew out of a theistic conception of human life which supported the notion that every person has equal dignity. This provided support for democratic forms of government. However, contemporary forms of democratic culture have a tendency to encourage an ideology of unrestricted freedom and individual autonomy which lead to cultural norms and legislation that are incompatible with human dignity (including the legalization and normalization of euthanasia). This not only results in the increasing acceptance of intrinsically evil actions, but it also undermines the very foundations of democratic culture.[63]

The very existence of a war between dignity and autonomy underscores the way in which procedural ethical theories of justice can undermine the "substantive moral insights," as Taylor calls them, that inspired them in the first place. It might be that the virtue of justice as understood by

Thomas can salvage the moral insights undergirding Kantianism ("universal attribution of moral personality") and utilitarianism ("no defensible distinction between different classes of human beings" and "each should count for one and only one") better than the modern theories can. We may now be in a situation in the ethical order isomorphic to that in the intellectual order identified by John Paul II in *Fides et Ratio*, where he noted that the hopeless skepticism, in the philosophical order, concerning the capacity of reason to know the truth means that faith has to come to the aid of reason. So too in the ethical order; the self-canceling project of liberalism is undermining its very foundation. Thus does a theological anthropology come to the aid of philosophical ethics by providing a foundation for human dignity.

Recovering this larger and deeper philosophical and theological context within which an account of precepts and virtues and of the dignity of the human person is intelligible would be far from routine. It would be radical in the etymological sense, a return to the roots of the moral life. For alerting us to the pressing significance of this task, a task at once theoretical and practical, we are all indebted to David Solomon.

Bibliography

Anscombe, Elizabeth. "Modern Moral Philosophy." In *Virtue Ethics*, edited by Roger Crisp and Michael Slote, 26–44. Oxford: Oxford University Press, 1997.

Finnis, John. *Natural Law and Natural Rights*. Oxford: Oxford University Press, 1980.

Geach, Peter. *God and the Soul*. London: Routledge and Kegan Paul, 1978.

Louden, Larry. "Vices of Virtue Ethics." In *Virtue Ethics*, edited by Roger Crisp and Michael Slote, 201–16. Oxford: Oxford University Press, 1997.

MacIntyre, Alasdair. *After Virtue*. 3rd ed. Notre Dame: University of Notre Dame Press, 2007.

———. "Plain Persons and Moral Philosophy: Rules, Virtues, and Goods." *American Catholic Philosophical Quarterly* 66 (1992): 3–19.

McDowell, John. *Mind, Value, and Reality*. Cambridge, Mass.: Harvard University Press, 1998.

McInerny, Ralph. *Aquinas on Human Action*. Washington, D.C.: Catholic University of America Press, 1992.

Schneewind, Jerome. "The Misfortunes of Virtue." In *Virtue Ethics*, edited by Roger Crisp and Michael Slote, 199–200. Oxford: Oxford University Press, 1997.

Simon, Yves. *The Tradition of Natural Law*. New York: Fordham University Press, 1999.

Solomon, David. "Christian Bioethics, Secular Bioethics, and the Claim to Cultural Authority." *Christian Bioethics: Non-ecumenical Studies in Medical Ethics* 11, no. 3 (2005): 349–59.

———. "Domestic Disarray and Imperial Ambition: Contemporary Applied Ethics and the Prospects for Global Bioethics." In *Global Bioethics: The Collapse of Consensus*, edited by H. T. Engelhardt, 335–61. Salem, Mass.: Scrivener, 2006.

———. "Filling the Void: Secular Bioethics and Academic Moral Philosophy." In *Secularism: Russian and Western Perspectives*, edited by David Bradshaw, 115–28. Washington, D.C.: Council for Research in Values and Philosophy, 2013.

———. "Internal Objections to Virtue Ethics." *Midwest Studies in Philosophy* 13 (1988): 428–41.

———. "Keeping Virtue in Its Place: A Critique of Subordinating Strategies." In *Recovering Nature: Essays in Natural Philosophy, Ethics, and Metaphysics in Honor of Ralph McInerny*, edited by John P. O'Callaghan and Thomas S. Hibbs, 83–104. Notre Dame: University of Notre Dame Press, 1999.

———. "MacIntyre and Contemporary Moral Philosophy." In *Alasdair MacIntyre: Contemporary Philosophy in Focus*, edited by Mark Murphy, 114–52. Cambridge: Cambridge University Press, 2003.

———. "Virtue Ethics: Radical or Routine?" In *Intellectual Virtue: Perspectives from Ethics and Epistemology*, edited by Michael DePaul and Linda Zagzebski, 57–80. Oxford: Oxford University Press, 2003.

Taylor, Charles. "Diversity of Goods." In *Philosophical Papers*, vol. 2, *Philosophy and the Human Sciences*, 230–47. Cambridge: Cambridge University Press, 1985.

Vogler, Candace. "Aristotle, Aquinas, Anscombe, and the New Virtue Ethics." In *Aquinas and the* Nicomachean Ethics, edited by Tobias Hoffmann, Jörn Müller, and Matthias Perkams, 239–57. Cambridge: Cambridge University Press, 2013.

PART TWO
NORMATIVE ETHICS

5

WHITHER MORAL PHILOSOPHY?

John Haldane

Moral Theory and Ethical Sense

Let me begin with a quote from the opening of a once highly influential essay published over a century ago by the English philosopher H. A. Prichard titled "Does Moral Philosophy Rest on a Mistake?":

> Probably to most students of Moral Philosophy there comes a time when they feel a vague sense of dissatisfaction with the whole subject. And the sense of dissatisfaction tends to grow rather than to diminish. It is not so much that the positions, and still more the arguments, of particular thinkers seem unconvincing, though this is true. It is rather that the aim of the subject becomes increasingly obscure. "What," it is asked, "are we really going to learn by Moral Philosophy?" "What are books on Moral Philosophy really trying to show, and when their aim is clear, why are they so unconvincing and artificial?"[1]

Prichard's diagnosis of the unconvincingness of ethical theory is that philosophers have been looking for arguments that would allow the derivation of claims of moral duty or obligation from nondeontological premises, but such searches he maintains must be in vain. The two principal routes they have followed in seeking obligation-generating assumptions have been (1) claims about what advantage would accrue in consequence to the agent (typically the promotion of his or her happiness) or (2) claims about what goods would be realized in the performance of certain actions. According to Prichard, however, the problem with these personal and impersonal modes of justification is that they fail to provide an intrinsic noncircular link to obligation. The first yields a prudential motive, not a moral reason. The second only provides a reason where the goodness of the action consists in its being the fulfillment of an obligation, and hence as a way of justifying claims of duty, it is circular. Prichard's conclusion is that while obligations can be recognized noninferentially they cannot be independently justified. As a matter of guidance, one may answer the question "Why must I?" by giving reasons, but the answers, if they are genuinely moral ones, will draw on a tight circle of synonyms: "It is your *duty*," "You have an *obligation*," "There is a moral *requirement*."

Prichard's argument assumes that there really are moral obligations to be accounted for, but a skeptic might take nonderivability to support the idea that no such obligations exist. The warrant for Prichard's nonskeptical conclusion, however, is what he takes to be the manifest fact of the sense of duty and the facticity of the objects of that sense. This part of his argument is akin to that developed by G. E. Moore in defense of common sense about the existence of the external world.[2] For just as Moore held that the belief that one is presented in experience with independently existing objects is more credible than any argument to the contrary, so Prichard maintained that the presumption of real obligations is more plausible than any denial or debunking explanation of such moral intuitions.

I will have more to say in response to Prichard's argument later on, but at this point I return to the opening passage, now reading it apart from the purpose it served in the context of his essay and seeing in it the expression of a feeling of dissatisfaction with moral philosophy that one might have on other grounds than those he diagnoses. I have in view especially the following sentences: "'What,' it is asked, 'are we really going to learn by Moral Philosophy?' 'What are books on Moral Philosophy really trying to show, and when their aim is clear, why are they so unconvincing and artificial?'" These questions stand out anew a century after Prichard posed them, now in relation to much that is published in journals and books or presented in symposia and conferences, which, it is expected, graduate students aspiring to become professional philosophers will read, absorb, and emulate in their own work.

In light of the scale and character of these productions, I want to raise the question of whether in recent decades moral philosophy has in some part lost its way and become disconnected from lived experience, the aspects of life out of which it claims to arise as reflection upon prephilosophical thought and practice. This is in part a historical question, and it is one that I think David Solomon is likely to have thoughts about. Certainly he has a long-standing interest in and has done much research on the historical development of English-language moral philosophy through the course of the twentieth century. Much of that interest is focused on British philosophy, particularly what went on in Oxford beginning in the late 1950s involving figures such as Elizabeth Anscombe, Philippa Foot, Iris Murdoch, and Bernard Williams, and of course he has a very deep knowledge of the thematic and dialectical developments in the work of Alasdair MacIntyre.

These figures, though differing in small or large ways in the manner of their approaches and the substance of their views, share certain common characteristics as thinkers, characteristics also shared by Solomon. They are all "serious" people, not grave—indeed far from it, for all have been alert to the humorous absurdities of human life and shared a taste and capacity for ironic wit. Rather, their seriousness is that of deeply reflective human beings for whom philosophy is a matter of thinking long and hard about matters that arise in the course of common life and not an intellectual parlor game or a series of puzzle-setting and puzzle-solving competitions. They are also people of broad literary imagination, historical perspective, and moral commitment. Indeed, I would say that for all those mentioned, moral philosophy is never far removed from generally recognizable moral perplexity and is to be checked against it, not in the manner of a theory being tested against individual intuitions, but as ideas being compared with experience. Something of this latter outlook is conveyed in the following passage from Bernard Williams: "There could be a way of doing moral philosophy that started from the ways in which we experience our ethical life. Such a philosophy would reflect on what we believe, feel, take for granted; the ways in which we confront obligations and recognize responsibility; the sentiments of guilt and shame. It would involve a phenomenology of the ethical life. This could be a good philosophy, but it would be unlikely to yield an ethical theory."[3]

Philosophers of this non-(if not anti-)theoretical type could hardly feel enthusiasm for much of the work that has become prominent in "analytical ethics" over the last quarter century, particularly the following:

1. That which projects the diversity and complexity of human existence via utility functions into a space of welfare distributions
2. That which converts any ethical consideration into a rights (or duties) claim
3. That which presupposes that the ethical belongs to either the ontology of natural science or to that of some "supernatural" domain
4. That which seeks to "scientize" moral philosophy whether through technicality or by subsuming it within some actual or, as it might seem, "pseudo" science such as evolutionary psychology
5. That which draws distinctions that make no difference—for example, between versions of a theory every instance of which falls to the same objection
6. That which demonstrates at length and with some ingenuity the possible defenses of a theoretical position without giving any convincing reason rooted in common experience to think that such a position may be true
7. That which seeks to turn every thought into a theory
8. That which proceeds without regard to the actual nature of human agents or to natural possibilities or necessities
9. That which makes philosophical ethics the handmaiden of social causes or cultural movements
10. That which proceeds as if moral philosophy began around or even later than the date to which the English poet Philip Larkin assigned the beginning of "sexual intercourse":

> Sexual intercourse began
> In nineteen sixty-three
> (which was rather late for me)—
> Between the end of the "Chatterley" ban
> And the Beatles' first LP.[4]

Manners and Modes of Moral Philosophy

Distaste or skepticism for or about 1 to 10 may be met with the counter that earlier moral philosophy tended to be conducted as if it were a branch of personal-cum-literary reflection or as moral counseling being in either case impressionistic and/or unmethodical and that by contrast, recent analytical ethics, whatever may be the verdict on particular examples, represent the effect of rigorous investigation and analysis and the application of a scientific outlook free of cultural prejudices and ideological biases.

So far as freedom from prejudice is concerned, there is a serious question whether contemporary academic moral philosophers exhibit pervasive *mauvais foi*, posturing as independent thinkers while conforming their opinions, methods, and modes of production to norms dominant within their peer group and congenial to their patrons, thereby securing approbation and advancement but also confirming themselves to members of an academic *petite bourgeoisie*. Such a possibility was an ongoing source of concern to philosophers of the earlier disposition such as Anscombe, MacIntyre, Williams, Stuart Hampshire, and Iris Murdoch, but the advocates of the new and improved versions of analytic ethics seem curiously unaware of this possibility. This may be because, unlike those earlier figures, none of whom engaged in Ph.D. research, the present generation of philosophers has been inducted into patterns of intellectual activity that are inwardly academic, in-group referential, and unremittingly publication oriented. This intensive professionalization of philosophy has meant that even when it looks beyond the academy, it generally does so through academic lenses facetted to facilitate systematization and heavily colored in the hues of one or another currently fashionable theory. This should be a cause not only of disappointment but of suspicion and even fear, for the co-option of academics to the fashions of the age means the transmission of those fashions and the habit of obeisance to students and thereby to those whom they in turn will influence.

As regards the matter or rigor of analysis and argumentation, there is an obvious question to be asked about what constitutes rigor. So far as it concerns care and thoroughness, it cannot but be a virtue of philosophical inquiry, but that does not mean that it requires formalization or the pluralization of merely logically distinct possibilities, whether as theories or as imagined examples disconnected from any reality-rooted sense of conceivability. A rigorous use of the imagination is valuable in philosophy, but it needs to be exercised under the discipline that distinguishes the imaginary from the merely fantastical.

On the matter of analysis and argumentation, there is no lack of this in the writings of Anscombe, Foot, or Williams, whom I select as earlier Oxford philosophers that Solomon particularly admires, and here I could add Peter Winch and David Wiggins, but for them, argument is proportioned to necessity and is not engaged in simply for its own sake. The point might be made by way of an analogy with the arts: facility—for example, in draftsmanship, in color contrast and harmonization, or in instrument playing or orchestration—is one thing; judgment about how much of these should be exercised and to what purpose and appreciation of when is too much and of what ends are banal are another.

One mark of argument inflation, explained in part by the market conditions of production, distribution, and exchange in which academics operate and by which they and their peers judge their success, is the growth in the length of academic papers and in the number of footnotes and references therein to peer group members. Anscombe's essay "On Brute Facts" and Peter Geach's "Ascriptivism" and "Good and Evil" did much to turn the tide in the 1960s and 1970s against ethical subjectivism and continue to be referred to more than half a century later, but they only run to four, five, and ten pages, respectively.[5] Likewise, Williams' "Practical Necessity" and "Internal and External Reasons," which gave renewed support to noncognitivism in the decade or so following the Anscombe-Geach revolution, run to only eight and thirteen pages but likewise continue to have influence.[6]

David Solomon himself demonstrates a significant capacity for rigorous analysis and argumentation in his early paper "Ethical Theory."[7] In this he takes on what at the time was an unengaged challenge to expound and assess the complex, highly distinctive, and difficult to categorize views of Wilfred Sellars on the nature and structure of ethical thought. In a letter to Solomon (written, I presume on the basis of the date, in response to a prepublication version of the essay), Sellars observes, "You have done an excellent job of tracing the dialectical structure of my thinking on these topics. You have been particularly successful in grasping what I was up to in 'Imperatives, Intentions and the Logic of Ought.'"[8]

In "Ethical Theory" Solomon sets out what he describes as "a [trilevel] model for understanding the general problematic of classical metaethics."

L1) statements of fact
↓
L2) moral judgments
↓
L3) actions

This serves to locate what he terms "the two fundamental problems in [Anglo-American] ethics": the problem of *justification*, or how to understand the arrow leading from L1 to L2, and the problem of *motivation*, represented by that proceeding from L2 to L3. This framework also provides for an interesting identification and contrast between broad groups of metaethical theories. In this scheme *naturalism* is specified as holding that there is an entailment between L1 and L2 because the meaning of ethical statements is fully accounted for by the empirical criteria of their application. In contrast *noncognitivism* denies that statements of fact imply moral propositions but holds that moral judgments are noncontingently related to actions because the former amount to expressions of commitment—in its simple prescriptivism version, someone who judges that doing A is good expresses thereby a subjective commitment to doing A. Prichard is then introduced as representing a further position in his version of *intuitionism*. According to this, moral judgments are truth apt and bear upon action but are neither equivalent nor reducible to statements of empirical fact, nor are they logically related to motivation.

I will return to the question of the nature of the three levels and the relation between them later, proposing an account that I believe Solomon may find congenial. While in a broadly naturalist tradition, it does not conform exactly to Solomon's logical characterization of that. By his own account, however, that characterization is somewhat limited and idealized, so the matter of conformity may not concern either of us very much if at all. At this point, however, I want to revert to the issue of the character of recent and contemporary moral philosophy and to the possibility that it is in a period of academic malaise.

In and Out of the Linguistic Turn

In the past couple of decades, there has been a fashion for returning to the works of what were hitherto somewhat neglected, or explicitly rejected, moral philosophers of the nineteenth and early twentieth centuries, such as T. H. Green, F. H. Bradley, G. E. Moore, and W. D. Ross, as well as Prichard. The reasons for this return are threefold. First, it is partly to do with the familiar phenomenon that when a subject seems close to exhaustion, it can be refreshing to look to its history. Second, there is the thought that work from the past may contain themes and ideas that can be redeployed today. Third is the possibility of understanding how and why more recent trends developed.

I have suggested that an important part of the answer to the last of these lies not with the internal dialectic of thought but with the sociology of academic professionalization. There is, though, a philosophical reason relating to the prior discounting of the figures listed. This is to do with the development among Anglophone philosophers from the 1930s of a heightened sense of the philosophical significance of the study of language—that is to say, of logical features of natural languages and of the discoveries such study might yield.

The origins of this development lie in the work of Frege, Russell, and Wittgenstein, but the method of linguistic analysis in application to ethical discourse was first brought to the attention of English-language philosophers by A. J. Ayer in *Language, Truth and Logic* (1936) and in the following year by C. L. Stevenson in "The Emotive Meaning of Ethical Terms" (1937) and then in developed form in his highly influential *Ethics and Language* (1944). This rapidly established "tradition" of doing moral philosophy by linguistic analysis was further advanced by R. M. Hare in a series of books beginning with *The Language of Morals* (1952) and continued with greater immersion in the philosophy of language (which had itself become increasingly sophisticated and quasi-technical) by the likes of Simon Blackburn, Alan Gibbard, Crispin Wright, and Mark Schroeder.

This line of development saw itself as novel and progressive, the former in bringing to light hitherto unrealized aspects of moral talk, the latter in achieving ever more subtle formulations of theses about the nature and import of such discourse. For the most part, the tendency of the analysts was subjectivist: either emotivist/expressivist: "x is good" = "hoorah for x," or descriptive/relativist: "x is good" = "I favor x." Both versions of this were retrospectively attributed to David Hume, though it is doubtful that he saw himself as giving any kind of linguistic or semantic *analysis*, and among the several things he says are statements that seem to be expressions of, or at any rate to be compatible with, different accounts of the logical status of moral statements.

In the first presentation of his sentimentalist/affective theory of morality in the *Treatise of Human Nature* (1739), Hume writes, "When you pronounce any action or character to be vicious, you mean nothing, but that from the constitution of your nature you have a feeling or sentiment of blame from the contemplation of it."[9] But forty years later (1777) in *Enquiries Concerning the Human Understanding and the Principles of Morals*, he writes, "The approbation or blame which then ensues [regarding human action], cannot be the work of the judgement, but of the heart; and is not a speculative proposition or affirmation, but an active feeling or sentiment."[10] The latter seems to equate favorable judgment with the expression of a sentiment, whereas the former identifies it with a judgment ascribing such a sentiment to oneself. To ask "Which is Hume's settled view?" presumes a kind of interest that makes sense in light of the "logico-linguistic turn" but is one of which I think Hume himself was innocent and of which is in any case tangential to his main point—viz., that while reason plays a part in morality, it is the servant (famously he says "slave," but that is rhetorical) of affective sensibility, which he is usually quoted as referring to as the "passions" but he also terms "humanity."

Since twentieth- and twenty-first-century philosophers tend to regard such a view as amounting to "emotivism" or "expressivism" and associate these terms with logico-linguistic "discoveries," they are apt to overlook the fact that Hume himself links his affective theory with ancient authors whose interests were anthropological rather than logical, as did his friend and follower in these matters, Adam Smith. On this account it may be that rather than side with or oppose Hume by means of some logico-linguistic strategy, we should try to consider his views as reflections on human psychology, setting aside his own not infrequent and sometimes incautious rhetoric and consider how they correspond to moral consciousness.

There were, of course, some contrary voices within the "linguistic school." Chief among these were the aforementioned Anscombe and Geach, who offered distinct but complementary observations about the informal logic of requirement and evaluation. Anscombe's point was that the category of descriptive statements, conceived in part to be contrasted with evaluative and prescriptive ones, was coarsely specified: not distinguishing between statements of (1) bodily movement, (2) action (intentionally characterized), (3) social performances, and (4) institutional exchanges. Such distinctions she deemed necessary for the purpose of interpretation so as to answer questions about what an agent did. But she also identified hierarchies in such descriptions, which she expressed in terms of the relationship of brute relativity: "It comes to light that the relation of the facts [that I ordered potatoes from a grocer, he supplied them, and he sent me a bill] to the description 'X owes Y so much money' is an interesting one, which I will call that of being 'brute relative to' that description. Further, the 'brute' facts mentioned here themselves have descriptions relatively to which *other* facts are 'brute'—as, e.g., *he had potatoes carted to my house* and *they were left there* are brute facts relative to 'he supplied me with potatoes.'"[11] One way of interpreting Anscombe's insight is to say that statements of fact may imply statements of requirement, but this way of putting things concedes too much to the neo-Humean orthodoxy that statements can be classified exclusively (though not exhaustively) as either descriptive or prescriptive, whereas it might be more accurate to think in terms of "descriptive/prescriptive entanglement" or even as aspect abstraction—a suggestion to which I will return. In any event she thought that in some contexts, the fact that certain things had occurred noncontingently (though defeasibly) justified the assertion that certain things ought to be done.

Geach's insight concerned the logically prior matter of evaluation. Beginning with Moore's attack on definitions of "good," which by means of the open-question argument he sought to show confused the "is" of predication ("happiness is good") with that of identity ("goodness = happiness"), linguistic philosophers had tended to the view that claims about goodness are logically independent of nonevaluative predications. What Geach showed in "Good and Evil" (1956), however, is that in its logically primary use, "good" is an attributive adjective and thereby a semantically incomplete term, the completion of which in an expression includes a sortal noun (or verb) such that "good-k" implies standards for the evaluation of things (or actions) of that kind. Thus in Geach's view, whether a is a good k depends on what ks are or are for.

This insight is easier to grasp than is Anscombe's, but both are irrefutable in their respective cores, even if one may quibble about outlying cases. Similarly discomfiting to semantic subjectivists (whether expressivists or relativists) is Geach's observation that whatever the analysis of the meaning of utterances in which "good" or "bad" or "right" or "wrong" (or more specific determinations) feature, as *used* rather than as quoted, inferences involving them must be uniform. Since inference is defined in terms of truth preservation from premises to conclusion, this requires treating them descriptively across the range of a discourse.

There is no question, I believe, that the development of analytical metaethics brought greater *logical* acumen and that there was real progress in understanding the relation between the logical properties of terms and statements, their potential inferential relations and their aptness for truth. Additionally, there was a recognition that there may be noncontingent, conceptual relations short of deductive entailment. This "discovery," explicitly championed by Geach but shared by Anscombe and deployed by Foot, is relevant to the earlier issue of whether the naturalist needs to be committed to saying that statements of fact may entail evaluative judgments or whether they are prohibited from saying that evaluative judgments are noncontingently related to motivation. At the same time, what was originally introduced in the context of defending the presumption of cognitivism from the logico-semantic versions of subjectivism later became a self-sustaining industry in which ingenuity was deployed in the fashioning of nonstandard logics, expressivist semantics, and other exotic blooms of philosophical horticultural specialism.

If the earlier British idealist and moral intuitionist figures I mentioned were neglected because they seemed logically unsophisticated, they have been recovered, I suggest, in part because of a sense that in moral philosophy, logical ingenuity will not achieve a great deal, and the preoccupation with it, and with philosophy of language, as with ontology, is a distraction from the business of addressing the issues of justification and motivation and of understanding the character and significance of moral experience. Here the point may be more effectively put by thinking about the experience of making and evaluating art. Suppose one is trying to work out a scheme of composition that, at one and the same time, will serve to stabilize a group of figures while also conveying a sense of tension primed for explosive movement or is trying to find a medium of representation that allows its formal properties to saturate the particular content that is to be expressed. It may be illuminating to understand how some courses of action would be better than others, some commendable, some facile, and so on, but what relevance could there be in being given a theory of the semantics of the terms in which such thought might be expressed or reported? What and how might it contribute to the business to hear about the ontological status of the features being deployed and evaluated?

The answers may not be "none," but the unobviousness of claims to relevance, to put it no more strongly, requires that they be demonstrated. Someone might respond first that philosophical aesthetics is unlike moral philosophy in that it is not concerned with the sphere of practical rationality, but that is evidently false, at least so far as concerns a large part of aesthetics—viz., the philosophy of art. Second, it might be claimed that metaethics, or meta-aesthetics, understood as being concerned with the logic, semantics, epistemology, and ontology of evaluative and/or prescriptive claims, should not be expected to illuminate the subject matter of ethics or aesthetics per se. Admittedly from *Language, Truth and Logic* onwards, that claim to purely second-order, nonsubstantive status has been a common refrain, but this should give us reason to wonder whether metaenquiries have anything to contribute to understanding the specific content of evaluative and practical thought. For the fact is that they are really enquiries in speculative philosophy happening to use examples from these domains as illustrations but without requiring interest in them per se, let alone as parts of lived human experience. It is no surprise, therefore, that the examples are so bland and sparsely specified as in discussions of the Frege/Geach problem: "If it is wrong to lie, then it is wrong to get your little brother to lie." This in turn prompts the suggestion that insofar as someone is trying to understand the *substance* of moral thought and argumentation, he or she may have little need for metaethics and the suspicion that it may be largely "epiphenomenal."

Return to the General Problematic

This is not to say that moral philosophy proper consists only in the identification of moral considerations and the casuistical resolution of problem cases where values and principles are in seeming conflict, for there are more abstract questions about the grounds of evaluative claims, the relation of the latter to prescriptive judgments, and the bearing of those on rational motivation. Here, therefore, I return to the issue raised by Prichard and to what Solomon termed the "general problematic of classical metaethics." Prichard's challenge to the idea that statements of requirement could be derived from statements of fact was that even where the latter might be cast in terms of good and bad, they could not establish moral ought-to-do-ness, for either they fail by only generating a prudential imperative or else they get things back to front because the intrinsic goodness of an action consists in its being the observance of an obligation. It should be clear, however, that this argument involves contentious presuppositions: first that there is a clear distinction between prudential and moral considerations, second that oughtness is prior to impersonal goodness, third and more specifically that notions of duty and obligation (obligatoriness) are the fundamental concepts of ethics, and fourth that the structure and content of actual moral thinking might be understood independently of the nature of the agents to which it applies.

It is a significant fact that things look very different in philosophy depending on where one begins, and part of the difference is that some perspectives seem to generate problems almost immediately. In epistemology, for example, one might begin by asking how we have certain kinds of knowledge, such as general knowledge about natures, or one might ask how we can ever know anything other than our own conscious states—and indeed whether we even have knowledge about those. Evidently the latter approach does more than invite skepticism; it seems to ensure its presence at the outset and then famously struggles to evict it.

In moral philosophy, if one begins with the idea that the ethical domain is composed of requirements, then an immediate question arises of what to say to someone who asks why he or she should do as the requirement states or who wonders whether and why those requirements apply to him or her at all. By making brute obligatoriness the nonconvertible currency of the moral economy, Prichard creates the possibility of rational skepticism and has no response to it other than reasserting claims of duty. If instead one begins with values and ideals, then the sceptics' task is made harder and appears as a recognizably speculative one. The kind of moral philosophy that begins, as Williams put it, "from the ways in which we experience our ethical life . . . [reflecting] on what we believe, feel, take for granted" invites questions about the correctness of an analysis, distinguishing, for example, between regret at having done something from remorse about the action and again between this and shame felt at what it implied about one's character. Asking "Was the shame I felt matched by remorse?" is one way of trying to improve one's moral consciousness, but it presupposes rather than prompts doubts about the applicability of the concepts involved. Perhaps moral skepticism remains a possibility, but it now looks forced and fabricated.

Suppose, however, without giving unnecessary hostages to fortune, one wants to turn from the particularities of moral phenomenology to something theoretical with which he or she may be connected. What might be the starting point? Well, we might recall something that Kant says in his *Critique of Judgment*: "In order to consider something good, I must always know what sort of thing the object is [meant] to be, i.e., I must have a concept of it. But I do not need this in order to find beauty in something. Flowers, free designs, lines aimlessly intertwined and called foliage: these have no significance, depend on no determinate concept, and yet we like them."[12] In fact, Kant allows that there is a kind of aesthetic judgment (of dependent beauty) that does require having a concept of the subject of which beauty is predicated, but his claim is that this is secondary to free beauty, in which there is pleasure at something independent of any conceptualization of it. While a sound pattern may (or may not) be conceived of as birdsong, the tones and their pattern may please simply on account of their phenomenal character. I am not altogether convinced that such experience is not concept dependent, but that is not to the present point. Rather, my interest is in the idea of dependent beauty, where the concept under which something is brought is the ground for an aspectual form of predication: for example, "*x* is beautiful qua horse," or more perspicuously "*x* is beautiful in respective of features belonging to it as a horse," features for which being a horse provides certain standards—for example, of overall shape, proportion, or integrity of parts. When Kant says that judgments of "good" are always concept dependent, he is not thinking of moral goodness in his own particular understanding of this but of the goodness of things that have functions or characteristic activities, things that can be thought of teleologically, and on that account be judged to act well or badly.

The introduction of teleology may be thought presumptuous, but it is present from the outset as the concepts are acquired. The mass of everyday (and scientific) sortal concepts are the products of abstractive inductions, formulations of general descriptive-cum-explanatory classifications. How they are passed on is through language, and it is helpful to think of how children are taught the meanings of these sorts of words. This typically involves certain kinds of ostensive activity, pointing at examples where it is presupposed that these are stereotypical. In fact, it is commonly done through using pictures, which are intended as abstract specifications (though their serving as such is not an intrinsic property, since they are themselves particulars but depend on a grammatical context in which singular and general terms are distinguished by use).

What a child learns, therefore, in learning the word *cat*, say, is an abstract generalization, moreover one that is articulable in various generic statements such as "cats have legs," "cats see," "cats meow," and so on. These are substance-involving predications, and they are also teleological in character: legs are the organs of walking; seeing is the activity defined in terms of its achieving a certain end, say the discrimination of light and dark; meowing is something cats do as part of their characteristic behavior with some unspecified purposes(s); and so on. What follows is that everyday concepts bring with them characterizations of the things falling under them that imply functions or activities that can be judged well or badly realized. We can go further, however, for it is implicit in these concepts that as well as distinguishing between (1) what belongs to the sortal per se and necessarily and (2) what may be predicated of it, there is a distinction within the latter category between what is proper to the sortal and what is purely contingent. For example,

1. it belongs per se to the sortal cat that cats are alive,
2. it belongs properly but not essentially to it that cats have eyes, and

3. it belongs only contingently that cats are to be found in North America.

It is not, absent some special story in which location is related to the preservation of a proper feature, a privation of a cat qua cat that it is not in North America, but it is a privation of it that it lacks eyes. It is not a privation but the ceasing to be of a cat that it lacks life. Sortal-dependent judgments of function or activity belong therefore not to the essence of a kind or primarily to purely contingent features of members of its extension but to proper characteristics, "propria." A cat's activity, or generalizing across functions its "life," is bad to the extent that it is lacking in certain propria or in the ability to exercise them effectively. Circumstances may lessen the disvalue of this or a situation may render the lack or defect circumstantially advantageous, but that is per accidens.

Pressing on, we may say that a category of natural evaluative judgments is introduced by characterizations of something as being an instance of an animate species-sortal. It is one thing, however, to say that an eyeless cat is defective qua cat, another to say that a myopic cat's seeing is defective (qua cat sight), and another still to say that a cat's abandonment of her kittens to escape some discomfort is bad qua nurturing role. The latter is couched in terms that imply knowledge and intention, but even if we were to reject the appropriateness of this, we may still say that, other things being equal, the action was defective with respect to the mother's role. Note that the badness is not derivative from the presumed harm in this case to the kittens, and in fact, none may have resulted; rather it pertains to the action as a failure of what was due given the mothering role and its functions.

The application of this structure to the human case is easy enough, though here questions of knowledge, intention, and voluntariness do apply in determining the appropriate action description and the issue of responsibility. There are additional features also. First, as with animate kinds generally, the primary operation of an organ, function, or activity is related to its role in the overall life of the animal, and there is therefore an issue of levels of description and evaluation. In the human case, however, the layering is greater and the interactions between them more complex, including weighing of functions and roles and of the goods to which they are directed. There are also cooperative functions brought into being to serve the interests of social interaction among which is a special category of "social acts." These involve expressed or implied undertakings that in the context of uptake by others and with appropriate mutual knowledge of the parties' beliefs and intentions constitute such actions as, for example, promises and orders and social institutions such as judicial courts, marriage, and adoption.[13]

There is, of course, a connection between the foregoing and what Aquinas has to say in response to question 94 of *Summa Theologiae, Prima Secundae*: "Whether the natural law contains several precepts or only one?"

> Since good has the nature of an end, and bad, the nature of a contrary, hence it is that all those things to which man has a natural inclination, are naturally apprehended by reason as being good, and consequently as objects of pursuit, and their contraries as bad, and objects of avoidance. Wherefore according to the order of natural inclinations, is the order of the precepts of the natural law. Because in man there is first of all an inclination to good in accordance with the nature which he has in common with all substances: inasmuch as every substance seeks the preservation of its own being, according to its nature: and by reason of this inclination, whatever is a means of preserving human life, and of warding off its obstacles, belongs to the natural law. Secondly, there is in man an inclination to things that pertain to him more specially, according to that nature which he has in common with other animals: and in virtue of this inclination, those things are said to belong to the natural law, "which nature has taught to all animals" such as sexual intercourse, education of offspring and so forth. Thirdly, there is in man an inclination to good, according to the nature of his reason, which nature is proper to him: thus man has a natural inclination to know the truth about God, and to live in society: and in this respect, whatever pertains to this inclination belongs to the natural law; for instance, to shun ignorance, to avoid offending those among whom one has to live, and other such things regarding the above inclination.[14]

The various inclinations or directional tendencies correspond to aspects of the proper nature of human beings, the sorts of things that are included in generics expressing it, such as "Humans seek to preserve their lives," "Humans engage in sexual intercourse," "Humans educate their offspring," "Humans live in society." In each case, the activity is directed to an end the realization of which is a good and contributes to the overall good of human life. It is clear that these statements are descriptive but also that they are normative or norm implying. The latter aspect shows in the fact that it is not an open question whether, in general, it is good for human beings to seek to preserve their lives or to live in society. It is no objection to this that it is not always for the best to live in society or that the claim that human beings do so has exceptions any more than it is an objection to the statement that cats have eyes that some do not. The statement pertains to the kind and is not logically equivalent to a lengthy conjunction of statements about individuals. Note also that the claim that human beings live in societies relates to a good to each and for all. It is not that social existence provides opportunities that an individual could not otherwise easily avail himself of and so has instrumental utility. Rather, the good is one partly constitutive of human well-being more generally, the partial and comprehensive goods consisting in the rationally controlled actualization of proper functions and activities.

Closing the Gaps

Recall Solomon's diagram:

L1) statements of fact
↓
L2) moral judgments
↓
L3) actions

And allow me to suppose that enough has been said to show that certain instances of L1—that is, propria-specifying generics—are both descriptive and normative, or directly norm implying: "Human beings eat" tells us both something of what human beings are (eaters) and what pertains to their good—viz., eating. It does not say that eating is always good or that in some circumstances it would be irrational to diet or to starve. A human's eating is under the governance of reason as evidenced in the fact that we make decisions about what, how, and when to eat—which is not to say that no such decisions are irrational. Does this amount to a transition from L1 to L2? That question cannot be answered without further specification of what is meant by "moral judgement."

"You ought to eat" and even "You must eat" may be justified in a given case by reference to general facts about what is required for the maintenance of human life and particular facts about the condition and circumstance of an individual, but they are liable to sound like nonmoral, practical judgments—indeed just the sort of thing that Prichard claimed only provided prudential motives and not moral reasons. I observed, however, that this distinction may be question begging. Certainly we can imagine situations in which the same judgments might be made and then sound like "moral judgements," but the difference may not be one of kind rather than one of intensity or urgency of need. Prichard's response will be that whether they are passing or vital, conceived in the way I have described, the judgments speak to something that the agent desires or needs and to that extent they remain prudential.

This, however, raises the question of what else is required for a prescription to be a moral one, once it has been allowed that practical reasons may be more or less weighty up to and including the point of pressing on the question of living or dying. Prichard speaks of "duty," and it might be thought that this introduces something not so far explained both on account of duties being generally (and perhaps always) other-regarding and because of the particular deontological register in which they are voiced. So far as the former point is concerned, I allowed that the relevant *proprium* ("Human beings are social animals") specifies a species good and recognition of this provides both self- and other-regarding reasons, or in Prichard's terms, both personal and impersonal reasons. Second, I also noted that among cooperative functions brought into being to serve the interests of interaction are "social acts" and associated institutions. The justification for creating these is that they facilitate life, and in that sense they are conditional upon an independently specified end, but it does not follow that one can rationally eschew that end—a matter I turn to next—and nor does it follow that the social acts themselves cannot create unconditional (though possibly defeasible) obligations. The point is simple enough, at least in general form. The fact that human beings are amorous and affectionate reproductive animals that generate altricial young gives reason for institutions that would facilitate that important aspect of life. So the justification of marriage, for example, is broadly instrumental. But the internal nature of the institution may involve noninstrumental requirements, such as fidelity. On that account, one can then speak of an unconditional duty, the explanation of which is the obligation acquired in entering into it.

Someone may allow this but insist that the surrounding framework of justification remains nonmoral insofar as it consists of various hypothetical imperatives to the effect that in order for certain goods to be attained, certain things have to be done. So even if something has been lifted into the sphere of the "moral" in the sense of the unconditional, it is only a small part of what might ordinarily be thought to belong to ethics in general. This form of objection insists again on drawing a special distinction between moral and other kinds of practical reasons, but given what I said about species-propria generics referring to the kind and not directly to the individual, it will not work to try to mark that distinction in terms of the impersonal/personal distinction.

What remains, I think, is the question of the character of the imperatives directly generated by reference to human nature. Put in terms of Kant's distinction, the point will be that moral imperatives are categorical, whereas those I have introduced (other than the derived "social act" dependent ones) are hypothetical. This is true. From "Human beings have altricial offspring," it follows that newborn humans will not survive without care, and from this that they need care, and from this that they ought to be cared for. The last is true even if an individual to whom that fact was pointed out had no interest in providing care. But since it is also true that human beings are social animals and that they are sympathetic animals, such a person does have reason beyond the impersonal reason deriving from the need to provide care where he or she may be in a position to do so. The following pair both derive from statements of need: "Given that they are altricial, human newborns ought to be cared for" and "Given that you are a human being, you ought to be social and sympathetic." Together and in relevant circumstances, these provide an agent with reason to provide help. What lies at the font of each is human nature, so while the conditionals are hypothetical, neither appeals to what an agent wants (and might equally well not want). Instead, both are assertoric, referring to needs, those of the patient's and those of a prospective agent. The needs in question derive directly from human propria, and one cannot rationally excuse oneself from these by saying that one chooses ends other than those one needs as a human being.

What though of the question of the relation between L2 and L3, where this concerns motivation? I have argued that certain noncontingent but nonessential features of human beings warrant ceteris paribus evaluation in respect of their deprivation (bad) or actualization (good). I have argued that the fact that something specified in highly general terms is good for a human being gives an agent defeasible reason to seek to protect or secure it. I have granted that the reasons are hypothetical but denied that they are merely instrumental in a rationally escapable sense, since one cannot rationally be indifferent to one's nature nor to what pertains to it. Suppose someone says, "I see that, but isn't it possible that I just acknowledge this without in fact being moved to act?" The seeming intelligibility of this response is, I think, illusory and derives from viewing what has been said from the perspective of something like theoretical anthropology. If one is in the position of a practical deliberator wondering what to do and whether this or that consideration provides reasons to act in one way or another, then the question is not whether to move from stasis into action for one is already in motion and seeking guidance as to how to redirect oneself. That being the case, recognizing that there is reason in the circumstance to achieve human good by doing such and such is thereby motivational. Of course, one may be confused, or in perplexity about which of several options to follow, or not really interested in acting at all, or depressed and inert, and so on. Absent such defeaters, however, to recognize that one ought to do some specific thing is, in the context of active practical deliberation, to have a motivational as well as a justificatory reason to do it.

The Primacy of Experience

No doubt there is more that could be said at the forgoing level of abstraction, but the main work so far as moral thinking is concerned, both in respect of forming generalizations about human good and evil and in connection with particular situations, lies in discerning what pertains to the human good and in judging in concrete situations how various elements of that good may be protected or realized. In this it is more than merely relevant but essential that one is oneself a human subject, for the meaning and import of features may only be visible to human eyes or appreciable to human sensibilities. So I return to the thought that what moral philosophy needs is not more theorizing but more input from reflective experience, and again I return to an artistic analogy. Aesthetics may take the form of applied philosophy of mind, general ontology, philosophy of language, and epistemology while hardly touching the surface of actual aesthetic experience. Alternatively, it could give attention to the content of such experience trying to understand what it is about music, say, and particular pieces that enables it and them to carry so much meaning. Similarly, a phenomenological approach in moral philosophy would look to explore the firmament of human value through the medium of reflection upon experience, noting and placing in relation various elements and identifying them for what they are and why and how much they matter. This may sound like a psychological exercise, but done in the way it needs to be, it is also conceptual and critical: distinguishing, for example, the range of character traits and dispositions and evaluating if and why they are either virtues or vices. It might also think about what it is to be in moral perplexity and how the character and situation of the deliberator might be necessary to determine a course of action, not presuming that what is determined is so for others in similar situations. There have been and are some philosophers whose personal experiences are so broad and deep and their imaginations and empathies so great that they can achieve much on their own account, but such are very few, and most of us would do well to read literary fiction, biography, history, and descriptive psychology, setting aside as unlikely to be of much if any help the copious products of contemporary metaethics. If they are to be studied for the purpose of understanding the human condition, it could be as examples of what happens when practitioners of an art or a science cease to use its methods to treat some independent subject matter and make the practice of the methods an end in itself, setting one exercise against another (what else could they be set against?) as professional performances self-consciously hoping to display inventiveness and ingenuity.

Bibliography

Anscombe, G. E. M. "On Brute Facts." *Analysis* 18, no. 3 (1958): 69–72.

———. "Modern Moral Philosophy." *Philosophy* 33, no. 124 (1958): 1–19.

Dunlop, F., and B. Klug, eds. *Ethics, Value, and Reality: Selected Papers of Aurel Kolnai*. London: Athlone, 1977.

Geach, P. "Ascriptivism." *Philosophical Review* 69, no. 2 (1960): 221–25.

———. "Good and Evil." *Analysis* 17, no. 2 (1956): 33–42.

Kant, Immanuel. *The Critique of Judgment*. Translated by Werner S. Pluhar. 1790. Reprint, Indianapolis: Hackett, 1987.

Moore, G. E. "A Defence of Common Sense." In *Contemporary British Philosophy*, 2nd ser., edited by J. H. Muirhead. London: Allen & Unwin, 1925.

Mulligan, K. "Promisings and Other Social Acts: Their Constituents and Structure." In *Speech Act and Sachverhalt: Reinach and the Foundations of Realist Phenomenology*, edited by K. Mulligan, 29–90. Dordrecht: Nijhoff, 1987.

Prichard, H. A. "Does Moral Philosophy Rest on a Mistake?" *Mind* 21, no. 1 (1912): 21–37.

Solomon, David. "Ethical Theory." In *Synoptic Vision: Essays on the Philosophy of Wilfrid Sellars*, edited by S. F. Delaney, Michael J. Loux, Gary

Gutting, and W. David Solomon. Notre Dame: University of Notre Dame Press, 1977.

Thomas Aquinas. *Summa Theologiae*. Translated by Fathers of the English Dominican Province. 2nd and rev. ed. London: Burns, Oates and Washbourne, 1920–1922.

Thwaite, Anthony, ed. *Philip Larkin Collected Poems*. London: Faber & Faber, 2003.

Williams, Bernard. *Ethics and the Limits of Philosophy*. London: Fontana, 1985.

———. *Moral Luck: Philosophical Papers 1973–1980*. Cambridge: Cambridge University Press, 1981.

6

PHILIPPA FOOT AND IRIS MURDOCH ON (NATURAL) GOODNESS

Michael D. Beaty

Two of the most remarkable intellectuals in the English-speaking world of the twentieth century are Philippa Foot and Iris Murdoch.[1] The two began a friendship at Oxford when men did not typically acknowledge women as their intellectual peers. Each became a formidable intellectual force, Foot in philosophy and Murdoch as a novelist and a philosopher. As is well-known, Murdoch and Foot were very close friends. Despite their friendship and their common projects, their philosophical interests and endeavors differed dramatically. In this chapter I compare and contrast their ethical perspectives. In each, I find an important component that is not in the other's fully developed view.

I

In her book *Natural Goodness*, Philippa Foot defends a kind of naturalistic theory of ethics,[2] one that clearly draws its inspiration from Aristotle and his natural teleology. In *The Sovereignty of Good*, Iris Murdoch says, "I offer frankly a sketch of a metaphysical theory, a kind of inconclusive nondogmatic naturalism, which has the circularity of definition characteristic of such theories."[3] In the same book, Murdoch refers admiringly to G. E.

Moore in several places, no doubt because she shares some of Moore's commitments. Both Murdoch and Moore are moral cognitivists and moral realists. Rarely, if ever, does Foot speak admiringly of Moore. Among intellectual enemies shared by Foot and Murdoch are the various versions of noncognitivism[4] concerning evaluative statements that were so pervasive from the mid-1930s until the publication of Rawls' *A Theory of Justice* in 1971, and some of which persist in sophisticated forms in contemporary metaethics.[5] It is fair to say that one of Murdoch and Foot's shared intellectual projects was to provide a definitive rebuttal to moral noncognitivism and moral antirealism. So at first blush, Foot and Murdoch appear to be moral cognitivists and moral realists and to embrace some form of naturalism about ethics. Despite these important similarities, there are deep and significant differences between the ethical theories each developed. To make these differences visible, in the next section I identify and discuss the primary features of Foot's ethical theory, and in the following section, I discuss similarly Murdoch's ethical perspective.

II

In *Natural Goodness*, Foot observes that her aim, for better or worse, is to propose and defend an account of human goodness that is "very different from that of most moral philosophers writing today."[6] In particular, she rejects, on the one hand, Moore's nonnaturalism and intuitionism and, on the other, the noncognitivist theories such as emotivism, prescriptivism, and expressivism. These noncognitivist theories had been the dominant metaethical responses to Moore's boast that he had refuted all forms of ethical naturalism.[7]

There are two primary parts to Foot's account of human goodness. First, she rejects Moore's nonnaturalism and intuitionism because it gets wrong the "real logical grammar of evaluations."[8] In short, she accuses Moore of misunderstanding the real grammar of goodness. Second, she argues that human goodness is a species of a more general kind, "the natural goodness and defect in living things."[9] And these two parts are conceptually tightly linked. To get a more robust appreciation of the force of her account, let's begin with Moore's famous rebuttal of "all forms of ethical naturalism."[10]

Famously, after insisting that "how 'good' is to be defined is the most fundamental question in all Ethics," Moore insists that it cannot be defined. Why? In retrospect, we can express his reasoning in something like the following way. Either "good" is meaningful or it is not meaningful, but not both, and everyone knows that "good" is meaningful. Now if "good" is meaningful, then it is either cognitively meaningful or merely noncognitively meaningful, but not both. But when we say something like "Pleasure is good," we make a truth claim. So "good" is not merely noncognitively meaningful. Thus "good" is cognitively meaningful. If "good" is cognitively meaningful, then "good" either refers to a complex set of natural properties or a simple natural property or a simple nonnatural property. "Good" does not refer to a complex set of natural properties, and it does not refer to a simple natural property. We know this because we can always ask, "But is pleasure good?" or "Is XYZ good?" So "good" refers to a simple, nonnatural property. And because "good" refers to a simple, nonnatural property, it cannot be defined, though it can be "seen."

Almost as famously, in insisting that "good" is both simple and indefinable, Moore compares "good" to predicates such as "yellow" and "red." Indeed, he says, "My point is that 'good' is a simple notion, just as 'yellow' is a simple notion; that, just as you cannot, by any manner of means, explain to anyone who does not already know it, what yellow is, so you cannot explain what good is."[11]

To sum up, Moore argues that "good" is a simple, nonnatural property. In doing so, he assumes that "good" functions like the predicates "yellow" or "red." Additionally, he provides the conceptual framework or categories for discussion in moral philosophy and metaethics for the next forty or fifty years. Put simply, "good" is either

1. cognitively meaningless, which prepares the ground for various versions of noncognitivism such as emotivism, prescriptivism, and expressivism;
2. a simple, nonnatural property, which encourages both nonnaturalism and intuitionism; or
3. definable because "good" picks out a complex set of natural properties, which provides the basis for theories of ethical naturalism of various sorts.

Now let's return to Foot in *Natural Goodness*. If one is a moral realist and thinks that "good" functions like "red," then it is not surprising that one supposes both that "good" cannot be defined[12] and that it picks out a nonnatural property. But why think that "good" functions like "red"? Foot faults Moore for taking as a standard form of predication "X is good." She puts the point as follows: "Fixing our eyes on the peculiarity of goodness

when predicated as a property in a sentence such as 'Pleasure is good'...
is to skew the enquiry from the outset. If in everyday life someone said to
us 'Pleasure is good,' we should ask, 'How do you mean?'"[13] She says, "For
the acceptance of this rarely appropriate form of words makes it hard to
see the real logical grammar of evaluations, in which, in most contexts,
'good' requires to be complemented by a noun that plays an essential role
in determining whether we are able to speak of goodness rather than badness, indeed, of goodness or badness at all."[14]

Foot makes two points. First, she claims both that any "X is good" phrase
is not only not a standard way of using "good" but also a "rarely appropriate
form of words." Perhaps this is just a modest way of asserting that "X is good"
is never intelligible. In her writings, I find no affirmation that "X is good" is
intelligible. Second, she insists that "X is good" is grammatically misleading.
The latter is her more important point. So instead, she claims, we should
consider predications of the form "X is a good K." Clearly, Foot is taking her
lead from what she identifies as "a sadly neglected article"[15] titled "Good and
Evil" by Peter Geach.[16] Thus she puts "good" in the class of attributive adjectives, like "large" and "small," rather than in the class of predicative adjectives,
like "red" and "yellow." What follows if she and Geach are correct? Here are
some possibilities:

1. Just as "large" can be defined, so can "good."
2. Like the phrase "X is large," the phrase "X is good" is incomplete. And just as "large" requires a noun or some substantive phrase to complete it for the sake of intelligibility, so does the adjective "good."
3. The properties picked out by the phrase "X is a good K" are determined by K. That is, the traits for which something is truthfully called "good" differ according to the K, the kind of thing in question. For example, a good carving knife is sharp. And a good butter knife is dull. These instruments serve different ends. Thus it is not surprising that their good-making qualities differ.
4. It is not intelligible simply to attach "good" to just any K. Is this a good rock? We hardly know what to say until we know by virtue of what aims or purposes the author regards the stone as good. We want to know, "good for what?"
5. Just as "large" has descriptive force and meaning, "good" has descriptive force or meaning.[17]
6. Because "good" has descriptive force or meaning, we can replace the phrase "X is a good K" with the traits picked out by the phrase

without loss of meaning. For example, for anyone who knows the end carving knives serve also knows that the assertion "That's a sharp carving knife" implies that "That's a good carving knife" and vice versa. Indeed, this linguistic insight explains why Foot (and Murdoch) insists that "good" is a thin concept in contrast to richer concepts such as courage, temperance, justice, and prudence.

7. Finally, the attributiveness of "good" demands a more intimate connection with its noun or substantive than does "large." For, whereas it is not possible for most Ks to be large—"X is a large K" means that X has more of the relevant size than the average-size K—it is possible for all Ks to be good. It is surely possible for most carving knives to be sharp.

Earlier, I claimed that Foot rejects Moore's nonnaturalism and intuitionism because she claims that Moore misunderstands the grammar of goodness. Following Geach, Foot insists that statements we take to be moral evaluations of good actions and good human beings share a logical grammar, an attributive use of "good" with statements like good carving knives, good carpenters, and good parents. However, Foot insists that the "grammar of good" is only half of the story. The other half is that the moral evaluation of human beings "shares a conceptual structure with the evaluations of characteristics and operations of other living things, and can only be understood in those terms."[18] Just as we speak intelligibly and insightfully about the "natural goodness and defect" of living things—plants and animals—so we speak intelligibly and insightfully about human moral goodness when we recognize that it too is a kind of species-dependent natural goodness. According to Foot, then, moral evaluations of human beings will reflect both (1) the natural goodness and defect of living things and (2) that logical attributive nature of "good." How does this work?

Let's begin with the attributive nature of "good." Think about any carving knife. It is an instance of a kind that shares some common properties. Each instance has a characteristic function. The characteristic function of carving knives is cutting meat smoothly and easily. Sharpness makes this end achievable; it makes it possible to achieve a high degree of success with respect to the end of cutting meat smoothly and easily. Dull knives thwart that end and so are defective. Being sharp is a good-making quality in a carving knife; being dull is a bad-making quality, a defect in a carving knife. To assert that some particular carving knife is good is to assert that it is sharp. "Being sharp" is a quality or characteristic that makes a carving knife good at its function or in its characteristic role. "Being sharp" is a good-making quality relative to the end or purposes of carving knives. This way of being good is a kind of instrumental goodness.

Note that to take the attributive nature of "good" seriously is to focus on the nature of the noun it modifies. To have more than a superficial knowledge of what is being asserted by claiming "X is a good K," we must know at least something about K. Sometimes the noun being modified by "good" is a kind or species of living things. It follows from Foot's account that we can evaluate all living things in a similar way to the way we evaluate the goodness of anything that has characteristic functions (with important differences, of course), such as artifacts (carving knives, garden tillers, fly rods), roles (carpenters, physicians, teachers), or kinds of living things.

Rather than having a cosmic designer that gives the kind of thing characteristic ends or functions, according to Foot, members of a living species have a shared natural history and life-form, which gives its individuals characteristic natural ends.[19] To speak intelligibly about oak trees, night owls, or deer, we need to speak about a species-dependent natural history and life cycle or life-form. On the one hand, what each living thing shares in common is a natural impetus toward self-maintenance by securing nourishment, by defending itself and its kind, and by reproduction.[20] These are natural ends intrinsic to the natures of all living things, and as such are natural goods. To speak of such natural goods is an intelligible way of speaking about all living things. Importantly, to realize these kinds of natural goods successfully, individual plants and animals will need certain natural traits whose ends include the securing of these natural goods, in a similar way that a particular carving knife requires some quality that enables it to realize its characteristic end—cutting meat smoothly. Foot notes that Elizabeth Anscombe called such traits "Aristotelian necessities."[21] Such necessities are forms of natural goodness.

The connection between the natural habitat of various plant and animal species and the traits needed to achieve their natural goods "determine[s] what it is for members of a particular species to be as they should be and do as they should do."[22] To flourish in their natural habitat, oak trees need deep, thick roots; shallow, thin roots are a defect. Owls need night vision; an owl is defective without it. Deer need a keen sense of smell, speed, and the kind of coloring that allows them to blend into the natural surroundings. A slow deer or albino deer is defective.

Because human beings are members of a living natural kind, a similar kind of natural normativity to that of plants and animals is true of human beings, claims Foot.[23] An animal is flourishing if it is living the kind of life that befits it. By fitting, Foot means, roughly, the kind of life made possible for members of its kind, given its species-dependent natural powers, capacities, or characteristics. Some natural characteristics are necessary for the flourishing of plants and animals. These characteristics will be "Aristotelian necessities" and provide a schema of "natural normativity" for plants and animals.

Similarly, argues Foot, some "natural" characteristics are necessary for a good human life, and they provide the conceptual framework for natural goodness, though she concedes a good human life and a human good are "deeply problematic"[24] in ways that plant and animal flourishing is not. It is problematic because there is such a diversity of human goods that constitute a good human life.[25] Despite this diversity of human goods, Foot suggests that it is possible to give some quite general account of what is necessary with respect to the human good.[26] "A good human life" plays the same role in determining goodness for members of the humankind that "flourishing" plays for determining goodness among plants and animals[27] and, I suggest, what "cutting meat smoothly and easily" plays in determining the goodness of carving knives. Indeed, she declares that Geach was correct to suggest that just as stings are necessary for the flourishing of bees, so virtue is necessary for the good life of adult human beings.[28] Foot adds, "Men and women need to be industrious and tenacious of purpose not only so as to be able to house, clothe and feed themselves, but also to pursue human ends having to do with love and friendship. They need the ability to form family ties, friendships, and special relations with neighbors. They also need codes of conduct. And how could they have all these things without virtues such as loyalty, fairness, kindness, and in certain circumstances obedience?"[29]

Yet while the human good maintains a common conceptual or logical structure to that of the flourishing of plants and animals, Foot says that the human good is sui generis.[30] By sui generis, Foot means that despite lots of similarities to "flourishing" for plants and animals, the human good, or good life for human beings, is unique in striking ways. It consists of more than survival and self-maintenance, development, and reproduction.[31] For example, human beings communicate in a written and spoken language, making truth as well as art and scholarship possible. But nonhuman animals are capable of enjoying neither the search for truth nor the goods of art and scholarship. Thus Foot argues that human beings are capable of enjoying a variety and diversity of goods unmatched by animals and plants.

In large part, the sui generis nature of human goodness can be explained as follows. While in most animals natural goodness is mostly a function of instinct, in human beings it is a function of reason, and—especially—the rational will, claims Foot. In particular, a good rational will is essential to a morally good human life.

Nevertheless, Foot insists that we can provide a natural history account of human goodness, a form of natural goodness. For, according to Foot, the same normative pattern for ascribing natural goodness to plants and animals is present, conceptually, in ascribing natural goodness to human beings. Indeed, some of the "Aristotelian necessities" for humans are virtues, such as prudence, temperance, courage, and justice, as well as promise keeping. Just as an albino deer is a defective deer, so a human being that cannot or will not keep promises or who is characteristically unjust is a defective human being. And just as a dressmaker who does not teach her protégées proper stitching is defective as a mentor, so parents who fail to teach their children to be just and promise keepers, or prudent and temperate, are defective as parents. This is because, among other things, they fail to teach their children to employ well "the rational human will," that feature that is unique for humankind and that has as its end purposeful, voluntary action.[32]

What she does not explicitly say but must assume is that a good human being exercises the rational will well. In doing so, he or she acts virtuously, for virtue is "goodness of the will."[33] And that to exercise the rational will well is to choose well in light of good ends, ends ordered rightly or fittingly or properly in relation to one another. The rational will's natural end is the human good, a kind of human flourishing,[34] or happiness, that only human goodness can achieve.[35]

In summary, for Foot, a good human life is one in which the human person exercises the rational will well and thus enjoys an appropriate variety and diversity of goods, ordered in a way that fits or befits a human life.[36] Foot insists that we need not appeal to some form of nonnaturalism or intuitionism to account for human goodness (human virtues and vices) or the variety of other moral norms (such as the obligatory nature of truth telling or promise keeping). Nor do we need to appeal to God nor the greatest happiness principle nor Kant to account for the objectivity of moral norms. So while Foot embraces both cognitivism and moral realism, her account is through and through a naturalistic ethical theory, for moral norms are forms of natural goodness. However, is it—armed with its attributive form of goodness and its enriched natural history account of human beings—an adequate ethical theory?

III

Murdoch thinks it is not. Indeed, she says, "The concept Good . . . is not a mere value tag of the choosing will, and functional and causal uses of 'good' (a good knife, a good fellow) are not, as some philosophers have wished to argue, clues to the structure of the concept. The proper and serious use of the term refers us to a perfection which is perhaps never exemplified in the world we know ('There is no good in us') and which carries with it the ideas of hierarchy and transcendence."[37] Notice Murdoch's scathing derision of attributive goodness of the form "*X* is a good *K*." It is, she boldly insists, both an improper and a nonserious use of "good." But why think these two charges are true? She suggests that we know the very great are not perfect, thus "we see differences, we sense directions, and we know that the Good is still somewhere beyond."[38] But we can see differences and sense directions without granting that the Good is somewhere beyond, in any robust Platonic sense of the Good. After all, we can compare two good NFL quarterbacks and see the differences in the level of their good-making skills such that one is far closer to perfection than the other one. For perhaps the precision of his passes, his downfield vision, and his ability to read the coverages are, though good, not as close to perfection as his rival's. And we can see what the lesser quarterback must do to achieve the level of goodness of the better quarterback and thus see the direction progress requires. For these differences and directions, no Platonic conception of the Good need be presumed. Similarly, often we can see the differences between the moral quality of two people's lives. Easily enough, we bring to mind two acquaintances, colleagues or friends, one of whom is temperate in speech, manages anger and frustration well, and exercises both patience and goodwill when in a verbal disagreement about something important to both, while another is lacking in all these areas. With respect to these differences, one is morally better than the other. Again, we see differences and can articulate the direction our one friend must turn and travel if that friend is to become a morally better human being. Indeed, we can make these judgments by appeal to the kind of natural normativity Foot calls natural goodness.

However, to appreciate more fairly and fully why Murdoch rejects the natural goodness account provided by her friend Philippa Foot, we need to investigate more fully Murdoch's ethical perspective. What are the essential elements of her view and how do they overturn my suggestion that Foot's account of natural goodness applied to human beings grounds judgments that patience, goodwill, justice, and temperateness in speech and behavior are, among others, virtues?

First, as I have already noted, Murdoch identifies her ethical perspective as "a kind of inconclusive non-dogmatic naturalism."[39] Given current understandings of naturalism, whether metaphysical, normative, or meta-ethical, Murdoch's claim that her ethical view is a form of naturalism is odd. Murdoch provides two clues to explain this characterization. One is found in a passage from the "Sovereignty of Good over Other Concepts." There she says, "I assume . . . that human life has no external point or telos."[40] Murdoch explains what she means: "There is no general purpose and externally guaranteed pattern or purpose of the kind which philosophers and theologians used to search," but rather, we are "transient mortal creatures subject to necessity and chance" and "there is . . . no God in the traditional sense of the term."[41] Murdoch's claim that her ethical theory is a form of nondogmatic naturalism is explained, in part, simply by its being, whatever else it is, a nontheistic ethical perspective. That is, it draws no support from, and is opposed to, all those ethical perspectives that rely on theism,[42] whether epistemically, normatively, or metaphysically.

But she means more than that. Near the beginning of "The Idea of Perfection," she discusses some of the ideas of G. E. Moore in considerable detail. She says, "Moore believed that good was a supersensible reality, that it was a mysterious quality, unrepresentable and indefinable, that it was an object of knowledge and (implicitly) that to be able to see it was in some sense to have it. He thought of the good upon the analogy of the beautiful; and he was, in spite of himself, a 'naturalist' in that he took goodness to be a real constituent of the world."[43] So we have identified a second way to understand her use of "naturalism" to describe her view. It is a form of moral realism. Of course, given these two ways of understanding her use of "naturalism," Moore's ethical theory is a form of naturalism. Yet famously, Moore is credited with offering a nonnaturalistic account of the Good or goodness—that is, a version of ethical nonnaturalism. By nonnaturalism, I mean (1) a form of moral realism and (2) cognitivism that (3) insists that there are some (at least one) moral realities, objects, or properties that are neither identical with nor reducible to natural objects or properties. Call this nonnaturalistic moral realism. In contrast, naturalistic moral realism holds that (1) some sentences that express moral claims such as "torturing innocent children is morally wrong" are true and (2) what makes such statements true are features, and only features, of the natural world. Clearly, Moore's ethical views were grounded in a nonnaturalistic account of the Good. Moreover, Plato's account or sketch of the Good was both nonnaturalistic and nontheistic. And as we shall see, Murdoch's own view seems to fit Moore and Plato's nonnaturalism better than standard understandings of naturalism in ethics, despite the fact that she calls her ethical perspective a form of nondogmatic naturalism. Indeed, like Plato and Moore, Murdoch is committed to nonnaturalistic moral realism.[44]

Second, Murdoch has a pessimistic view about the prospects for a life of moral goodness for human beings. Her moral pessimism is grounded on several assumptions, ones she thinks are easily granted or demonstrated. One, she "assume[s] that human beings are naturally selfish."[45] Insisting that we have much to learn from modern psychology, especially Freud, she emphasizes the way in which the individual is, in large part, a psychic bundle of energy that resembles a machine that is relentlessly looking after itself. She suggests that because the self is so divided, both against itself and others, there are insuperable barriers to goodness for human beings.[46] Indeed, she declares, "In the moral life the enemy is the fat relentless ego."[47] And despite the emphasis on the centrality of reason, choice, and will among many moral theorists, she insists, regarding the ego, that "the area of its vaunted freedom of choice is not usually very great. One of its main pastimes is daydreaming. It is reluctant to face unpleasant realities. Its consciousness is not normally a transparent glass through which it views the world, but a cloud of more or less fantastic reverie designed to protect the psyche from pain. It constantly seeks consolation, either through imagined inflation of self or through fictions of a theological nature. Even its loving is more often than not an assertion of self."[48] From Freud, she says, we "learn to picture the mechanism as something highly individual and personal, which is powerful and not easily understood by its owner."[49] And also we learn that this mechanistic bundle of energy has a life of its own and from which, often in ways that surprise its owner, acts of will or choices emerge in ways that are unclear, both to the self whose acts they are and to those affected by those acts.[50] Perhaps this is but a gloss on Nietzsche (and amplified by Freud), who said, "We are unknown to ourselves, we knowers, we ourselves, to ourselves, and there is a good reason for this."[51]

The second assumption grounding Murdoch's moral pessimism is that in addition to pervasive and deeply rooted selfishness or egoism, she insists that "goodness [in men and women] is rare and hard to picture."[52] She defends her claim by insisting that we know very little about morally good men and women. Insightful and useful information about those in history that have traditionally been thought of as morally good (Socrates, Jesus, Saint Francis of Assisi) is "scant and vague."[53] With respect to contemporary candidates for moral goodness such as friends or public figures, she suggests that the sources of their moral goodness are likely to be obscure to us, or after an investigation, we discover their goodness is frail and fragile (perhaps like our own), and thus we don't get much help from these sources either.[54] Notice that she makes three distinct though related points. One, the sources of moral goodness of the morally good are obscure. Two, we have difficulty picturing moral goodness in ourselves and others. Three, we discover that the moral goodness of our moral exemplars is frail or fragile.

Murdoch asks, "How can we make ourselves morally better,"[55] given the powerful efficacy of our fat, relentless egos; our inability to picture moral goodness; and our frail, fragile hold on moral goodness? More directly she asks, "Are there any techniques for the purification and reorientation"[56] of our naturally selfish egos? The simple answer Murdoch provides is attention of the right sort.[57] By attention she means "a just and loving gaze directed upon an individual reality."[58] Attention is natural to human beings and is a source of energy, if we attend to objects of the right sort. Consider how much moral help one gets when one attends to the character and actions of morally virtuous people, or to objects of beauty, or to religious icons or moral parables, Murdoch suggests. Notice the tension between her defense of the importance of attention and her claims that our understanding of moral goodness is obscure and its hold on even the best of us is fragile. She observes that it is a psychological fact that bad objects of attention corrupt while good objects of attention improve people. So "we can all receive moral help by focusing our attention upon things which are valuable: virtuous people, great art, . . . [and ultimately] the idea of goodness itself."[59]

The most important element of moral formation (or transformation) and the supreme object of attention, of our loving gaze, is the Good. Like Plato, for Murdoch the Good is the supreme object or concept necessary to live the morally good life and to become a morally good human being. Yet she claims that "where virtue is concerned we often apprehend more than we clearly understand and grow by looking."[60] While Foot need not deny that we grow morally by seeing, no doubt she would, like Aristotle, insist that we grow more by doing. By practice, we acquire the sorts of habits or dispositions to behave that make us, and our work, good. We become just by doing just actions, temperate by acting temperately, and so on.[61]

Murdoch offers a rich, complex account of the Good, which reverberates with Platonic themes. And yet, it is also a puzzling account, as I have already suggested. Let me say more about its richness and complexity. Murdoch maintains that the Good is a unifying concept or a unitary form.[62] All virtues, for example, are forms of goodness and find their unity in the Good.[63] More generally, all forms of excellence are unified by the Good. The Good includes degrees of excellence, with perfection being the highest.[64] For even if some state of our character is good, we easily admit that it could be better until a state of perfection is reached, wherein no further development in goodness is possible. The Good transcends the natural world understood as an empirical set of conditions and happenings. The Good exists necessarily and, thus, is incorruptible or indestructible.[65] Because the Good is transcendent, it lies beyond the empirical world[66] and exercises its authority from beyond.[67] The Good is like the sun in that it is an object of vision, though it cannot be looked at directly, only indirectly.[68] Like the sun, it provides light or enlightenment by virtue of which the rest of reality is visible.[69]

The Good not only illumines the natural world; it is also an object of desire, and thus it is magnetic, drawing us to it.[70] Both desired and desirable, the Good is mysterious, indefinable, and nonrepresentable.[71] Its mysterious, indefinable, and nonrepresentable nature lends itself to the charge of obscurity. But Murdoch explains the indefinability and nonrepresentable features of the Good in terms of (1) the unsystematic variety of the world, (2) the pointlessness of human virtue,[72] and (3) human frailty.[73] Despite the limitations imposed by human frailty and the random variety of the world, Murdoch maintains that contemplation of the Good is essential to the morally well-lived life, however pessimistic she is about the moral transformation of most individuals.

IV

Consider now some important similarities and differences in Murdoch's and Foot's ethical perspectives.

Foot's defense of human moral goodness as a kind of natural goodness is a version of moral realism and moral cognitivism. We can identify it as a naturalistic moral realism. A moral realist insists that there are moral truths and, thus, moral knowledge. Second, Foot's view is a teleological normative theory. By teleological, I mean that character traits are justified by their place in a framework that presumes some end or ends justify the goodness of certain traits (and actions), either as means to, or a constituent of, the end. Let's call Eudaimonism the teleological ethical view that the end of human life is human flourishing that consists in the enjoyment of a variety and diversity of human goods, some of which function as Aristotelian necessities, or virtues. Foot's naturalistic moral realism is or at least approximates a eudaimonistic ethical theory. I say approximates because she is reluctant to identify eudaimonia, or human flourishing or human well-being, as the ultimate or supreme end of human action. But there is the human good whose general contours are sufficiently clear, she maintains, so that some virtues and some rules of conduct are justified by their relationship to the human good. Her eudaimonistic-like framework grounds her natural normativity or natural goodness. More specifically, her attention to the biologically grounded, natural-history life cycle both of the human and nonhuman species provides the explanation and justification of moral judgments in terms of normative natural goodness.

Murdoch's ethical perspective is a version of moral realism and moral cognitivism. In contrast to Foot, it is a version of nonnaturalistic moral realism. Is Murdoch committed to a form of ethical eudaimonism? Murdoch scholars disagree. Those who do not think that her ethical perspective is eudaemonist include Philip Cafaro[74] and Tony Milligan.[75] In contrast, Doug Henry argues her view is a version of eudaimonism.[76] While traditional forms of eudaimonism identify human flourishing to be the end that justifies the normativity of human virtues and vices and other ethical norms, Murdoch speaks rarely, if at all, about human flourishing as an end. She does, however, see the Good as the proper ultimate object of human attention, and from it one can naturally construe human perfection as an end. If her view is a version of eudaimonism, it is only implicitly so. Whether or not Murdoch's ethical perspective is eudaimonistic, on her view normativity is not simply or fundamentally a teleologically derived, and biologically attentive, natural normativity as it is for Foot.[77] In contrast to Foot, Murdoch emphasizes the importance of what psychology, especially Freud's, teaches us about human beings. Murdoch thinks the facts about our propensity for selfishness, for self-deluding fantasy, and for irrational consolations are truths about the human condition that must be admitted and addressed by any realistic ethical perspective. And these facts point toward the need to go beyond the natural world for normativity, she claims. For Murdoch, an appeal to the Good is necessary for normativity, and this appeal must be to something nonnaturalistic.

Another important difference between Foot and Murdoch is their stance toward the possibility of human beings living morally virtuous lives. Given our natural condition, Murdoch is pessimistic about human beings, while Foot is more optimistic.[78] For Murdoch, whatever chance human beings have to overcome our natural selfishness is a function of our being transformed, and thus overcome, by a source of goodness and light that transcends the natural world and, from its transcendent location, exercises authority over our fat, relentless egos. Moral progress is daunting and requires a nonnatural source of moral authority. One possible meaning of "authority" is the issuing of categorical demands and imperatives. For Kant, this kind of authority was necessary to distinguish morality from prudence or selfish behavior. And Kant reasoned that such authority was, then, independent of one's desires or interests, one's appetitive or sensible nature, or one's mechanistic ego. In short, there are reasons to act that are independent of one's fat, relentless ego. For Murdoch, the Good as a magnetic center that transcends the empirical world functions similarly.

In contrast, for Foot, human moral progress requires no nonnatural resources. At the same time, she insists that the account of normativity she defends is a form of practical reason, one that provides the agent reasons to act that are independent of his actual desires or interests. In other words, she insists that her account of natural normativity provides reasons to act that are more than mere hypothetical imperatives.[79]

V

In this section, I identify and discuss an important puzzle in Murdoch's perspective and argue that Foot's view is superior precisely because it has the conceptual resources to articulate and explain what Murdoch cannot explain within her perspective. Then I point to an important strength of Murdoch's perspective that is missing or underdeveloped in Foot's ethical perspective.

To begin, let me identify the puzzle. On Murdoch's view, the Good is indefinable, mysterious, obscure, and nonrepresentable. Yet the Good is that which both grounds and justifies the claim that the virtues Murdoch identifies (e.g., truth telling, humility, and courage, among others) are genuine virtues, aspects of human goodness, and more fundamentally, aspects of the Good.[80] If the Good is indefinable, obscure, mysterious, nonrepresentable, how can one be justified in asserting that truth telling, humility, or courage is an aspect of the Good and thus of human goodness? I can say that having four right angles is a characteristic of squares because I can represent a square via a definition. So its nature is conceivable by me and is neither obscure nor mysterious. In contrast, for thousands of years, the moon was visible, but its surface and internal or deep structure(s) were invisible or scarcely visible to the naked eye. Hence the real nature of the moon's surface was obscure and mysterious. Precisely because of this obscurity, accurate knowledge about the moon's real nature (and characteristics) was not available. Thus the moon's characteristics were unrepresentable, unknown, and, hence, mysterious. Similarly, if the Good is indefinable, unrepresentable, obscure, and thus mysterious, one has no justification for claiming that justice, truth telling, and humility are aspects of the Good and of human goodness. In contrast, Foot's appeal to the attributive nature of "good" and to natural normativity provides an explanation of human goodness by means of a familiar form or pattern of reasoning and, to that extent, is rationally preferable to Murdoch's appeal to the Good as mysterious, unrepresentable, indefinable, and obscure.

Murdoch is not without a possible response. The ancients believed the moon was perfectly spherical and farther from the earth than it is. While they were wrong about those two claims, they had some justification for their views. Their justification was primarily based on their views about the perfection of the heavens and was independent of accurate observations of the moon. They did have some independent observations that were true: the moon is round; it is white; it brightens the night. Call these surface-level claims. Given this analogy, Murdoch might have some justification for saying that the judgments that truth telling, humility, and courage (and others as well) are virtues are true surface-level claims with respect to the Good.[81]

Nonetheless, clearly Foot's explanation of why certain human traits are virtues and others are vices has far more explanatory power than does Murdoch's and, to that extent, is a superior account. Let me explain. If we return to the analogy, despite the truth of these surface-level claims (the moon is round, appears white, and often brightens the night), the real nature of the moon was obscure to its ancient observers, and thus, its real nature remained unrepresentable, thus obscure and mysterious. If we use this analogy to understand Murdoch's account of moral goodness, then being a morally good human being is being truthful, humble, courageous, and so on. But these are merely surface-level claims, and the real nature of human goodness is mysterious, unrepresentable, obscure, and indefinable.

In contrast, just as the goodness of a carving knife consists in being sharp or the goodness of an NFL quarterback consists, in part, in the preciseness of his passing, so the moral goodness of human beings (being a good human being) consists, in part, in being courageous, humble, honest, temperate, persistent, resilient, compassionate, and so on. These latter claims (being sharp, being a precise passer, being courageous) are not merely surface-level truths. Each attribution identifies a deep truth about the relevant subject's goodness. That truth is the relation between the end or good sought and, with respect to human virtues, both the means and some of the end's constituents. In contrast, Murdoch's picture of the relation of the virtues to the Good is nonilluminating.

On Foot's account, there is a deeper structure, and we have access to it in an illuminating way. It is the combination of the attributive nature of good (X is a good K) and her appeal to natural normativity. Given the human good (our natural end), the moral virtues are just those acquired characteristics that are the means to, or the constituents of, that end or good. What Foot makes clear is that nature of the deeper structure. Thus neither the end nor the relation of virtues to the end is mysterious, obscure, unrepresentable, or indefinable.

Murdoch does not provide as sufficiently rich a conceptual framework within which an account of the virtues (and vices) can be articulated. Moreover, this lack of conceptual clarity undermines the moral realism and cognitivism of Murdoch's ethical perspective. For how can we know that truth telling or humility is a really genuine human virtue if the Good is indefinable, obscure, and mysterious? This lack of conceptual clarity is a defect in her account.

In contrast, Foot's naturalistic eudaimonism provides a conceptual framework within which it is possible to explain why truth telling, courage, and humility, for example, are virtues. The key elements are (1) the notion of a good human life (or a good life for human beings) and (2) the characteristics that are necessary for, or conducive to, or constituent of, the achievement of that kind of life.

For example, in addition to survival, longevity, and reproduction, a good human life characteristically includes the use of language to explore and describe the world and its constituents accurately. Most of the time we simply want an accurate picture for its own sake. This is one of the ways human beings differ from nonhuman animals. Sometimes describing parts of the world accurately is necessary for achieving the ends or purposes that are a means to, or a constitutive of, a good human life (e.g., how to build shelter, how to improve the conditions that make physical or mental health possible, how to resolve conflicts). Sometimes it may be a matter of life or death. So whether exploring parts of the world (e.g., a neurological map of the brain) for its own sake or for the sake of eliminating disorders of the brain, truth telling is a virtue, an acquired character trait that makes its bearer and its work good.

A good human life includes making one's way in a dangerous world. For some, it includes protection of the vulnerable and weak (one's children or your neighbors' children). For these ends, courage is a virtue. Some possible ends of human action are unworthy of our efforts or significant sacrifices of time, money, or physical or mental energy. Knowing what ends to pursue, under what conditions, with what limitations, and the like requires more than knowing some facts. A life that is good for a human being necessarily includes the acquisition of knowledge, of understanding, and of practical wisdom. By practical wisdom I mean (1) knowing what the genuine human goods are and how they are properly ordered with respect to one another in a good human life and (2) knowing what particular decision to make in light of one's efforts to live a good human life. The acquisition of knowledge, of understanding, and of practical wisdom requires humility from the learner. Humility is a proper stance toward one's intellectual shortcoming or limitations.[82] The proper stance includes recognizing one's strengths and one's limitations and being willing to submit to another source of authority in order to gain what one lacks. Humility is an essential virtue with respect to the acquisition of knowledge, understanding, or practical wisdom. Since few, if any, human beings are complete with respect to the knowledge they need in order to make wise decisions across a wide range of diverse circumstances as one traverses the stages of human life—from adolescence to young adulthood, then mature adulthood, and finally old age—humility is a virtue, an Aristotelian necessity, for human beings.

How might Murdoch respond? Perhaps she would say that not only are truth telling, courage, and humility virtues; temperance, prudence, justice, and many others are as well (charity or love, generosity, patience, resilience, persistence, and others besides). But each of these exemplifies an excellence. Unlike sharpness in a knife, insofar as the human virtues are a kind of excellence, they are intrinsically, not merely instrumentally, good. If so, then there must be some further way in which each of these is related. But whatever it is they share in common, it is not a natural property or set of natural properties. Thus the best explanation of the way in which they are all excellences is that they exemplify goodness, or the Good. That is, she may claim that there must be some further way of explaining and justifying why each of these characteristics is in fact an excellence, a way of being intrinsically good, and doing so requires a nonnatural property, which transcends (is distinct and nonidentical with) all empirical objects and their properties. But this response simply begs the question in favor of a Platonic explanation. What Foot shows is that we can account for a variety of human excellences by reference to a conceptual scheme of natural normativity and the attributive nature of "good."[83]

Despite my criticism of Murdoch, her account has something compelling that is absent in Foot's *Natural Goodness*. Murdoch reminds us that being a good human being is very hard work indeed. Many, perhaps most, of us are failures in one way or another. Sometimes our efforts to improve our character are admirable and successful, even though, to be sure, perfection exceeds our grasp. At other times, our efforts, however admirable, have meager success or are largely unsuccessful. Still other times, some people are so utterly at odds with what is good for them and for others—at odds with the human good—that their efforts to become morally better are pitiful and pitiable. Others seem resolutely opposed to human goodness. They are evil.

The ways of being at odds with one's own good are many, but one important way is to love some genuine goods too much and others too little. Murdoch is pessimistic about human beings loving themselves or others well because of our fat, relentless egos and our propensity for self-deception and, worse, hatred of the good. On Foot's account of moral goodness, the resources for becoming morally good are merely and only human. As Aristotle reminds us, if one gets off to a bad start (bad parents, bad kinfolks, bad community), then one is utterly without hope. No further help is within our sight or within our reach. For Plato and Murdoch, the Good is real and transcends the natural world. By transcends, clearly Murdoch means (1) what is outside, distinct from, the natural world; (2) what not only is distinct from but surpasses all other forms of natural goodness; (3) what refers to a perfection never exemplified in the natural world; (4) but what is both attractive and energizing (a magnetic center).[84] It is within our sight, she contends.

One hopeful possibility of attention to the Good is that those who turn and attend to the Good properly may find themselves aided by a kind of Goodness that supplies power to become what one is not yet, a power of neither our own making nor our own doing. Thus one may find resources outside oneself (and one's community) to become good. Murdoch makes the point this way:

> I think there is a place both inside and outside religion for a sort of contemplation of the Good, not just by dedicated experts but by ordinary people: an attention which is not just the planning of particular good actions but an attempt to look right away from self towards a distant transcendent perfection, a source of uncontaminated energy, a source of new and quite undreamt-of virtue. This attempt, which is a turning of attention away from the particular, may be the thing that helps most when difficulties seem insoluble, and especially when feelings of guilt keep attracting the gaze back towards the self. This is the true mysticism which is morality, a kind of undogmatic prayer which is real and important, though perhaps also difficult and easily corrupted.[85]

In Foot's account of natural goodness, there are no nonnatural resources available for the pursuit of human goodness. For many human beings, this is not good news but rather a counsel of despair.

Conclusion

I have provided here a comparison of the ethical perspectives of two highly influential intellectuals, Philippa Foot and Iris Murdoch. A definitive comparison requires much more work than I have accomplished in this chapter. Still, I have shown that Foot's account of natural goodness provides an attractive conceptual structure and richly articulated account of the human good-making natural characteristics—that is, the human virtues—and of other human moral norms as forms of natural goodness. Foot's project requires a sufficiently rich and accurate understanding of a good life for human beings (a good human life) and the relation of that natural end to justice, temperance, courage, and practical wisdom, for example, to explain why they are virtues, Aristotelian necessities. In contrast, I have argued that Murdoch's account of moral human goodness is much less specific and articulate with respect to the virtues. Indeed, Murdoch fails to provide a conceptual structure to explain why truth telling, courage, and humility are virtues, except that "the mind which has ascended to the vision of the Good can subsequently see the concepts through which it has ascended (art, work, nature, ideas, institutions, situations, etc., etc.) in their true nature and in their proper relationships to one another."[86] But if the Good is obscure, mysterious, indefinable, and unrepresentable, then it seems implausible to think that seeing it illuminates, explains, justifies the claim that being courageous, just, and truthful are aspects of being a morally good human being. If I am right about this, Foot's view is superior to Murdoch's because of its greater explanatory power.

Still, Murdoch's view has one feature that is especially salient and points to an important lacuna in Foot's account. Murdoch's discussion of the all-too-human tendency to selfishness, to false consolations, to deluded forms of thinking, or to other self-entangling forms of human frailty and imperfection is an important dimension of any rich and robust account of the possibility and limits of human goodness.

Bibliography

Adams, Robert M. *Finite and Infinite Goods: A Framework for Ethics*. Oxford: Oxford University Press, 1999.

Aristotle. *Nicomachean Ethics*. Edited by Roger Crisp. Cambridge: Cambridge University Press, 2000.

Cafaro, Philip. "Virtue Ethics (Not Too) Simplified." *Auslegung* 22, no. 1 (1997): 52.

Foot, Philippa. *Natural Goodness*. Oxford: Clarendon, 2001.

Geach, Peter. "Good and Evil." *Analysis* 17 (1956): 33–42. Reprinted in *Theories of Ethics*, edited by Philippa Foot, 64–73. Oxford: Oxford University Press, 1967.

Henry, Douglas V. "Iris Murdoch's This-Worldly Eudaimonism." Paper presented at Conference on *Iris Murdoch and Virtue Ethics: Philosophy and the Novel*, Universita degli Studi Roma Tre, Rome, Italy, February 20–22, 2014.

Milligan, Tony. "Iris Murdoch and the Virtue of Courage." Paper presented at Sixth International Iris Murdoch Conference, University of Kingston, U.K., September 2012.

Moore, G. E. *Principia Ethica*. Cambridge: Cambridge University Press, 1993.

———. "The Subject Matter of Ethics." In *20th Century Ethical Theory*, edited by Steven M. Cahn and Joram G. Haber, 12–32. Upper Saddle River, N.J.: Prentice Hall, 1995.

Murdoch, Iris. *The Sovereignty of Good*. London: Ark Paperbacks, 1986.

Nietzsche, Friedrich. *On the Genealogy of Morality*. Edited by Keith Ansell-Person. Translated by Carol Diethe. Cambridge: Cambridge University Press, 1994.

Smith, Michael. "Moral Realism." In *The Blackwell Guide to Ethical Theory*, edited by Hugh LaFollette, 15–37. Oxford: Blackwell, 2000.

Sturgeon, Nicholas. "Ethical Naturalism." In *The Oxford Handbook of Ethical Theory*, edited by David Copp, 91–121. Oxford: Oxford University Press, 2006.

Whitcomb, Dennis, Heather Battaly, Jason Baehr, and Daniel Howard-Snyder. "Intellectual Humility: Owning Our Limitations." *Philosophy and Phenomenological Research* 94, no. 3 (2017): 509–39.

7

DAVID SOLOMON ON EGOISM AND VIRTUE

Irfan Khawaja

Introduction

It's often useful to revisit and discuss a classic paper in philosophy, whether for purposes of historical or conceptual perspective. David Solomon's "Internal Objections to Virtue Ethics" (1988) certainly qualifies as a classic in the literature on virtue.[1] It opens with an account of the essence of an ethics of virtue (EV) and then states and answers three fundamental and well-worn objections to the very legitimacy of the enterprise. Solomon's paper is probably one of the clearest, most concise accounts of where the literature and profession on EV was in 1988, and in reading it today, we can profitably ask not just where the profession was but, with the benefit of hindsight, where it went and whether it made progress along the way.

My aim here is to focus primarily on Solomon's response to one of the three objections, the so-called self-centeredness objection. As is perhaps obvious, the objection asserts that EV entails or at least promotes an ethic that is in some sense problematically focused on the self—more problematically so than its would-be competitors, Kantian deontology and consequentialism.[2] I want to suggest that Solomon's response to the objection fails, not for lack of ingenuity, but for lack of fundamentality. In other words, it doesn't answer the right objection in the right way. This failure arises in part from an ambiguity in Solomon's formulation of the objection, in part from a failure to ask why the problem the objection poses is in fact problematic, but ultimately from his insistence on drawing a sharp distinction between "internal" and "external" objections to EV and focusing on the former in contrast to the latter. Like so many apparently innocuous distinctions in analytic philosophy, I think this one conceals more than it clarifies.

Preliminaries

Let me begin by summarizing some of the essential features of Solomon's argument, a task eased by the elegance and clarity of the paper.

Solomon's first task is to get clear on the essential features of an EV. He starts by distinguishing three grades of interest in virtue and associates EV with the third, strongest grade: "EV entails the view that normative theory must have a structure such that assessment of human character is, in some suitably strong sense, more *fundamental* than either the assessment of rightness of action or the assessment of the value of the consequences of action."[3] "An EV, according to this third view, is a normative theory that takes *foundational* claims to be claims about the agent, or about human character. It takes judgments of character or of agents as *basic* in that it construes the *fundamental* task of normative theory to be to depict an ideal of human character."[4] Solomon continues,

> Given this general characterization a virtue ethics will typically have three central goals:
>
> 1. to develop and defend some conception of the ideal person;
> 2. to develop and defend some list of virtues that are necessary for being a person of that type;
> 3. to defend some view of how persons can come to possess the appropriate virtues.[5]

On this view, "the concept of a virtue is in important respects a more *fundamental* notion than the concepts of 'the right' or 'the good' where the good is seen as attaching to objects as possible consequences of our action."[6]

I've italicized the words that I regard as both crucial to Solomon's argument and also its weakest element. The task at hand is to contrast the essence of EV with the essence of deontological and consequentialist theories. The claim is not that deontologists and consequentialists cannot concern themselves with virtue. Nor is the claim that advocates of EV cannot concern themselves with rigid injunctions/prohibitions of the deontic type or with inquiry into the expected value of the intended consequences of human action a la consequentialism. The issue concerns what is "fundamental," "foundational," "basic," or "central" to each theory, and Solomon's point is that virtue is *fundamental* (etc.) *only* to EV. For now, I'll simply note that the preceding four concepts are not necessarily equivalent, that it's not clear what they mean, that Solomon doesn't explain their meaning, and that it wouldn't have been (and still isn't) easy to find clear analyses of them in the literature (whether the literature of 1988 or of 2017). But a great deal turns on what they mean, for if we cannot spell that out, we can't clearly distinguish EV from its rivals, much less explain why EV is to be preferred to them.

Solomon's second task is to address objections, distinguishing between internal and external ones, setting the external ones aside for separate treatment, and dealing for the present with internal ones. Here is Solomon's characterization of the idea of an external objection:

> By an external objection to an EV, I mean an objection that comes from outside ethics proper. . . .
>
> Typically, such objections will raise broadly epistemological or metaphysical difficulties with an EV. The primary external objection to an EV claims that an EV cannot be sustained because a necessary condition for the success of such a theory is a certain metaphysical or theological underpinning which, given the rise of distinctively modern science and the decline of classical theology, is implausible.[7]

Here is his characterization of the idea of an internal objection: "Internal objections to virtue ethics differ from external objections in that they come from within ethical reflection itself. They claim that there are general considerations connected to the point of ethical theory or to the structure of the moral point of view that make a virtue ethics untenable. As a consequence of being internal they ultimately depend upon arguments that support the claim that ethics really is the way they say it is. There is always the possibility, given their internal character, that these objections can slip into being question-begging."[8] As with all philosophical distinctions between "the internal" and "the external," the clarity of the distinction presupposes an account of the boundaries involved between "inside" and "outside." In this case, the boundaries involved are disciplinary, between the ethical and the nonethical.[9] But the distinction in question is a very blurry one. For one thing, it's not clear whether metaethical issues are "broadly metaphysical" or whether they "come from within ethical reflection." For another, it's not clear whether issues in moral epistemology or moral semantics are "broadly epistemological" or are internal to ethical reflection.

This last objection might seem quibbling, but I think it raises a basic issue of coherence in Solomon's paper. Solomon's first task was to identify the essence of EV. The second task was to distinguish internal from external objections. The combination of tasks presupposes that you can identify the essence of EV and defend it against standard objections, at least provisionally, while bracketing external considerations. There are some topics in ethics that are like that, but not, I think, the self-centeredness objection.

The self-centeredness objection claims that EV is "overly" focused on self. Clearly, the objection presupposes that something about EV makes this case and likewise presupposes some norm distinguishing excess from optimum with respect to self-regard. To understand the objection, we need to ask what would make EV so self-centered and, in particular, what it is about this thing that produces *excess* in the way of self-centeredness.

Prima facie, the most obvious answer is that EV gives a certain pride of place to individual well-being that is absent from most (or all) other ethical theories and that something about this focus produces excessive self-centeredness. The argument might go as follows: According to EV, virtue is central to EV because *well-being* is central to EV. A commitment to virtue is, after all, not a self-standing feature of an EV but gets its rationale and content from the teleological contribution it makes to well-being. Well-being is an ultimate end, and virtue *serves* this end. It's this tightness of fit between virtue and well-being that generates the self-centeredness problem. In other words, something about well-being—about virtue's teleological relation to it, about the motivations activated in pursuing it—simultaneously makes EV taxonomically distinctive *and* makes EV problematically self-centered.

If that were the objection, the essential issue involved should be clear. Either we have to deny that well-being is as central to EV as the objection suggests or we have to admit that it *is* central and contest the supposition that its centrality poses the problem that the objection suggests. In the latter case, we would need to query the supposition that tightness of fit generates the relevant problem. Tightness of fit would only generate a problem if there were something problematic about the very nature of well-being—something about the phenomenon itself that explained why something teleologically promotive of it, like virtue, would be tainted by causal association with it. The dispute would then be one between critics of EV, who insist that there *is* something problematic, and defenders of EV, who insist that there is *not*. Note, however, that that would be a dispute about *the nature of well-being, its relation to virtue, and how we know about both*, a dispute that seems to straddle the boundary between internal and external considerations. The objection would no longer be internal, and neither would the response.

This, of course, is not the way Solomon's paper actually proceeds. The paper's focus on internal considerations requires us to think of ethical issues as though they could be abstracted from metaphysical and epistemic ones so that those questions can be bracketed and given a separate treatment. But its focus on questions of essence and definition redirects us back to the external questions it insists on bracketing, practically in the act of bracketing them. The paper's central definitory claim is that virtue is more central to EV than it is to deontology or consequentialism, but this claim can't simply be a matter of stipulation. Something about the *world* makes virtue that central to human conduct—so central that deontology and consequentialism get ethics systematically wrong by ignoring it.

Talk about *what makes virtue central to human life* sounds metaphysical. But the metaphysical thing in question—well-being—seems both to provide the underlying explanation for why virtue seems so self-centered and to demand consideration in metaphysical terms. Either something about (the nature of) human well-being generates the self-centeredness objection or it's not clear what the objection is supposed to be. In focusing so assiduously on internal considerations, Solomon skirts all this, but in doing so, it seems to me that he sets things up to skirt the essence of the objection itself.

The Self-Centeredness Objection(s) and Solomon's Response(s)

The self-centeredness objection turns out to be the first of three objections to an EV. Let me state the whole objection in full, essentially verbatim from Solomon's paper, then come back and comment on it.

The self-centeredness objection, Solomon tells us,

> alleges that an EV tends to focus too much attention on the agent. As we noted in discussing the structure appropriate to an EV, such

theories demand a focus on the character of the individual agent. What gives point to the task of acquiring the virtues is that one supposes that one should become a person of a particular kind. One wants to change one's character from "the way it is" to "the way it ought to be" in the language of Alasdair MacIntyre. This view demands that the moral agent keep his or her own character at the center of his or her practical attention. To many persons, this requirement that each agent keep his or her character as the central focus of practical thought seems to import an *unjustifiable degree of self-centeredness* into ethics. If one supposes that the point of moral reflection *essentially involves a concern for others* (or at least that the interests of others be taken into account in practical thought, or that one move away from *a narrowly prudential view of one's action*), then it may appear that an EV cannot satisfy this requirement.

This attitude toward an EV is reflected in the claims frequently made that Aristotle, Plato, and other classical virtue theorists are ethical egoists of some sort. The thought behind such claims seems to be that for classical virtue theorists, it is rational for an agent to acquire the virtues only insofar as it is a good for that agent that he or she acquires them. But if the rationality of virtue acquisition is thus grounded in the needs of the agent, so the argument goes, the needs, wants, and desires of others have, from the point of view of morality, an *insufficiently prominent status*. Many twentieth-century Kantians have argued that this agent-centered feature of classical virtue theory makes it impossible to account for genuine moral obligation.[10]

Once again, I've italicized the phrases that I myself regard as fundamental to the objection. I'll return to them later.

Solomon's response to the self-centeredness objection consists of eight paragraphs spanning about two and a half pages of text. In form, the argument proceeds as follows: Solomon offers a preliminary response to the objection as previously stated (para. 1), then considers the possibility that the preliminary response is inadequate (para. 2). In considering the possible inadequacy of the response, he then slightly modifies the objection and offers a response to this slightly modified objection (para. 2). He then gives a more elaborated example intended to illustrate this latter response (para. 3). Having done so, he uses the example to suggest that EV has "partners in crime": deontology exemplifies the same feature as EV (paras. 4–5), as does utilitarianism (paras. 6–7). He then concludes that if the self-centeredness objection is a problem for EV, it is at least as much of a problem for its rivals. And so, "it is difficult to see that the special features of the asymmetry in the case of an EV should constitute a serious objection to theories of that type."[11]

I see two problems here. For one thing, even on its own terms, Solomon's argument does not in fact *answer* the self-centeredness objection. The objection asserts that EV is problematically self-centered. Solomon's argument only shows that EV is *as* problematically self-centered as are deontology and utilitarianism. Even apart from the plausibility of that claim (which I find implausible), it's perfectly compatible with Solomon's argument that all *three* theories are equally problematic and that all three fail. Solomon's argument here resembles, without quite exemplifying, a tu quoque fallacy.

A second problem concerns the move from paragraph 1 to 2. Paragraph 1 attempts to answer the *original* version of the self-centeredness objection; paragraph 2 reformulates the objection and answers *that*. There are, then, two *different* versions of the self-centeredness objection under consideration here. If the two are sufficiently different from one another, however, we confront the danger of equivocation over the meaning of "self-centeredness objection." As it happens, I think that the two versions *are* sufficiently different from one another; the first version is the more important one, and the first version goes unanswered.

Solomon concentrates on what might be called the *problem of asymmetrical concern*. The problem here is supposed to be that the agent is overly focused on self to the exclusion of others, which commits the agent to "an asymmetry that arises between an agent's regard for his own character and his regard for the character of others."[12] It's worth noting that on this version of the problem, we get no explanation for *why* the EV agent is excessively self-focused. Nor is there any implication that the agent is self-focused because being that way benefits him. The excessive concern for the agent in EV arises simply because it's a defining feature of EV to put the agent's character at the center of the normative picture, full stop.

There is, however, a slightly different problem lurking in Solomon's formulation of the self-centeredness objection, which I'll call *the problem of self-benefit or egoism*. The problem might be stated as follows: If "the rationality of virtue acquisition is grounded in the *needs* . . . of the agent," virtue *serves* those needs. If virtue serves those needs, then virtue gets its rationale and content from some conception of human needs. And if that is so, then EV conceives of virtue as inherently self-beneficial. Indeed, it seems to hold morality hostage to an egoistic constraint on the content of virtue: virtue must, so to speak, meet Glaucon's challenge to qualify as virtue at all. Put in this way, the self-centeredness objection is that being so fixedly concerned with one's *needs* is incompatible with what morality requires of us. Morality requires impartiality, but a fixation on need-satisfaction is incompatible with impartiality.

In fact, that understates things. A fixation on need-satisfaction gives free rein to conflict-generating behavior. For if I am out to satisfy my needs and you are out to satisfy yours, there will be some point at which our self-confined regard for our needs puts us in conflict with one another—the inevitable point at which mutual and simultaneous need-satisfaction is impossible. If we *both* insist on our own need-satisfaction up to and past that point, we are headed for conflict, and if EV does so, EV promotes conflict. So the assumption at the heart of this second version of the self-centeredness objection is not simply that EV generates asymmetries between self and other per se but that it generates *conflict-generating asymmetries rooted in self-benefit*.

Pace Solomon, few have ever thought it a problem that agents must be more concerned with their own characters than they are with the character of others per se. It's just obvious that each of us is better placed to be concerned for our own character—both causally and epistemically—than we are to be *equally* concerned for the character of others. For that reason, each of us has more responsibility for our own character than we do for others and so have more reason to be concerned with it.

What's *not* obvious is that we ought to be the ultimate beneficiaries of our own actions via some architectonic conception of well-being, self-benefit, or need. What's even less obvious is the implication that the benefits we confer on others have to travel through the benefits we confer on ourselves—or else aren't (morally) worth undertaking. Neither deontology nor utilitarian consequentialisms face a version of this problem, but we can see why an EV based on individual well-being would. If the rationality of virtue acquisition is rooted in (the individual agent's) needs or well-being, then virtues like justice and benevolence must benefit the agent. If they don't, they must not be virtues. And if they are not virtues, EV subverts morality as such.

That, as I see it, is the *real* self-centeredness objection, insofar as there is one. The problem is not *being focused on self* per se but *being focused on self for the sake of benefiting the self*, where focus on self-benefit is what explains the excessive nature of the self-focus that critics find objectionable in EV.

With this in mind, consider Solomon's first-round response to the objection: "The particular virtues characteristic of an EV may be as other regarding as one might wish. While each agent may be expected to devote primary practical attention to the development of his or her own character, that attention may be required to turn the agent into a person fundamentally concerned with the well-being of others. Classical virtues like justice, Christian virtues like love or charity, and Alasdair MacIntyre's favorite modern virtue, Jane Austen's amiability, all have a predominantly other-regarding character."[13] This response seems to me to both misconstrue the objection and misplace the burden of proof.

Misconstruing the objection: The objection (as I understand it) asserts that EV takes the rationality of virtue acquisition to be rooted in the needs of the agent and thus produces a conception of virtue that subordinates virtue to need-satisfaction. Solomon's answer makes no clear contact with this problem. Is Solomon

1. *granting* that EV takes the rationality of virtue to be rooted in the needs of the agent and suggesting that virtue being rooted in the needs of the agent is compatible with a conception of virtue that is not thoroughly self-beneficial?

Or is he

2. *disputing* that EV takes the rationality of virtue acquisition to be rooted in the needs of the agent altogether?

Either way, I think he faces a dilemma.

Regarding (1), it seems to me incoherent to say that virtue acquisition is rooted in the needs of the agent and yet gives rise to virtues that are not self-beneficial. "Rooted" is a metaphor for "justified by the contribution x makes to the agent's needs." If virtue is justified by the contribution it makes to the satisfaction of the agent's needs, then once we insert the trivial truth that need-satisfaction benefits the agent, we get the conclusion that virtue is self-beneficial. I suppose there are hairs to split here, but in general, the inference seems pretty clear.

Regarding (2), suppose then that we deny that the rationality of virtue acquisition *is* rooted in the needs of the agent. In that case, we can either

(a) dispense with an account of the rationality of virtue acquisition altogether or (b) rely on an account that is rooted in something other than the needs of the agent. Option (a) seems hopeless. If we dispense with an account of the rationality of virtue acquisition, it is not clear that it is rational to acquire virtue. In that case, the price of the answer to the self-centeredness objection becomes an irrationality objection: EV seems irrational. By contrast, option (b) is certainly a possibility. The defender of EV could produce a nonegoistic, non-self-beneficial account of the rationality of virtue acquisition, one that rationally demands that the agent acquire and practice self-sacrificial virtues. But Solomon's list of candidates hints at the problem here—a problem that I suspect would become more explicit if Solomon were more explicit about the content of the candidates. The classical defense of justice *is* rooted in well-being.[14] The Christian virtues like love or charity may not be, but to adhere to the internal/external distinction, Solomon would be forced to invoke a nonmetaphysical conception of Christian virtue that was somehow purely internal to ethical reflection. It's not clear to me what this would be.

Misplacing the burden of proof: Recall, as well, that the first item on Solomon's list of desiderata for an EV was that it must "develop and *defend* some conception of the ideal person." Solomon describes this whole conjunction as "basic," but that is misleading. A conception of an ideal person cannot be *basic* if it requires a further and separate *defense*. If I develop some ideal, *p*, and then seek to defend it by some defense *q*, then insofar as *q* is distinct from *p*, *q* is more basic than *p*. But if *q* isn't distinct from *p*, it's not clear how it can function as a defense *of p*.

If so, an EV requires not just an articulation of an ideal of the person but a defense of that ideal as more basic than the articulation. Suppose Solomon rebuts the self-centeredness objection by invoking Christian love and charity. For the rebuttal to work, he would need to *defend* these other-oriented ideals, not just invoke them. But the defense would in Solomon's view have to be internal to ethics, not external to it, and it simply is not clear to me how that would go or if it even makes sense.

I should stress that my objection to Solomon is not that he fails to provide a defense of the nature of virtue or of Christian virtue per se but that he fails to see that he cannot *answer* the self-centeredness objection unless he *has* one. In other words, my objection concerns the misordering of conceptual priorities involved, not the brevity of his exposition. It's not an *answer* to the self-centeredness objection that there happen to be conceptions of virtue out there that are not self-centered. In that case, the critic might simply rejoin that there are conceptions out there that *are*. What would answer the objection is that it is the non-self-centered rather than self-centered conceptions of virtue *that are in fact central to EV*. But this presupposes a way of demonstrating that one conception of virtue rather than another is in fact central to EV, which presupposes in turn an account of that which makes virtue central to EV. And *that*, I am insisting, is not an "internal" inquiry.

If I am right, we cannot address the self-centeredness objection until we first have in hand an account of the *metaphysical* nature of virtue, an account isomorphic in structure and content to the discussion of eudaimonia and *arête* in *Nicomachean Ethics* I or of virtue and happiness in Aquinas' *Summa Theologiae*. We need to know why human beings need the virtues (or virtue) before we can tackle the supposed problem of the self-centeredness that arises from acting on them. After all, if the justification of virtue really turns out to be need based or egoistic, the self-centeredness objection would simply beg the question against EV rather than state a bona fide objection to it. If we ought to be virtuous because virtue benefits us, it cannot be an objection to EV that it makes us "self-centered." In that case, "self-centeredness" would be a feature of the theory, not a bug. If on the other hand, there is some *other* self-sacrificial reason we should be virtuous—say, a distinctively Christian one—then the answer to the self-centeredness objection would have to be that it's mischaracterized what EV was about in the first place. In that case, you can't talk virtue unless you first invoke Christ. But the mischaracterization in question is a matter of mischaracterizing the relation between virtue and its *metaphysical* basis (in Christ)—an external consideration that couldn't be grasped by restricting our inquiry to internal ones.

What we *can't* do is to answer the self-centeredness objection from a standpoint that is neutral as between accounts of the relation between virtue and its underlying justification. Doing so puts us in the position of simply holding up our favorite conception of virtue to EV in an ad hoc fashion against the objection, which I think is what Solomon ends up doing.

Having said all this, I think it's clear *why* Solomon adopts the procedure he adopts. The project of providing an underlying rationale for virtue is a colossal task, one that was nowhere near complete in 1988 and is nowhere near complete in 2017. Prima facie, it might well have seemed as though the self-centeredness objection ought to be answerable by a defender of EV without the defender having to travel through the metaphysics of morals to answer what seems a fairly narrow and local objection.

One apparently plausible way of delimiting the task is to divide the terrain between considerations that are internal to ethics and those that are external to it, focusing on the former and leaving the latter for another occasion.

That's the analytic way: when a problem seems too big to handle, you cut it up into smaller pieces, and if you slice finely enough, it ought at last to become tractable. My objection here is that the analytic way is not always the right way. If, logically speaking, an answer to the self-centeredness objection presupposes an account of the relation between virtue and its rationale and questions about *that* relation are not internal to ethics in Solomon's sense, then the self-centeredness objection is not really an internal objection to EV. And no answer to it can be entirely internal either. Once you figure out why we need virtue, you can figure out what to say to the self-centeredness objection. But if you have no idea why we need virtue or what justifies virtue in the first place, any answer to the objection will involve some question begging and/or some groping in the dark. As I see it, the distinction between internal and external objections divides the terrain up artificially, and does so in ways that distort the issues at hand.

Conclusion

It's fitting, I think, that I should end on what is ultimately a quasi-Anscombian note. Anscombe famously opened her essay "Modern Moral Philosophy" by asserting, "I will begin by stating three theses which I present in this paper. The first is that it is not profitable for us at present to do moral philosophy; that should be laid aside at any rate until we have an adequate philosophy of psychology, in which we are conspicuously lacking."[15] Much later in the paper, in considering some problems related to the nature of justice, she says, "Now I am not able to do the philosophy involved—and I think that no one in the present situation of English philosophy *can* do the philosophy involved."[16]

I think something similar ought to have been said about the self-centeredness objection in 1988 and still has to be said about it today. It wasn't profitable for us to discuss the self-centeredness objection in 1988 or at present; that ought to have been laid aside until we had an adequate account of the relation between well-being and virtue, which itself would have obliged us to have produced an anthropology and psychology adequate to the debate. The self-centeredness objection itself was too far downstream in 1988 to have generated a satisfying debate. And without pretending to Anscombe's stature, I think it can still be said that I am not able to do the philosophy involved, and I think no one in the present situation of Anglo-American analytic philosophy can do it either. The literature is simply focused on the wrong things, and Solomon's paper shows why. As with "Internal Objections," the ubiquitous methodological assumption is that we must focus on small, analytically tractable problems that are internal to ethics rather than large, metaphysical ones external to it. What I would challenge, as Anscombe did, is the assumption that narrowness of focus yields analytic tractability.

As it happens, Elizabeth Anscombe's "Modern Moral Philosophy" was the first piece of philosophy I read as a graduate student at Notre Dame—in David Solomon's seminar on twentieth-century ethics, a seminar in which his legendary generosity, tolerance, openness, geniality, and patience were always in vivid operation. The seminar was a formative, memorable intellectual experience, one that I take as a standard in my own teaching to this day. I was at the time a callow, ill-informed, ill-educated Ayn Rand–intoxicated philosophical bigot, and twentieth-century ethics seemed to me a morass of pointless, uninteresting confusion. I doubt that anyone but David Solomon could in that state have made Moore, Prichard, Ross, or Hare seem interesting to me. In consequence, I'm happy to say that twentieth-century ethics now seems a morass of pointless, *interesting* confusion. That may seem to some a distinction without a difference, but it has for me meant the difference between perpetual alienation and authentic engagement, something to be grateful for—*a lot* to be grateful for. I'm very grateful to have the opportunity to say that at last to my own philosophical benefactor, the gift of a self-centered person to a self-abnegating one, but mutually beneficial, I hope, all the same.[17]

Bibliography

Anscombe, Elizabeth. "Modern Moral Philosophy." *Philosophy* 33, no. 124 (1958): 1–14.

Nagel, Thomas. *The View from Nowhere*. Oxford: Oxford University Press, 1986.

Solomon, David. "Internal Objections to Virtue Ethics." *Midwest Studies in Philosophy* 13 (1988): 428–41.

Williams, Bernard. *Ethics and the Limits of Philosophy*. Cambridge, Mass.: Harvard University Press, 1985.

8

YOU OWE IT TO YOURSELF

Candace Vogler

Introduction

David Solomon is an expert in the history of contemporary Anglophone moral philosophy.[1] As far as I know, Solomon is the ethicist best able to explain the intellectual roots, links, and quarrels that have animated philosophers interested in whether there might be a sound, systematic account of matters of right and wrong, good and bad that could be theorized in so-called analytic philosophy.[2] But in my experience, Solomon also is one of the very few Christian philosophers who think deeply about the relations between faith and academic practice, both in disciplinary philosophy and in North American higher education more generally. In moral philosophy, one of the places that strong lines of Christian intellectual tradition diverge from nontheist moral philosophy centers on understanding the scope of moral obligation. Contemporary nontheist work on moral philosophy draws its fundamental inspiration from Immanuel Kant's practical philosophy. In this chapter, I will argue against one of the pillars of contemporary neo-Kantian moral philosophy—the thought that I have a fundamental obligation to govern myself, an obligation rooted in practical reason and owed, in the first instance, to myself as a rational being. I mean the argument to provide indirect support for a contrary claim—that while I am responsible for trying to meet the challenge of the ethical rationally and humanely, any obligations I have to improve myself in this regard cannot be understood as things I owe to myself.

An Awkward Situation

> *Pooh-Bah*: Of course, as First Lord of the Treasury, I could propose a special vote that would cover all expenses, if it were not that, as Leader of the Opposition, it would be my duty to resist it, tooth and nail. Or, as Paymaster General, I could so cook the accounts that, as Lord High Auditor, I should never discover the fraud. But then, as Archbishop of Titipu, it would be my duty to denounce my dishonesty and give myself into my own custody as first Commissioner of Police.[3]

Do I have any duties to myself?

The claim that I do is perfectly familiar from advertising and intimate conversation. In these settings, claims that I owe myself things are meant to inspire me to make a better life for myself. But moral philosophy sometimes sounds a somber note in this otherwise uplifting chorus of voices urging me to be my own advocate. Kantians sometimes argue that I have duties to myself and that discharging these is (in some sense) prior to acknowledging obligations to anyone else.

Now it isn't obvious how I am to see myself as simultaneous debtor and creditor, as the one who owes such-and-such and the one to whom that very thing is owed, as having a directed duty to myself to do A, and a right against myself that I do A. Suppose I fail. Should I forgive myself? Is it enough if I offer myself a good excuse, or should I demand more by way of compensation *in foro interno*? And why think that I need to be able to sort through *those* questions in order to honor my obligations to other people?

For many neo-Kantians, as for Kant, it is built into the characteristic operations of practical reason that I hold myself accountable to moral requirements. Holding myself accountable makes no sense unless I can fail to do what I should do. For Kant, morality's reach extends beyond the sphere of adult human beings with their wits about them because nonhumans might count as practically reasoning beings capable of straying—that is, as addressees of imperatives. Not all neo-Kantians follow him in this. But however wide or narrow the relevant class of practically reasoning beings, Kantian ethics accepts the commonplace that morality enjoins conduct quite apart from personal projects, goals, inclinations, and tastes; quite apart from personal relationships; and quite apart from the vicissitudes of mood and fortune. Morality does not get its grip on me via such contingencies. It is not mediated by what happens to matter to me. Instead, morality enjoins conduct immediately. Morality is nonaccidentally developed and deployed by practically reasoning beings as such.

I have no interest in questioning the thought that morality is simultaneously possible and problematic for sane adults. I have no interest in dislodging the thought that obligations are crucial to morality. My concern is with the suggestion that positing duties to oneself is a good way of capturing a practical orientation alert to the demands of morality. After all, one normally thinks of ethics as involving more than one living thing. For example, the traditional stock of moral obligations comes into play when different adults going about their own business find themselves at cross-purposes. Morality inhibits our tendency to run roughshod over each other in such circumstances. To their credit, parties to moral interaction do not wrong each other. They abide by action-guiding constraints recognized as such by each and every party to mutual, reciprocal ethical congress.[4] It is because they are of one mind about such things that it is to their credit when they act well. It belongs to modern moral philosophy to hold that two strangers meeting on a road who are as different as you please might show due restraint in their dealings with each other. The possibility of moral interaction exceeds the boundaries of customs and culture as well as the limits of the parties' private concerns.[5]

Providing an account of morality in these terms is not easy. My first question is, How is positing duties to oneself meant to help? My second question is, Does talk of duties to oneself add to our understanding of acting well more generally? It is a strange thought after all—the thought that I owe myself things. Why go in for it?

An Argument

Explicitly or implicitly, neo-Kantian moral philosophy rests on the thought that, above all, I owe myself *rational self-governance*. It is an oddity of such views that what I owe to myself is unlike what I normally take myself to owe to others.[6] If I were elected, appointed, or born to high office, if I were the sole head of a tribe or some other corporate body, then I would be obliged to govern and perhaps even to make law. As it happens, my station in life is not like that. Instead, I owe *payment* to my creditors; *support* to my dependents; *service* to my employer; *aid* to others in need; persistent *unwillingness* to commit acts of murder, rape, or fraud against anyone to everyone; and so on.

The thing that neo-Kantians who accept talk of obligations to oneself think that I owe to *myself*—governance—may involve actual episodes of practical *reasoning* (if the theorist suggests that "self-legislation" is the name of something that I do on specific occasions), or else practical reasoning that meets certain standards (if, for example, the theorist urges that adequate reasons for acting are reasons that will apply to any similarly situated person facing circumstances like mine and I am obliged always to seek such a ground for my doings), or failing these more stringent requirements, plain openness to reason. In effect, I owe myself an adequate justification for what I do, or did, or propose to do. In this sense, what I owe to myself is steady and effective exercise of my own practical reason.

David Velleman has explored this aspect of Kantian moral philosophy as thoroughly as any prominent contemporary Anglophone neo-Kantian. He writes, "The requirement to act for reasons ... seems to come as close as any requirement can to having intrinsic authority, in the sense of being authoritative by virtue of what it requires. This requirement therefore comes as close as any requirement can to being inescapable.... The requirement that bears this mark of morality is the requirement to act for reasons; and so we seem to have arrived at the conclusion that 'Act for reasons' is the content of our duty."[7] What will such a requirement amount to in practice? Is it the requirement that I never engage in idle action—that I never pick up a piece of straw and chew on it while walking, or draw designs on the margins of a handout while listening to a talk, or pet the cat on impulse? If asked why I do any of these, I might answer, in all sincerity, "No reason."

A moral prohibition on idle action is, to say the least, counterintuitive. Doodling comes out paradigmatically immoral. Going to great lengths to plan and execute fraud, less obviously so. And happily, I think it *can't* be that Velleman means that I am inescapably bound, qua moral agent, never to engage in idle action. If there are hands doing the devil's work, then insofar as *working*, these hands are not idle. And Velleman is on record chiding moral philosophy for relying upon the moral psychology of the bland, earnest agent who always is concerned with acting for the sake of something she deems worthwhile.[8] He writes, "I can still care about doing what makes sense even if I don't care about the good. This possibility is demonstrated by my capacity to be guided by what makes sense in light of a counter-evaluative mood such as despair, since what makes sense in light of such a mood just is to do what's bad rather than what's good."[9]

To argue that I am inescapably bound to act for reasons, then, is to argue that I am bound to act in ways that make sense. Even things that we do just because we feel like doing them are subject to reasons-for-acting review, and practically reasoning beings may have to act in ways that could make sense. It makes sense to doodle on the handout while listening to a talk. Breaking off *giving* a talk in order to squat down and doodle on the floor at the base of the podium does not make sense. There might be a story. I might have my reasons. But the episode will *attract* reasons-for-acting-seeking questions even if everyone present is too polite to ask. In this sense, it seems reasonable to think that Velleman holds that I am inescapably obliged to act in such a way that I could be asked to explain myself.

Velleman goes on to argue that, although I am inescapably obliged to act in such a way that you can ask after my reasons, I am not, myself, the source of the authority attaching to my reasons. Nothing can count as a reason for acting unless a community of practically reasoning beings recognizes the action-guiding authority of the consideration. Regard for reasons, Velleman points out, is inextricably bound up with regard for persons.[10] Regard for persons is regard for beings who have the status of personhood, a status that belongs to members of communities of practically reasoning beings who share a framework for practical reasoning. Velleman writes, "Being an autonomous person is thus impossible without belonging to the community of those with access to the same sources of autonomy"—that is, the same rational requirements governing action.[11] And due self-regard is likewise rooted in personhood: "The value of our individual personhood here and now is inseparable from the value of participating in personhood as a status shared with our selves at other times and with other people, whose access to the same framework of reasons is what lends those reasons authority."[12]

Because I owe myself reasons for acting, and because reasons for acting take their normative force from a framework for practical reasoning that I share with other like-minded persons, in acting for reasons, I hold myself to community standards. Accordingly, Velleman thinks, it is by discharging my obligation to myself that I hold myself morally accountable.[13] So he has provided an account of morality rooted in the requirement that I act for reasons and taken it that meeting this requirement is something that I owe to myself.

Now I am inclined to think that the traditional prohibition on procuring the judicial condemnation of a man I know to be innocent, along with other such directed duties, yield requirements that are authoritative *by virtue of what they require*. They are certainly not "escapable" in the sense that their authority depends on some interest or inclination that I just happen to have. Nor are they escapable in the sense that they are only in effect for those subject to the rule of a specific governing body—the municipality of Chicago, for example. Limited jurisdiction and dependence on contingent projects, plans, and inclinations are the two escape routes to a requirement that Velleman discusses explicitly.[14] And Kant and Velleman alike regard traditional prohibitions on (for instance) murder as universally obligatory.

The kind of inescapability that Velleman uses as a basis for his argument is the inescapability of acting in ways that make sense. Noticing that we can question the authority of our own inclinations and that we can (in principle, if not always in practice) emigrate in order to escape the authority of the local governing body, Velleman writes,

> Suppose, then, that we attempted to question the authority of reasons themselves, as we earlier questioned other authorities. Where we previously asked "Why should I act on my desire?" let us now ask "Why should I act for reasons?" Shouldn't this question open up a route of escape from *all* requirements?
>
> As soon as we ask why we should act for reasons, however, we can hear something odd in our question. To ask "Why should I?" is to demand a reason; and so to ask "Why should I act for reasons?" is to demand a reason for acting for reasons. This demand implicitly concedes the very authority that it purports to question—namely, the authority of reasons.[15]

I think that this *can't* be the right place to lodge the argument about the inescapable authority of moral requirements.

Whatever inescapability attends the prohibition on taking murderous means to my ends, for instance, is compatible with the recognition that my killing Frank won't count as *murder* unless I have reasons for killing someone. It isn't *murder* if I fall off a cliff trying to rescue Jane and Frank breaks my fall. In paradigmatic cases, if I *murdered* Frank, then it is pretty apparent that I took myself to stand to gain by Frank's death. Perhaps I stood to inherit a fortune from his estate. Perhaps I was robbing a convenience store, had no special bone to pick with Frank, but Frank was blocking the exit.

Velleman argued that the requirement that I act for reasons is inescapable and that *no* consideration can count as a reason for acting if it is idiosyncratic or temporary. In his view, this shows that I must take it that I assess my own actions and actions-in-prospect from a shared framework for practical reasoning, and it is the supposition that I am not alone in this that lends authority to the considerations that weigh with me. But even if moral reasons meet the requirement of universally accessible common knowledge, a great many frankly immoral considerations do as well. For example, "those who stand to gain by wrongdoing have a reason to wrong others." And because of this, "those intent on wrongdoing as a means to private advantage have a reason to disguise their intent and work to escape detection"—a prudential consideration that takes its force from the fact that *everyone knows* that the prospect of gain is the most common reason for wrongdoing. In this sense, the way in which the prospect of gain underwrites misconduct is universally accessible common knowledge among practically reasoning beings.

Trying to ground morality in a distinctive requirement that I act for reasons is initially puzzling because, as Velleman knows perfectly well, there are reasons for wrongdoing. Although it is true that it must be in principle possible for other persons to see the sense in what I do if there is reason in my actions, this is *nowhere near* enough to establish that if I have recognizable reasons for acting, then those are reasons to act morally.

Velleman can reply that purported reasons for immoral conduct will show themselves to be inadequate upon further reflection. That's fine, but the problem with his account seems much worse than any that can be got around by saying more about reasons and persons. Consider: Velleman accepts the philosophical commonplace that intentional actions, *as such*, are subject to reasons-for-acting-seeking review.[16] In this sense, positing a distinctive obligation—an isolable practical requirement with inescapable universal authority—that I act in such a way that I can be asked my reasons for so acting is rather like positing a special, distinctive nutritional requirement that I eat things that are edible. We might posit such a requirement on the grounds that we cannot so much as *begin* to consider the finer points of my diet unless and until I stand prepared to eat edible things. One wants to say, but how does it count as *eating* if the stuff you are ingesting orally isn't even a *candidate* for being edible! Far from providing a special, extranutritional requirement, the demand that I stand prepared to eat things that are, for my kind, edible is the demand that I eat stuff that counts as food. And this is the same as pointing out that I need to eat now and then. Swallowing stones or arsenic or paper clips is not, in the relevant sense, *eating*.

Just as I can always be asked to provide reasons for my intentional actions, I can only do what it is in my power to do. *No one* will argue that I owe it to myself only to do what it is in my power to do, even though "Act in such a way as only to do what it is in your power to do" looks to be universally inescapable simply by virtue of what it says in roughly the way that "Act in such a way that you can be asked to provide reasons for your actions" does. That it is in my power to act, that you can ask after my reasons for acting—these things are already built into the part of the command that says *Act*. You have, in effect, ordered me to act in such a way that I can rightly be said to have acted afterward. I take it that this *cannot* give the content of a duty. A duty is the kind of practical consideration that can operate as a principle of action. As Douglas Lavin once put it, "An agent is subject to a principle only if there is some kind of action such that if the agent did it she would thereby violate the principle."[17] Are there any kinds of action I can do on purpose such that I cannot be asked why I did a thing of that kind? Velleman's argument suggests that he agrees with Elizabeth Anscombe. The answer is no. Accordingly, there is *no basis* for a duty here.

In short, it's not just that one needs more detail about what makes some practical consideration reason *enough* for action before one knows what to make of Velleman's account of the ground of morality. One needs some explanation about why it makes sense to posit an *obligation* to act for reasons. I mean, given that wrongdoing has its reasons too, how is this not just a lopsided wheel spinning idly in an account of moral conduct?

Velleman notes in passing, "Defenders of Kant's moral theory often seem embarrassed by his account of having obligations to oneself, which is said to be odd or even incoherent."[18] Velleman finds the notion unproblematic. But the attempt to explain the authority of morality in an inescapable and universal duty that I have *to myself* seems to have led to trying to ground morality in something that is true of all my intentional actions—namely, that they are subject to reason-for-acting-seeking review.

Unlike Velleman, Kant thought that there *was* something puzzling about the claim that I owe things to myself. It is worth a look at why he thought this and a suggestion about how he worked to solve the puzzle.

Kant

Velleman's neo-Kantianism turns on the explicit rejection of Kant's thought that *I* am the source of *all* my obligations. This thought gives rise to Kant's puzzle about how I can have obligations to myself. In the *Tugendlehre*, Kant rehearses two complaints against the idea:

> If the I *that imposes obligation* is taken in the same sense as the I *that is put under obligation*, a duty to oneself is a self-contradictory concept. For the concept of duty contains the concept of being passively constrained (I am *bound*). But if the duty is a duty to myself, I think of myself as *binding* and so as actively constraining (I, the same subject, am imposing obligation). And the proposition that asserts a duty to myself (I ought to bind myself) would involve being bound to bind myself (a passive obligation that was still, in the same sense, an active obligation), and hence a contradiction. One can also bring this contradiction to light by pointing out that the one imposing an obligation (*auctor obligationis*) could always release the one put under obligation (*subiectum obligationis*) from an obligation (*terminus obligationis*), so that (if both are one and the same subject) he would not be bound at all to a duty he lays upon himself. This involves a contradiction.[19]

Kant also thought that if I have no duties to myself, then I have no duties at all: "For I can recognize that I am under obligation to others only insofar as I at the same time put myself under obligation, since the law by virtue of which I regard myself as being under obligation proceeds in every case from my own practical reason; and in being constrained by my own reason, I am also the one constraining myself."[20] That is why the claim that I have duties to myself gives rise to an antinomy for Kant.

The short form of Kant's solution to the antinomy in the *Tugendlehre* is straightforward: what generates the apparent contradiction is that I am to be at one and the same instant legislator and subject to legislation, active and passive, source imposing the obligation and person thereby bound, hence capable of obliging and releasing myself at will. If it is so much as conceivable that I have obligations to myself, then I must be viewing myself in two different ways—qua rational organism (insofar as subject to law) and qua being endowed with noumenal freedom (as legislator). In short, Kant's solution to the antinomy turns on exactly the points that Velleman rejects: the claim that I am the source of the authority of the reasons that guide my action and the claim that my authority stems from noumenal freedom.

It is not easy to understand noumenal freedom. This is in part because noumenal freedom itself cannot be a content for thought. And some ways of getting around this point seem not to do the trick here. For example, it is true that I deliberate about *what to do* but not about *whether to do something of my own free will*. If I'm wondering what to do, then I'm wondering what to do under my own steam. On the face of it, this may dissolve the active-passive problem. An implicitly acknowledged source of my own actions (otherwise, apparent episodes of practical deliberation can't be practical reasoning at all), I *govern* myself, and since the actions thereby governed are, of course, *mine*, in governing myself I am also the one *governed*. It is not clear how the "two aspects of a single subject" thought dissolves the problem of being in a position to oblige and release myself willy-nilly, however. Kant's suggestion is that in obliging myself, I both show due respect *to* and place myself at the service *of* the humanity in my own person. The humanity in my own person is not fickle. I am its bearer, its advocate, and its steward. I owe it my concern. It is at once me and more than I am.

In what sense am I my humanity? In what sense is my humanity more than I am? And why is legislation the preferred metaphor for practical reason? We need an answer to these questions before we know what to make of Kant's solution to the antinomy he finds at the heart of his account of obligation.

I will not attempt a reading of Kant's account of law beyond mentioning that Kant thought that everything in nature operates in accordance with laws and that laws are universal in the sense applicable without exception to everything in their domain.[21] Neither will I attempt a full-blown interpretation of Kant's account of practical reason. Instead, I will give a nonstandard reading of one bit of Kant's *Groundwork of the Metaphysics of Morals*, the bit that is most obviously relevant to the suggestion that the practical reason I bear is my will and is also more than my will.

Having, he thinks, established that it belongs to ordinary moral thinking that the good will is the only thing that is always and everywhere good and that the good will acts not just in accordance with duty but from duty, the problem is to explain acting from duty—that is, acting from, and in accordance with, a very special kind of reason for acting. This kind of reason enjoins conduct *directly* and *immediately* rather than by way of any interest or inclination that a practically reasoning being might have. Because the law that governs the operations of the good will has to apply to every practically reasoning being for whom ethical conduct is at once possible (such that the being is capable of having a good will) and problematic (such that the being is capable of immoral action), it cannot take its force from *anything* about an individual practically reasoning being that isn't common to all such beings. It turns out that the list of merely contingent facts about an individual practically reasoning being is long. Obviously, my plans, projects, tastes, hobbies, personal relationships, profession, citizenship, sex, gender, political views, and religious affiliation are among the things that I do not share with all other practically reasoning beings. For Kant, even the fact that I am a *human being* rather than a practically reasoning bird or sea mammal or Martian is a mere contingency. If there is a law that governs the operation of practically reasoning beings for whom ethical conduct is at once possible and problematic, then that law *cannot* enjoin action by way of any of these contingencies. For such a law to get a grip in the way Kant thinks that it must, it must get its grip *without* appeal to things that belong to me, but not to you, and not to any practically reasoning dolphins that may inhabit the waters off our shores.

Suppose, then, the will stripped bare of every contingent interest, inclination, habit, incentive, plan, purpose, project, and so on. Suppose, that is, factoring out *absolutely everything* that serves to distinguish your practical orientation from mine, ours from the Martians', the Martians' from the parrots', the parrots' from the nonhuman primates', the nonhuman primates' from the dolphins', and so on. Suppose the bare finite, dependent locus of practical reason.

Far from being a special status conferred upon practically reasoning members of communities sharing substantive reasons for acting, the naked will is more like the lowest common denominator across finite, dependent rational beings—the will unallied with any of the things that make one practically reasoning being's field of practical engagement different from another's. In acting solely from and for the sake of duty, the good will acts from *this* source, from itself as such, and not for the sake of any of the aspects of its life that distinguish *its* life from the lives of other practically reasoning beings. And this provides a kind of framework for understanding the universality that is supposed to be captured in the universal law formulation of the categorical imperative. Since we have factored out everything *but* a will devoid of contingent incentives, *anything* it wills it wills without reference to, or stake in, anything that distinguishes it from any other finite, dependent locus of practical reason. Accordingly, every finite, dependent locus of practical reason that acts from and for the sake of a reason that enjoins action *immediately* and *directly* acts from *exactly* the same source as any other. There is *nothing else left* for any such locus of practical reason to act from, under the suppositions.

On this way of trying to cope with Kant, my *humanity* consists in the possibility that I might act from this source, a source shared by any and every finite, dependent locus of practical reason as such. In this sense, then, I am my humanity (insofar as ethical conduct is possible and problematic for me). Humanity is my nature.

Unsurprisingly, Kant takes it that no individual practically reasoning being can ever be certain (in its own case or about any other such being) that it has acted, will act, or is acting, strictly from and for the sake of duty. Bare willing is not part of *any* finite, dependent rational being's experience of itself. And the possibility of acting strictly from and for the sake of duty depends on the possibility that I am free, a thing that *frames* practical reasoning but can't be a content of practical reasoning, or of experience, or of thought. In this sense, my humanity is other than myself as I know and experience myself.

Duties to myself are duties to myself qua bearer of humanity. There is no danger that I will oblige and release myself willy-nilly. Rather, every time I acknowledge any duty, I recognize a reason for acting that enjoins conduct directly and immediately and will do the same for any finite, dependent, free locus of practical reason.

My humanity is not a thing that can release me from the need to respect *it*. To think otherwise will be rather like entertaining the possibility that the English language could release me from the need to obey the constraints of idiomatic usage and grammar in speaking English. I am a native speaker of English. I think, read, dream, write, and converse in English. In this sense, English belongs to me—is mine, is in me, qua native speaker. But in using English, I am constrained by the requirements of the very language that informs thought, writing, and speaking for me. In this sense, I am governed by my own mother tongue. I could learn another language and stop using English. But I can't remain a language user without using some language or other. Abstract humanity is rather like an abstract capacity for language use in this sense. And self-legislation becomes rather like abiding by the constraints of *some natural language or other* in speaking, thinking, writing, conversing, or otherwise engaging in linguistically competent activity.

That's all well and good for linguistic capacity, I might think, but why go in for even *taking* myself to be morally accountable?

For Kant, it is cosmically impossible that there might exist *any* practically reasoning being that did *not* have in it a tendency to develop and deploy *exactly* the same sorts of moral thoughts as I do and from *exactly* the same source—the very practical reason that it and I alike must bear in order to be so much as capable of acting upon rudimentary instrumental thoughts about how to get what we happen to want. Every actual or possible practically reasoning being, in this view, is *as such* bound by considerations of duty, and in exactly the same way, and from exactly the same source. That source is the free, finite, dependent locus of practical reason *as such*, something that we cannot experience, cannot observe, cannot ever be certain has informed any given act that we ourselves perform, and cannot track with certainty in the doings of others. And in *this*, my Kantian humanity is utterly unlike my own, or anyone else's, facility with any language.

As near as I can tell, Kant thought that he needed all this (and more besides) in order to ground morality. Grounding morality is very difficult. If Kant's system works, then he has done it. But the cost of accepting Kant's solution to the philosophical problem is high. I once knew a man who was good at calculating how to get what he wanted, could make conversation, acted on the basis of maxims—that is, calculative representations of his actions-in-prospect—and gave every indication of being *incapable* of holding himself morally accountable (although many of his stratagems depended upon his understanding that his fellows were susceptible to moral practical considerations). True, the man was criminally insane. True, we can't *know* that our impressions of such a man's will are veridical, if will is what Kant claims it is. Still, Kant seems to be arguing that some kinds of sociopaths *cannot* exist. And this is, as Michael Thompson puts it, metaphysically alarming.[22]

What's gone wrong here?

One possible culprit is the thought that morality must arise from my duties to myself. Somehow, morality must take hold of me qua isolated agent capable of deliberating about what to do and potentially alert to what immorality might do for me. Kant's system may not provide a way of talking me out of wronging others, but it at least tries to show that in wronging others, I also violate myself qua being capable of so much as considering taking immoral means to my ends. But requiring the will *to set* the conditions for sound willing is disconcertingly like requiring a legislator to pass a law that enjoins law abidingness. In this sense, Velleman's tendency to liken it to a rational requirement that I meet such requirements as are constitutive of reason isn't wrong. As near as I can tell, what makes Kant's efforts in this direction less perplexing than Velleman's is Kant's account of *the* will—finite, dependent practical reason—as constitutively determined by a self-imposed duty to act from, and for the sake of, duty and *my* will as a particular bearer of this will. *The* will sets standards that *my* will must obey.

I take it that Velleman is right to be concerned about taking Kant's account on board. But Velleman tries to translate Kant's thought about *the* will into thought about a community of practically reasoning beings sharing a framework for practical reason. The effort looks to fall prey to objections about the substance of common knowledge in communities of practically reasoning beings (since everyone knows there are reasons for wrongdoing) and to objections about the content of the alleged duty to oneself (since "Act in such a way that you can be asked why you did what you did" looks to be a long-winded way of saying "Act"). I take it that we have yet to be given compelling reasons to think that a practical orientation alert to the demands of morality finds secure grounding in thought about what we might owe to ourselves.

This brings me to my second question: whether there are independent grounds for thinking that I have duties to myself in the first place.

Possible Sources of the Intuition

I mentioned at the outset that "You owe it to yourself" is a familiar form of words and that those of us who have been inspired to take a holiday or leave a partner in response to advertisements or advice from friends may think, "They're right—I deserve better than this." A great many people who have no interest in producing a less demanding version of Kantian moral philosophy are perfectly happy to posit duties to themselves. In closing, I want to speculate about the source of the intuition that I have duties to myself. My speculation will rest in part on trying to provide an intellectual diagnosis of anxiety that may have no distinctively intellectual source. Solomon has always been better at developing this sort of understanding than I ever will be, but I offer up the effort in part based on having tried to learn from his example.

I suspect that practical isolation of some sort may be the secret of the intuition's force. The most important form of isolation, the one that seems to me to underlie advice from friends, is the sense that what I do is, to some extent, up to me and that, given this, I am to some extent responsible for how things go for me. This point works in tandem with the truism that I can deliberate about what to do but not about whether to do it under my own steam, even when I am trying to figure out how to get someone else to do something. What I decide, what weighs with me and how, and what

I do—these things are, to some extent, *mine* even when I have very little control over the options available to me and even though it is not in my power to *ensure* that things will go well for me, no matter what I do. Call this "step 1."

Step 2. This step has two cases. In the first, other people are concerned about me; in the second, I am on my own. In the first case, those who are concerned about me may have thoughts about what I should do in order either to improve my circumstances or to maintain and build upon those things in my life that are going pretty well. In the second case, I may take it upon myself to have an imagination for what I might do in order to make my life better (e.g., make some friends) or maintain and build upon the things that are in good order in my world (e.g., look after my health)—that is, I may think that there are things that I should do on my own behalf. People who know me can have thoughts about what I should do. I can have thoughts about what I should do. The question becomes, "What is the status of this *should?*"

Notice that the arena of concern in both cases is the sphere of *self-interest*, even though my intimates can have personal stakes in what I do and what comes of it, such that what's in *my* self-interest is also in *theirs*. I strongly suspect that, at the point one feels compelled to posit duties to oneself, it isn't credible to think that the action in question is one that I owe to *anyone else*. Otherwise, we would be discussing what I owe to somebody else—my children, say, or my parents, or God, or my employer—and, if we agree about the duty, the question becomes one about whether I was going to discharge my duty to so-and-so and, if so, how I am going to do that.

I confess that I don't quite know how we get from step 2 to positing duties to oneself, unless it's via some thought that action must be taken in this matter, that I am the best (perhaps even the *only*) individual in a position to do what's necessary, and that if *no one* is obliged to do something about the situation, then nothing will be done. As Solomon will be the first to point out, this thought does not provide a ground for positing duties to oneself. I don't know whether the thought suffers more from its tendency to overestimate the pull of duty or from its tendency to underestimate the pull of self-interest. It seems to me to suffer from both. I don't know how best to characterize the fear in the thought either.

In the case where we are inclined to posit these duties for others, it might be the fear that comes of our impotence to get other people to take action on their own behalf. Noticing that it is up to each of us, what to do is not always a liberating and joyful experience.

In the case where I self-reflectively move to expand the sphere of my duties to cover self-interest, it could be that I am trying to learn to be my own advocate, or I could be experiencing a kind of shapeless regret.

My speculation will involve three scenarios. What they all share is the supposition that the agent who is supposed to posit duties to herself or himself is, in crucial respects, alone and is also alert to the demands of duty more generally. The first scenario features a dutiful person surrounded by friends who want only the best for her. The second features a dutiful person who has broken ties with a tight-knit community and now must keep track of himself in ways that family and neighbors kept track of each other back home. The third features a dutiful person experiencing remorse over indefinitely many things he did not do. They are scenarios of mounting, increasing isolation in the face of an understanding that, after all, at the end of the day, sane adults are responsible for themselves.

Scenario 1: Friendly Ambitions

Friendly advice couched in terms of obligations to myself normally involves situations in which the good up for discussion is only practicable *for me*. It might be that no one else *can* do the thing I am told I must do; I am the only one who can implement my new exercise regime, for example. Or although the vicissitudes of fortune might always alter my circumstances, the only *legitimate* source of relief for me rests in what I can do for myself. No one else owes me what my friends think I deserve. In telling me that I deserve better and owe to myself to change, my friends are trying to convince me to demand more from life than I have.

Scenario 2: Culture Shock

Suppose, in the second scenario, someone who has left home to seek a better life. In the old town, definite ties of kinship and community tended to support the daily reproduction of material and social life through networks of obligation, attachment, and expectation. Now surrounded by strangers, the person whose daily life used to be shaped and structured by what he owed to others and whose material and social needs were met by what they owed to him retains a sense of duty while losing the whole field of specific obligations that shaped his old life. No one here owes him food or shelter. No one owes *him*, specifically, anything that is not subject to the terms of some new undertaking—a lease, say, or a job contract. His needs are, if anything, more acute than they were back home. He decides that he must owe *to himself* the things that were formerly provisions of community.

Scenario 3: Reflective Regret

Suppose now, a solitary episode of reflection. I can ask myself questions like these:

- Do I have good enough reasons to do what I want to do?
- Have I done enough?
- Should I have done something other than what I did?
- Am I misguided in the things that I have taken to be choice worthy?
- Do the many things that I work for and care about fit together, and is the result a life that I take to be worth living?

All these questions involve aspects of my life that may be invisible to other people in socioeconomic circumstances like mine. Provided that I am fairly steady, reasonably reliable, and not much inclined to outbursts, fragmentation in my larger practical orientation may never show itself to others. No one else may notice that I am brought up short when trying to determine which of several things that matter to me should take precedence here and now, for example. By the same token, provided that the things that I appear to value are things that it makes sense to value, my doubts about how I live may attract no notice at all.

Should I have acted differently? Notice that if I could have done even one thing other than what I did, then *indefinitely many other options* also were there for me. Who can compass the vastness of what I might have done?

Whether I have *reasons enough* to do what I do and whether I *do enough*, given the reasons that I have—it is not at all clear what kind of calculation of sufficiency and inadequacy is involved here. How much reason is reason enough? And even given sufficient reasons for action (whatever those might be), who is to say that I have done enough in the service of things that I care about where "enough" is meant to capture more than what's needed to attain my specific goals?

In short, when I engage in this kind of thought, I rapidly find myself considering things that *never happened*, things that I never started or never tried or never considered. Suppose I conclude that I have squandered my days with many things. When I reflect upon what I ought to have thought and did not think, what I ought to have said and did not say, and what I ought to have done but did not do, I will likely see that I have wasted many opportunities to make a better life for myself. Perhaps I am the *only* human being who can experience disappointment in the face of my imagined omissions. Much of what I have failed to do or say or think was of no concern to anyone else, after all.

If only I hadn't let myself get so caught up in details! This is not the kind of regret that fastens on a specific event or circumstance or type of action. Any particular occasion I seize upon in memory—a moment when I might have left petty concerns to the side for the sake of something more important—will slip into indefinitely many other moments when I could equally well have changed course.

In what sense might reflection on such topics seem to suggest that I owe things to myself?

There are, I suspect, three crucial points at issue here. First, *ex hypothesi*, my failures to live up to whatever standards are at issue in finding myself disappointing have not involved wronging anyone else. *I did not owe anyone else* the things that I might have thought or said or done for my own sake.[23] Second, *no one else owed me* whatever I think I might have got, if only I had thought or said or done different things. Third, because my flirtation with despair involves my representation of myself as a good person, it will feel as though there *must have been a duty here* and someone must have *failed* to discharge that duty. But there is only one person involved in my meditation, so any practical failure should have been prevented by the only person who could have acted differently—the single agent at issue here, the one who is reflecting upon her own life, me. And surely someone must set things right again, insofar as this is possible. (I am the only one who *can* repair those damages that are reparable; I am the only one who can see to it that I lead a finer life in the future.) Under the circumstances, it is natural to think that I have shirked my duty to myself.

At this point, notice, friends' and advertisers' invitations to seek better things for myself intersect with the mood of moral philosophy in urging me to develop my capacities for rational self-governance more fully—all in the name of duty.

But what, exactly, is it that I am supposed to have done differently?

It is one thing if the problem is that I have been attempting to habituate myself to some specific regime of self-control. I should have gone to the gym last week. I should not have had cake last night. Regimes of this kind are built of scheduling. If I intend to keep to a schedule, and I don't, then I have failed to do what I intended to do. Since I haven't changed my mind about the schedule and since my failure to follow the schedule had nothing to do with some sort of emergency that rightly disrupts schedules indefinitely, I should get back on schedule. In this sort of situation, normally, the schedule involves my free time—that is, portions of days or weeks when I am not obliged to be at work, say, or looking after children. We do not need to postulate duties to make sense of my finding ways of spending my free time that are beneficial to me. The theater of concern, here, is the theater of self-interest. Kant, at least, thought that human beings were strongly inclined to pursue self-interest and private advantage. That was part of the reason he thought that linking our obvious skill in doing things on our own account to holding ourselves accountable to moral precepts was a good strategy for grounding morality.

Now people with time on their hands and deep attachments to using their free time well do all kinds of things to keep to schedules. If they are likewise deeply attached to pretending that they are required to do whatever it is that they have decided to do with themselves, then they may well use talk of owing themselves healthy food and time at the gym as at once a crutch and a blunt instrument. The crutch gives people who are afraid of seeming selfish permission to follow the schedule. The blunt instrument can be used in attacking oneself inwardly when one fails to keep to the schedule. This technique for self-control may be psychologically efficacious. So might a self-talk strategy built out of frank concern with health or one that was all made of considerations of pleasure. Different temperaments move in different ways. And of course, people can band together for the sake of making better use of their spare time and undertake *joint* fitness projects so that they owe it to each other to exercise together. There are many ways to keep to a schedule. The fact that elevating intention to the status of duty is useful for some people does not mean that this self-management technique illuminates anything of philosophical interest. Duty talk, like pleasure talk and self-interest talk, is a way that people can hold themselves in check and keep themselves in a world. Vivid fantasy may also do the trick.

If much of my time, my income, and my assets are mine to do with as I please, there is no obvious place for talk of duty to get any traction (except in the sense that I am in an excellent position to find ways of being of use to someone else, and this is somehow not even occurring to me). Philosophically, if not psychologically, it seems to be enough to deploy the machinery of intention and planning to understand how things are, what is going wrong, and what kinds of things might improve my situation. If I am horrified at the thought that I am the chief beneficiary of my own efforts to improve my life, then this is a psychological fact about me, one that I might try to explore with a trained professional, using some of my discretionary income in my free time.

But what of my more amorphous concern about what might be and what might have been, if only I had thought or said or behaved differently? Ethically significant omissions are not just any old things that I didn't think or say or do. They are not even just any old things that could have made some difference to others, had I behaved differently. Ethically significant omissions fasten onto specific kinds of acts that were called for in specific kinds of circumstances, sometimes on the part of specifically positioned individuals. The shapeless and pervasive sense that things might have gone otherwise for me if I had behaved differently rests in a truism without enough content to ground a specific conclusion about what I ought to have done or what I ought to have avoided doing. At root, it expresses no more than the fact that I am partly responsible for how things go with me and that, in some matters, I am the only one who can have an impact on how things go with me. This isn't a description of a sphere of obligation. It is the kind of thing that has to be in place before anything as definite as a sphere of obligation can emerge.

In short, where the shapeless "might have been" is concerned, there is no specific act that I ought to have performed, there are no specific words that I ought to have spoken, and there is no specific thought that I ought to have entertained; in short, *there is no content to this duty*. Like Velleman's duty to act for reasons, my meditations on what might have been yield no more than an undirected exhortation to pay more or different attention to my own life—a thing that is too indeterminate to guide action.

Concluding Remark

Where does it come from, then, this thought that there is a gap in our understanding of moral conduct that can be filled if I owe myself things?

It is, I suspect, difficult for some basically good, reasonably materially secure adults who are, for whatever reason, alone and at liberty to tend to the business of prudence unless they can see prudence as somehow necessary to something other than plain self-interest. Humans are naturally social beings. It is built into the sentimental education of many of us to see ourselves knit into a social world by, among other things, duties. If there are things that we can do on our own account that will provide us with better lives and if it feels as though the kind of "ought" that attends such things is of a piece with the kind of "ought" that attends morality, we will be strongly tempted to extend our willingness to abide by moral constraint to the theater of self-interest.

I have no quarrel with people doing what they need to do in order to look after themselves, particularly in settings where no one else owes them any help. But I do not think that positing duties to ourselves helps us to account for either prudence or morality. I expect that Solomon will agree.

Bibliography

Anscombe, G. E. M. *Intention*. Cambridge, Mass.: Harvard University Press, 2000.

Kant, Immanuel. *Grunglegung zur Metaphysik der Sitten*. Abschnitt 2. Akademieaugabe von Immanuel Kants Gessamelten Werken, Band 4.

———. *The Metaphysics of Morals: Doctrine of the Elements of Ethics*. Translated by Mary Gregor. Cambridge: Cambridge University Press, 1991.

Lavin, Douglas. "Practical Reason and the Possibility of Error." *Ethics* 114, no. 3 (2004): 424–57.

Linsky, Leonard. *Semantics and the Philosophy of Language*. Chicago: University of Illinois Press, 1952.

Scanlon, T. M. *What We Owe to Each Other*. Cambridge, Mass.: Harvard University Press, 1998.

Thompson, Michael. "What Is It to Wrong Someone? A Puzzle about Justice." In *Reason and Value: Themes from the Moral Philosophy of Joseph Raz*, edited by R. Jay Wallace, Philip Pettit, Samuel Scheffler, and Michael Smith, 333–84. Oxford: Oxford University Press, 2004.

Velleman, J. David. "A Brief Introduction to Kantian Ethics." In *Self to Self: Selected Essays*. Cambridge: Cambridge University Press, 2006.

———. "The Guise of the Good." *Noûs* 26, no. 1 (1992): 3–26.

Part Three
ETHICS AND CULTURE

9

DIGNITY AND THE CHALLENGE OF AGREEMENT

Bryan C. Pilkington

Attempting to make sense of claims like "Human dignity is inviolable. It must be respected and protected"[1] and "Dignity is a useless concept ... and can be eliminated without any loss of content"[2] calls out for careful work on this murky concept. Among other mistakes, ranging from oddly poor arguments to seemingly purposeful uncharitable readings of good-faith attempts to understand dignity, critics of the use of dignity have failed to account for tensions within the concept and between distinct accounts of dignity.[3] The most striking mistake has been a failure to notice a tension between dignity's *meritorious* and *egalitarian* elements. Better and more philosophically rigorous work has since followed the now well-known lambasting of dignity by Ruth Macklin and Steven Pinker, and though discussions of dignity can be traced back to a variety of sources—Pico della Mirandola is a favorite of some, Immanuel Kant a favorite of many—I focus here on more recent philosophical work on the increasingly discussed, sometimes supported, and much maligned concept of dignity.

Introduction

Though difficult to solve, the problem of dignity is relatively easy to articulate: What is dignity and why should we take it seriously? Critics argue that dignity[4] is eliminable from our moral and political discourse without serious consequences, even accusing those who employ the concept of dishonesty and sleight-of-hand.[5] Yet dignity is relied upon to do serious moral and political work, as evidenced by its inclusion in numerous international human rights documents and national constitutions.

In what follows, I argue that we face a challenge in employing dignity in this manner. I worry that either accounts of dignity lack sufficient content to do the work required of dignity in the moral and political realms or they become—once fully articulated—accounts about which agreement is untenable. I'll briefly discuss a tension that is at the heart of this disagreement, consider two attempts to alleviate the tension, and offer a suggestion as to why the failure to alleviate this tension coupled with the challenge of agreement makes dignity a hard concept to employ in the documents in which it is expected to do so much work.

Dignity and Its Tensions

Some think that the properties necessary for the possession of dignity are biological, others claim they are psychological, still others that they are social. Some tie dignity to the possession of a soul, others refuse to entertain anything but naturalistic claims to dignity. Some argue that the possession of dignity is binary (i.e., either you possess it or you fail to possess it), but others claim that dignity possession admits of gradation (e.g., most readers of this chapter are more dignified than its author, yet few are as dignified as David Solomon). However, I believe much of the disagreement over dignity is rooted in a less noticed tension, the tension between two of dignity's essential elements: merit and equality.

Given these challenges, critical resistance to appeals to dignity is not surprising. Why bother with appeals to dignity when, it is claimed, another concept does just as well? I believe that an examination of the kinds of situations in which dignity is commonly invoked shows that dignity allows for a more accurate assessment of what is going on psychologically, conceptually, and rhetorically than reflection on other concepts. I have in mind here instances like what happened to Rosa Parks in 1955, to children at the Willowbrook State School in the 1960s, to residents of Hiroshima and Nagasaki in 1945, and, more recently, to victims of torture (at Guantanamo Bay, for example). In evaluating situations like these, we might invoke concepts other than dignity. A person's freedom, autonomy, privacy, or bodily integrity—to pick out a few—might have been violated. However, it is the treatment of human beings as less than what they are that motivates many to ground our treatment of others on what Martin Luther King Jr. called the "solid rock of human dignity."[6]

In light of these considerations and the centrality of situations like these to our lives, dignity not only is a plausible candidate to fill the conceptual role necessary for our evaluation of these cases but also proves to be an ineliminable part of our understanding of our shared human experience. However, the focus of this chapter is neither a full characterization and defense of these claims or the more general instances in which reflection on dignity proves useful, nor a response to particular criticisms of dignity's use, nor even an argument for the benefits of dignity over a particular rival concept. Rather, here I attempt to elucidate the tension between dignity's meritorious and egalitarian elements and explore attempts to alleviate the tension between them. This is an important step in arriving at a satisfying account of dignity, which must be achieved prior to comparing its merits and defects to other rival concepts. I now move to discuss dignity's essential elements.

Merit and Equality

The tension between merit and equality exists because dignity is employed both as a ground for the equal treatment of all human beings and as the concept that marks out what is characteristic of the best human lives. As mentioned earlier, dignity serves as the foundation of human rights in many international agreements and national constitutions and of our treatment of other people. These rights are said to apply to all human beings and to apply to them equally. However, dignity has also been used to denote a certain kind of life or certain projects and activities within that life that are best or most fitting for human beings.

We might think of John Stuart Mill's distinction between the higher and lower pleasures, of the sorts of entertainments enjoyed by swine as opposed to humans or by the fool as opposed to Socrates, as capturing this idea. Rolling around in mud is a fine thing for pigs to do, but not for human beings. For Socrates to spend his days as the fool spends his would not be for Socrates to live a life emblematic of dignity. We can notice the tension between merit and equality emerging in these two examples. When we understand dignity to apply to human beings as contrasted with other beings, we can speak of these human beings as equals. What keeps us from locating dignity not in the first distinction but in the second? What keeps us from understanding dignity as applying only to the excellent among us—Socrates, Mozart, Marie Curie, Jackie Robinson, or Benazir Bhutto—who might have merited dignified treatment by their lives, actions, or projects?

With respect to merit, there are some distinctions, rights, or kinds of treatment owed to people because they have "earned it." They have done something or are something such that they deserve the relevant distinction, right, or treatment. There are other distinctions, rights, or kinds of treatment given to all regardless of desert. With respect to equality, many accounts of dignity take the concept to apply to all human beings. Many of these latter accounts take dignity to be the basis for human rights or the general treatment of ourselves and others.

The tension between merit and equality arises with respect to dignity because of the history of the concept and its usage. Though it has been used to single out persons of special distinction, it is now used to undergird claims applicable to everyone. If dignity denotes something one achieves because of characteristics, activities, or powers that one possesses or engages in, how can one also achieve dignity without these characteristics or powers or while unable to engage in these activities? This question is one articulation of the tension between dignity's essential elements. Notice that if the possession of dignity is tied to achievements of a certain kind, requires engagement in certain activities, or relies on the possession of certain powers (which are not shared equally by all), then our egalitarian sympathies (and the use of dignity as a foundation for human rights or of our treatment of others) will not be satisfied. To the contrary, if dignity is not connected to achievements, engagements, or possessions of these kinds, we both lose the historical character of the concept and must wonder, In virtue of what should we treat people in the special way that dignity demands?

There may be interest in dropping either dignity's meritorious or egalitarian element, as doing so would quickly alleviate the tension. But we should not do this, at least not so quickly. Consider again dignity's connection to human rights. Suppose that we do appeal to an *exclusively equal* (and thus not meritorious) *dignity* and that there is widespread agreement that such an appeal is warranted. In order to elucidate particular rights from this appeal, we must know more; we must know about the content of this *exclusively equal* dignity. Reflection on what it is to live a good human life, what it is to meet the standard of dignity, is necessary for successfully connecting dignity to human rights because we must be able to specify the content of the relevant rights. If I claim that you should treat all people equally, you know that much, but you do not yet know how to treat them except that it ought to be in the same manner. To say only that human beings are inviolable is not enough. If we rely solely on *equal* dignity to inform our treatment of others and to ground human rights, we will lack specific articulations of these rights and support for those articulations; we will also lack a measure for adjudicating between the competing articulations, when they arise, and we will ultimately fail to agree.[7]

Alternatively, we might leave out dignity's egalitarian element. Might *exclusively meritorious dignity* alone successfully play the role that dignity is called to play in human rights discourse? I think not. If human rights are to apply to everyone, dismissing equality will not allow dignity to serve as the ground for these rights and our treatment of others.

Another way of putting the question with which we are faced is to ask, How might *all* human beings *merit* being treated with dignity? I now consider two possible answers to this question; though very different, both proponents endeavor to take seriously the tension between dignity's meritorious and egalitarian elements.

Nobility for the Common Man

In his Tanner Lectures, Jeremy Waldron offers a very nice response to our question. Everyone is equal before the law; the law treats everyone with dignity. By using the law as a model, we might come to understand how the tension between merit and equality can be resolved. Waldron attempts to salvage dignity by constructing an account that carefully attends to the history of the concept and employs resources borrowed from the legal realm. His primary insight[8] is drawn from conceiving of the contrast between merit and equality within dignity in light of the contrasts between rank-ordered as opposed to egalitarian considerations and noble as opposed to antiaristocratic considerations. He attributes a very high rank to everyone.[9]

Historically, the law distinguished between commoner and noble and afforded the latter special treatment in accord with her *dignity*. Consider one illustrative example from Waldron:

> In 1606, in London, a carriage carrying Isabel, the Countess of Rutland, was attacked by serjeants-at-mace pursuant to a writ alleging a debt of £1,000.... The Star Chamber held that the

> "arrest of the countess by the serjeants-at-mace ... is against the law, and the said countess was falsely imprisoned" and "a severe sentence was given against [the creditor], the serjeants, and their confederates." The court quoted an ancient maxim to the effect that "law will have a difference between a lord or a lady, &c. and another common person,"... There are two reasons, the court went on, "why her person should not be arrested in such cases; one in respect of her dignity, and the other in respect that the law doth presume that she hath sufficient lands and tenements in which she may be distrained."[10]

The law now treats everyone as if they were members of the nobility, extending this special legal standing to all, hence the title we may use for this view: *nobility for the common man*. Waldron claims that we have made a similar move in the moral realm. We now think of everyone as members of a "single-status community."[11]

There is much in Waldron's account with which to be pleased. First, his focus on status is novel and imputing the same moral status to all means granting everyone the same basic rights and liabilities, allowing for variances based on circumstance. Second, according to *nobility for the common man*, dignity serves both "as source and as content," which is to say that the ground of human rights is connected with the content of those rights in the correct manner. Finally, nobility for the common man relies on an independent, ordinary definition of dignity, which is to say that it avoids philosophical stipulation and connects current uses of dignity with the concept's rich history. Given my earlier claim that we should retain dignity's meritorious and egalitarian elements, at least as long as we can, I'm amenable to Waldron's position. Without the connection of source and content and absent the connection to current attributions of dignity and the concept's history, we risk the loss of any motivational force, which appeals to dignity hope to harness. Rights dependent on dignity as a source cannot float free from that source and retain their motivational force.

Since we are all part of the single, high-status moral community, in this view, dignity's egalitarian and meritorious elements appear to be satisfied. The focus on nobility allows a perspective, according to Waldron, from which to understand the concept and its normative implications.[12] He recommends engaging in an "unwieldy" thought experiment in which we take all rights and privileges that have ever applied to any noble and apply them to all rights holders. Once we rid ourselves of contradictory results (e.g., each person cannot have the right to speak first) and unattractive results (i.e., positional goods or goods that become less effective when more people possess them [e.g., voting rights in a small council as opposed to voting rights in large democracies]), we will hold on to rights that retain the viability and value of the original noble right (e.g., the right not to be struck).[13] Every candidate for a dignity-based universal human right is added to the list, then the list is whittled down by universalizing the rights and retaining those that do not end up unattractive or contradictory. We are now in a position to see, more clearly than before, how the elements of merit and equality are supposed to come together in this account. Merit is tied to nobility, high status, and the related rights and privileges, and by universalizing these rights—already tied to merit—equality is accounted for.

Unfortunately, the apparent satisfaction of dignity's meritorious and egalitarian elements is only apparent. There is a difference between granting a high rank to people and *explaining why* they have merited this high rank. To illustrate this, consider another example from Waldron. He draws our attention to Gregory Vlastos' "Justice and Equality," in which Vlastos suggests that we might think of all people as members of a single, high-ranking caste. Waldron claims that reflection on the transvaluation of dignity gives us the following interpretation of that suggestion: We might interpret the thought through an emphasis on deference as part of the language of respect associated with dignity and the offices that historically conferred dignity on their inhabitants. Thus deference owed to the inhabitant of a dignity-conferring office—for example, a judgeship—is extended beyond that office. The deference owed to the judge is on display not only in the courtroom but in other areas of life as well. Similarly, we should not limit our deference in response to the dignity of ordinary people only to those instances in which they merited such deference. Rather, we should think of their dignity as extending beyond the limits of their merit, as it extends beyond the dimensions of a judge's courtroom.[14] Thus we would treat others with an "extensive and diffuse deference," illustrating, it would seem, both dignity's meritorious and egalitarian elements.

But this argument goes by too quickly. Though the judge example might illustrate a useful way to think about our treatment of others, it does not give us a reason to treat people with this deference. Waldron claims people possess dignity, but he has not shown this. The manner in which he constructs the example is telling. We move from the judge *qua judge* in the courtroom to the judge outside of the courtroom. The implicit suggestion is that this latter judge is a judge *qua person*. This leads us, more easily, to extend the dignified treatment of the person who merits it in one instance (because of the office she holds) to her at all times.

Two problems exist. First, we might move from treating as her dignity demands a person who holds a dignity-conferring office *in that office* to treating that person in *that* manner all the time. However, it does not follow that we should treat others likewise, especially those who lack the relevant meritorious characteristics. Thus the example shows—at most—that those who merit treatment with dignity in some instances should be treated with dignity in all instances. (This is similar to Waldron's historical claim about dignity's transvaluation; he offers a description of how this has happened but neither an argument for nor an explanation of the change.) However, and this is the second problem, the example cannot take us even this far. A judge might merit special deference beyond the courtroom in virtue of her holding that office, but she might also be treated with dignity outside of the courtroom because of what she does outside of the courtroom (even if related to her office). For example, suppose she has worked hard to learn the law and embody a certain degree of impartiality. Because of this, she may hold a prominent place in her community with respect to other aspects of its life. She is treated with dignity not because she is a judge but because of the meritorious activities she performs (or characteristics she displays) inside *and* outside the courtroom. (And this is to ignore entirely the manner in which we might treat bad judges and judges who act badly outside of the courtroom.)

These problems show that Waldron has not given us reason to extend the treatment associated with dignity to all people. We might call this criticism the "noble's challenge," highlighting the importance of this missing explanation. Throughout the time and places where nobility garnered special treatment, there were reasons, albeit bad ones, for such treatment. Take, as an example, the divine right of kings. If God had bestowed a special designation (and the relevant accompanying skills) on a monarch, there would be an explanation as to why she should receive special treatment. There is a difference between offering reasons, albeit bad ones, and not offering reasons at all. Claiming that anything else would offend against our democratic sensibilities is not enough. The noble of old may challenge us: "What makes these others special?" In formulating answers to this question, we can feel the absence of merit in Waldron's account and see the need for a more robust perspective than he can offer. By tying merit to nobility but failing to account for it, Waldron does not give us a new perspective; he just speaks as though he has.

This failure is unfortunate but not terribly surprising. This is because, though thinking about ourselves and others as equal before the law, and now morality, is a fine idea, doing so without first answering questions like, "Who counts as one of us?" and "In virtue of what does one have equal standing before the law?" leaves something out. Consider Waldron's claim of transvaluation. Waldron acknowledges that the change in values was perhaps aided by the work of Catholic thinkers and others, such as John Locke, even though Waldron contrasts his view with the ontologically based Catholic account.[15] To emphasize the importance of the equality of the members within a particular rank, such as Locke does, and to suggest that we can "draw on this idea of the special rank accorded to all humans in the great chain of being" and within "Catholic dignitary teaching"[16] but then to leave out any conclusions that might follow from relying on these rich accounts appears to me to be a mistake. We cannot rely on these elements to do work in the argument but then avoid them in the conclusion. If we miss the reason for the change in thought about dignity, we might miss something crucial in accounting for the meritorious and egalitarian elements of dignity, and this is just what I believe *nobility for the common man* does.

Equidistance

Another promising account that might serve to alleviate the tension between the meritorious and egalitarian elements of dignity—that is, between an account of dignity that applies to all people to the same degree and an account of dignity that highlights the great achievements of individual human beings—comes from Gilbert Meilaender. In *Neither Beast nor God: The Dignity of the Human Person*,[17] he eloquently describes two concepts: human dignity, a shorthand phrase or a placeholder for a particular vision of human life, and personal dignity, the idea that we are all equal persons whose comparative worth cannot and ought not be assessed.[18]

Human dignity, as the title of his book aptly suggests, is a vision of life focused on human beings as neither beast nor God. It is a vision for a life that is characteristically human and commends engaging in activities and undertaking projects that take seriously our humanity. This is why much of his book is devoted to topics like birth, breeding, childhood, loyalties, and death. Features emblematic of our experience as human must be accounted for when characterizing a full and successful life. Human dignity serves as a standard by which we might judge the merit of human lives. We are offered a substantive account of what a human being is,[19] and once such a vision has been specified—even if there are various articulations of this vision—there will be lives that fail to be characteristically human, pursuits deemed not worthwhile, and, to borrow a phrase from Meilaender, activities that fail to "honor our human dignity."

Human dignity is a normative concept. Whatever the norms are, there will (almost always) be human beings who fail to measure up. Contrast this with personal dignity, which aims to capture the idea that we are all equal persons whose comparative worth cannot and ought not to be assessed. Personal dignity accounts for the inviolability of all people.[20]

This account faces the same reconciliation or alleviation challenge that Waldron's account faced. Can human and personal dignity be—to borrow another term from Meilaender—"transformed" in such a way that they can coexist within the same account of dignity?

Meilaender offers a few resources to support this transformation. Presently, I will briefly mention two, but first consider a big-picture note on the project. One of the challenges for accounts of dignity, if we wish them to inform human rights and play a role in international declarations and national constitutions, is that they must be able to gain support from diverse parties to these agreements. This was a possible benefit of Waldron's legal account; it did not rely on what John Rawls referred to as *controversial philosophical and religious doctrines*,[21] although it appeared that it may have relied on some implicitly in the posited transvaluation. On the contrary, Meilaender's conception of humanity, which directly informs his account of dignity, is rooted in a Judeo-Christian context and anthropology. He writes, "I doubt whether we can understand dignity well without at least a modest anthropology—without some notion of what it means to be the sort of creature a human being is. And I, at least, do not think that this understanding can possibly be right if we abstract the human beings we seek to understand from their relation to God."[22]

Now we might rely on this anthropology in two ways. First, we might invoke the divine in a very simplistic sense. Second, we might take on board Meilaender's entire anthropology or, at least, a substantial portion of it. Meilaender argues that we have lost the context in which the concepts of human and personal dignity make sense together. He claims, "It may be that we cannot make good sense of an egalitarian and non-comparative understanding of dignity, to which our civilization has in many ways been committed, if we abstract it entirely from the context of the religious beliefs that formed it."[23] This context is one in which the equal distance between all human beings and God allows for the alleviation of this tension. I suspect that this second way of relying on this anthropology will cause obvious problems for agreement, so I first explore the simplistic way.

Consider the following passage from Meilaender:

> Here, then, is our problem, from which we cannot for long continue to avert our gaze: Our society is committed to equal human dignity, and our history is in large part a long attempt to work out the meaning of that commitment. Christians and Jews have an account of persons—as equidistant from God and of equal worth before God—that grounds and makes sense of this commitment we all share. A society that rejects their account but wishes to retain the commitment faces, then, a serious crisis in the structure of its beliefs. And often, in fact, we do little more than posit an equality about which we are, otherwise, largely mute; for the truth is, as Oliver O'Donovan has assertively put it, that this belief "is, and can only be, a *theological assertion.*" We are equal to each other, whatever our distinctions in excellence of various sorts, precisely because none of us is the "maker" of another one of us. We have all received our life—equally—as a gift from the Creator.[24]

Call this the equidistance argument (EA). Meilaender uses a mathematical metaphor—the relative distances between beings and God, following Kierkegaard's thought that "eternity never counts,"[25] to help explain how the tension between merit and equality might be resolved. Given that all human beings are equidistant from God, any difference in their human dignity, in merit, becomes negligible. Even if there are great disparities in how successful a life is in terms of those characteristically human features, when one life is compared to God, it is no better than any other life. By extending dignity's comparison class to include God, we might be able to make room for both merit and equality.

It should be noted that EA does not block interpersonal comparison. If it did, an advocate of EA would fail to take seriously the importance of merit and, in so doing, give up on human dignity. The transformation would then consist of personal dignity simply blotting out human dignity.[26]

This resolution is, unfortunately, flawed. In relying on EA, we would be unable to distinguish human beings from other beings as possessors of dignity and, in so failing, would not remain true to the content and motivating assumption of Meilaender's account of human dignity. It is not clear, having brought in the idea of equidistance, how human dignity can adequately characterize human beings as creatures that are neither beasts nor God. For Meilaender human dignity is a placeholder for "larger understandings or background beliefs not easily articulated in shorthand ways."[27] However, introducing God into the comparison class—oddly enough—endangers this anthropological vision. For if it is in relation to God that our excellences are to be compared, then they become irrelevant to our treatment of others. We need reasons to uphold human dignity and for it to inform our treatment of others. Many features of any number of creatures seem able to fill this role once the comparison to God is made.

To be clear, the objection I raise against EA is that in order to make room for personal dignity, we must sacrifice human dignity. Human dignity becomes impotent in exactly the way we want to avoid. Consider the following illustration as support for this claim. Compare a human being who is engaged in characteristically human pursuits in a characteristically human way to one who is not. Suppose the former engages in such pursuits excellently and the latter engages in other pursuits in a mediocre way. The first is emblematic of human dignity; the second is not. In comparison to God, both have the same dignity, but notice that this is supposed to be a claim of equal *human* dignity and not a claim about equal *personal* dignity—a claim about merit, not equality. The claim is that in comparing the executions of those characteristically human features, none of us comes close to doing them as well as God could. This is surely right, but it is a claim made exclusively within the realm of human dignity, the realm of merit. Were it a claim about personal dignity, other arguments in support of human dignity would be needed. The challenge for EA is that the very pursuits—those characteristically human pursuits—must be deemed no better than the noncharacteristically human pursuits; otherwise, we need an additional argument for the conclusion that the two concepts come together.

In other words, it has been shown that in comparison to God, our characteristically human features do not matter, but it still must be shown how the two concepts relate to each other. The more we press on this, the further apart they appear. Consider human and nonhuman animals. Suppose some highly intelligent, highly advanced, nonhuman animal[28] is compared with the two humans mentioned in the previous example. It follows from the aforementioned argument that they all possess the same human dignity (and if we take the argument to be offering a claim about personal dignity, though I have argued that this is mistaken, then they all possess the same personal dignity). Once we make comparisons to God, all differences are negligible. We are *all* on equal footing.

Consider a final example. Suppose that due to further advancements in biotechnology, there is a genetically modified human being who extends greatly, and in so doing even reshapes, what was once thought of as characteristically human pursuits. (We might suppose that this being can fly, reproduce asexually, and develop into an adult at an exceedingly rapid rate. It seems reasonable to assume from Meilaender's point of view that some of the characteristics and pursuits of this being would be objectionable to human dignity and others not.) It follows from EA that this being possesses the same human dignity as any other. Arguments against genetic enhancement (and even against hybridization) rooted in claims about essential or characteristic humanity cannot be made from a standpoint that relies on EA, and this goes hand in hand with the blotting out of human dignity and, in turn, the loss of content for our treatment of others with which I have expressed much worry.

Continuing to unpack the passage I quoted earlier, we might find resources to salvage EA. We might rely on the claim that "we have all received our life—equally—as a gift from the Creator."[29] Emphasizing the idea of a creator might help to bolster EA, call this variant EA(C), because EA(C) allows us to employ the equidistance metaphor without relying so heavily on what is characteristically human. This is not to denigrate what is characteristically human. Rather, in relying on what is characteristically human to be the measure that becomes equalized in order to maintain the equal personal dignity of all, we lessen the worth of human dignity. We have faced this problem already. If human dignity is to inform our treatment of others, we need a more robust account of it than EA admits. Instead of the characteristically human, the measure by which we compare ourselves to God in EA(C) becomes the sharply demarcated distinction between the created and the creator. We are all—regardless of our differing levels of human dignity—of the created class, so we all possess personal dignity to the same degree. Interpersonal comparisons with respect to human dignity are safeguarded, since there is no need to reduce their importance in an effort to salvage personal dignity.

Unfortunately another—and not dissimilar—problem arises. Humans are not the only beings within the class of the created. The question now becomes not how to include those without human dignity but how to exclude those beings we generally take to lack personal dignity. An account that gives personal dignity to all animals, and even plants and rocks, surely includes too much. However, with only the distinction between creator and created, we do not yet have the resources to adequately answer this question. Thus both EA and EA(C) fail in a similar manner.

Conclusion

In conclusion, what we are left with is the opportunity to explore rich traditions, the contexts in which dignity might be at home and which might possess the resources to make sense of its meritorious and egalitarian elements. The legal-moral analogy failed because it failed to offer a reason to extend dignity to all. The simplistic appeal to the divine failed because we lost dignity's meritorious element in an attempt to salvage its egalitarian one. There is an interesting similarity between what we might describe as the legal assertion—that all are equal in dignity before the law—and the theological assertion just discussed. These assertions, though bold, need not be bald. If made within a rich context that helps to inform an account of our dignity, we might yet make sense of the meritorious and the egalitarian. I am hopeful that as further and more careful work—like that of Meilaender and Waldron—continues, stronger accounts of dignity might arise, supported by the rich traditions of which they are a part. However, whether we are able to reach meaningful agreement about dignity, such that it can be employed in the manner addressed earlier, is another matter. In order for dignity to be a worthwhile moral concept, we need more than superficial agreement; a mere modus vivendi would not be satisfying. If we take dignity seriously—both human and personal, both meritorious and egalitarian—we must rely on an account of human dignity to inform our treatment of others. Positing equal dignity is not enough. Even if this gives us equal treatment, we need to know what kind of equal treatment is appropriate. And without something like human dignity, we will lack sufficient content or support for well-grounded human rights.

Bibliography

Crosby, John. "The Twofold Source of the Dignity of Persons." *Faith and Philosophy* 18, no. 3 (2001): 292–306.

King, Martin Luther, Jr. "Letter from a Birmingham Jail." In *A Testament of Hope: The Essential Writings and Speeches of Martin Luther King, Jr.*,

edited by James M. Washington, 289–302. New York: Harper Collins, 1991.
MacIntyre, Alasdair. *After Virtue*. Notre Dame: University of Notre Dame Press, 2007.
———. *Dependent Rational Animals: Why Human Beings Need the Virtues*. Chicago: Open Court, 1999.
———. "The Essential Contestability of Some Social Concepts." *Ethics* 84, no. 1 (1973): 1–9.
———. *Whose Justice? Which Rationality?* Notre Dame: University of Notre Dame Press, 1998.
Macklin, Ruth. "Dignity Is a Useless Concept." *British Medical Journal* 327 (2003): 1419–20.
Meilaender, Gilbert. *Neither Beast nor God: The Dignity of the Human Person*. New York: Encounter Books, 2009.
Nozick, Robert. *Anarchy, State, and Utopia*. New York: Basic Books, 1974.
Pilkington, Brian. "The Problem of Human Dignity." Ph.D. diss., University of Notre Dame, 2012.
Pinker, Steven. "The Stupidity of Dignity." *New Republic*, May 28, 2008.
Rawls, John. "Justice as Fairness: Political Not Metaphysical." *Philosophy and Public Affairs* 14, no. 3 (1985).
Taylor, Charles. *The Ethics of Authenticity*. Cambridge, Mass.: Harvard University Press, 1991.
Taylor, Richard. "Time and Life's Meaning." *Review of Metaphysics* 40, no. 4 (1987): 675–86.
Vlastos, Gregory. "Justice and Equality." In *Social Justice*, edited by Richard B. Brandt, 31–72. Englewood Cliffs, N.J.: Prentice Hall, 1962.
Waldron, Jeremy. *Dignity, Rank, and Rights*. Oxford: Oxford University Press, 2012.
———. "Dignity, Rank, and Rights: The 2009 Tanner Lectures at UC Berkeley." New York University School of Law: Public Law and Legal Theory Research Paper Series, 2009.
———. "Dignity and Rank." *Archives Européennes de Sociologie* 48 (2007): 201–37.
———. *The Dignity of Legislation*. Cambridge: Cambridge University Press, 1999.
———. "The Dignity of Legislation." *Maryland Law Review* 54 (1995): 633–65.
———. "Does 'Equal Moral Status' Add Anything to Right Reason?" *New York University Public Law and Legal Theory Working Papers*, 2011.

http://lsr.nellco.org/nyu_plltwp/292. Originally prepared for delivery at the 2004 Annual Meeting of the American Political Science Association, Chicago, September 2–5, 2004.

———. "Torture and Positive Law: Jurisprudence for the White House." *Columbia Law Review* 105, no. 6 (2005): 1281–1750.

10

AGAINST THE "AUTONOMY" AND "BEST INTEREST" DEFENSES OF MEDICALLY ASSISTED DEATH

Raymond Hain

Those who would defend medically assisted death (primarily, for purposes of this essay, voluntary euthanasia and physician-assisted suicide[1]) have two strategies at their disposal. First, they can argue that their opponents accept as morally licit, under specific conditions, various practices that do not differ in any morally relevant respect from medically assisted death.[2] According to this strategy, those who permit the discontinuation of artificial life support (such as a breathing machine) must also, on pain of inconsistency, permit voluntary euthanasia and physician-assisted suicide. The second strategy defends medically assisted death on its own terms by means of two interrelated arguments: voluntary euthanasia and physician-assisted suicide are morally permissible when they are the result of the autonomous choices of individuals and/or when they are in the best interest of patients. This essay focuses on this second strategy that defends medically assisted death on its own terms, and I will argue that while proponents must rely on both autonomy and the best interest of patients, doing so results in destructive contradictions that arise from the very argumentative strategies employed.[3]

My argument for this has three parts. First, the argument from autonomy requires that I recognize the autonomous capacities of a patient and respond to that patient's choices with respect. But recognizing the autonomy of a patient involves imposing my own conception of rational agency on that patient, and since this conception consists, in part, of judgments about the acceptability of medically assisted death, the recognition of autonomy involves imposing on the patient my own judgments about medically assisted death. In this way, the argument from autonomy shows too much, since we have no way to prevent the killing of those who manifestly do not wish to die and do not agree with our judgments about if and when medically assisted death is appropriate. Second, we might think that the argument from a patient's best interest can rescue us, for according to this argument, a patient should die only if death is in that person's best interest. Because the value of a person's life cannot be determined by the presence of any particular suffering (given any two patients experiencing the same objective factors contributing to their suffering, we might always get two contradictory conclusions about the value present), it is the patient's own judgment that life is no longer worth living that should be decisive. It now seems that the argument from a patient's best interest has not shown enough, for it cannot prevent the irrational suicide of the heartbroken young adult. Third, advocates of medically assisted death claim that both strategies are necessary and sufficient to justify medically assisted death. But this is problematic, since each strategy moderates the other not by providing a solution to its excesses but by contradicting its central claims and so destroying its overall force. The argument from autonomy requires the imposition of judgments about when life is no longer worth living, whereas the argument from a patient's best interest insists that it is the patient's own judgment about when life is no longer worth living that should be determinative. And so the arguments from autonomy and a patient's best interest are failures.

I begin with the argument from autonomy. Appeals to autonomy in defense of medically assisted death are at home in a variety of moral traditions (James Rachels draws upon John Stuart Mill's writings, for example, whereas Mary Warnock looks to Kant[4]). Here is Robert Young's recent formulation: "Respect for persons demands respect for their autonomous choices, as long as those choices do not result in harm to others. . . . It is in the interests of competent persons to make important decisions about their lives in accordance with their conceptions of how they want to lead those lives. In exercising autonomy, or self-determination, each of us takes responsibility for our life and, since dying is a part of life, choices about the manner of our dying, and the timing of our death, are part of what is involved in taking responsibility for our life."[5] My autonomous choice for death should therefore be respected, and if I solicit and receive help in carrying out my particular choice, the actions of those who help me should likewise be respected. This is not an argument that the choice for death is itself a moral one. Instead, it is an argument that you are morally required to allow me the freedom to choose death and likewise morally required to allow others to help me die. In this way, the concept of autonomy allows an indirect defense of medically assisted death. It likewise makes it possible for us to permit voluntary euthanasia and physician-assisted suicide while avoiding moral responsibility for the actual choices for death. Indeed, the authors of "The Philosophers' Brief" (submitted to the Supreme Court during its 1997 deliberations on voluntary euthanasia and physician-assisted suicide) drew on these features of autonomy in order to argue that in respecting the choices of citizens to die, we need not "make moral, ethical, or religious judgments about how people should approach or confront their death or about when it is ethically appropriate to hasten one's own death or to ask others for help in doing so."[6]

Critics of this argument typically respond that autonomy is not an absolute good; we should respect the autonomy of agents only when the exercise of that autonomy respects the larger moral order of which autonomy is itself a part (and the harm principle is only one of many legitimate restrictions on autonomy).[7] But even if this criticism fails, there is a deeper problem connected to the understanding and application of autonomy. Once we speak of respect for autonomous choices, we are already referring to an interpersonal relationship; one person must recognize that an autonomous choice has been made by another rational agent and then respond with respect. This recognition and response, despite the claims of "The Philosophers' Brief," entail moral judgments about the value of human life and the permissibility of medically assisted death. If I judge that you are making an autonomous decision to die that requires my respect, this is only possible if I have *already* made a series of judgments about the value of human life and whatever joys or sufferings it claims as its own. Any defense of voluntary medically assisted death grounded in autonomy depends for its force on these deeper substantive claims about the value of human life, and in this way, the argument from autonomy cannot itself justify the permissibility of voluntary euthanasia and physician-assisted suicide.

How can this be shown? Here is the simplest case. As of 2017, laws permitting medically assisted death require that the patient's health be significantly restricted in some way. According to Oregon's Death with Dignity Act, a person must be suffering from a terminal disease that will result in that person's death within approximately six months.[8] In the Netherlands, a patient must be enduring "lasting and unbearable" suffering.[9]

Assuming that the patient will not harm others in choosing death, our reasons for restricting the patient's autonomy must be centered on the particular patient in question. The autonomy of that person consists in rational control over the structure of his or her life. But in the case at hand, my autonomy will be respected (I will be allowed to structure my life as I see fit) only if I am experiencing significant suffering. Let us suppose, as is the case in Oregon and the Netherlands, that we must apply objective medical criteria in order to determine if such a situation is present. If we depend on such criteria (e.g., suffering from a terminal illness or seriously debilitating chronic depression), then the presence of these factors is necessary if my autonomous choice is to be respected. We now need to explain why it is only then that a request for medically assisted death should be respected and so why the criteria for permissible medically assisted death are not merely arbitrary. These criteria have no obvious connection to autonomy itself, as if autonomous choices for death could only be made by persons suffering from intolerably burdensome situations. Indeed, if there is any intrinsic connection between these criteria and autonomy, it would be the reverse; suffering from an intolerably burdensome condition tends to reduce the autonomy of patients, since emotional and physical pain, as well as the close proximity of death, can easily cloud one's judgment. The only plausible nonarbitrary reason for selecting these criteria is the obvious one: certain forms of suffering justify the choice to die and so likewise justify the provision of help in dying. If intolerably burdensome situations could never make the choice of voluntary euthanasia or physician-assisted suicide a good and rational one, then it would be senseless to make our respect for your autonomous choice dependent upon them.[10]

A more sophisticated argument from autonomy does not depend on objective criteria for an intolerably burdensome situation. Robert Young, in opposition to current legal statutes, argues that the patient's own judgment whether or not such a situation is present should be determinative: "There is . . . no single, objectively correct answer, applicable to every individual, as to whether, and, if so, when, life becomes an unwanted burden. But that fact simply points up the importance of individuals being able to decide autonomously for themselves whether their own lives retain sufficient quality and dignity for them to judge that further life will be worthwhile. In making such decisions, competent individuals are entitled to decide about the mix of self-determination and personal well-being that suits them."[11] Nevertheless, he adds that the judgments of competent individuals who are seriously debilitated should "other things being equal . . . carry the greatest weight"[12] in determining whether or not an intolerably burdensome situation is present. This muddies the water, but other advocates of this position are less ambivalent. Mary Warnock says simply that "it is the value of the life as it is lived by the person, not any value that it has in someone else's eyes, that is crucial in determining whether he should go on living."[13]

According to this way of thinking, we can recognize (and then respect) a particular choice as an autonomous one without implying any judgment of the content of the choice. But in order to do this, we must determine whether the agent is genuinely able to act autonomously. "Autonomy" includes both cognitive and volitional elements; an autonomous agent must have the knowledge necessary to engage in genuinely rational deliberation concerning possible actions, and that agent must likewise be able to act freely in response to his or her rational judgments. To "respect autonomy," therefore, involves granting someone who possesses cognitive autonomy the freedom to carry out the rational actions the agent has chosen, thereby making it possible for the agent to act with full autonomy. But what makes someone cognitively autonomous and therefore deserving of the freedom to act as he or she chooses? Here are some of Young's criteria:

> It is clear that a competent health care decision maker must have at least the following capacities: the capacity to understand his health care situation; the capacity to understand the options open to him (including not only the various possible modes of treatment, but the possibility of not having any treatment at all); and the capacity to make an assessment of the risks and benefits associated with the various options for treatment, including nontreatment. In addition, he must have a minimally consistent and stable set of values to which he can appeal in exercising the various capacities just adumbrated.[14]

Since it is of course impossible for any agent to know everything, the autonomous agent must know a certain subset of truths about the world that bear on the decision at hand—the "relevant truths." Nothing is peculiar in itself about Young's chosen subset; it is likely that any account of autonomy will include them. What is crucial here is that Young must leave aside all propositions similar in form to this one: medically assisted death in this case brings about more harm than good to all parties involved. Young might think he is limiting himself to descriptions of causes and effects that have nothing to say about real harms and benefits (we leave individuals to decide for themselves about harms and benefits). You can know that the needle will penetrate your flesh, that chemicals introduced into your body will cause sedation, that sedation will be followed by death, but it is not required that you know anything about the goodness or badness of any of it. But judgments about goodness and badness cannot be left entirely to one side; deciding which truths are "relevant" already brings judgments about harms and benefits into play, since it is only by appeal to what we all might agree are potential benefits or harms (dying is usually a harm, for example) that the choice of relevant information can be made. Even more, a person who understood all the causal patterns in question and understood that death is usually a harm but whose values and choices did not reflect this understanding of death would not be considered an autonomous agent; autonomy requires knowledge of the relevant information *and* possession of the values that underpin the selection of relevant information. An agent who did not see (and value) death as at least prima facie harmful would not be considered autonomous, no matter the other "relevant information" or "stable values" he or she possessed. Young argues that a patient must have a consistent and stable set of values, which is a purely formal criterion, but Young's own selection of relevant information presupposes a specific set of values, the most basic of which is that death is a serious harm and, generally speaking, to be avoided.

Therefore at least some knowledge of the harms and benefits attached to the options before an agent is required for autonomy, as well as the values that specify the relevant knowledge. And how will we decide which judgments about harms and benefits (and their corresponding values) are the right ones? Young and Warnock and others will argue that an autonomous agent must understand that death is, at least prima facie, a serious harm. Opponents of medically assisted death will agree but will argue that an autonomous agent must also understand that medically assisted death always brings about more harm than good to all parties involved. How can I make an autonomous decision, it will be argued, when it is the case that medically assisted death always brings about more harm than good to all involved and I do not know this? I am missing a crucial piece of information. Supporters of medically assisted death construct their account of autonomy such that no one would *reject* the implied judgments about harms and benefits (death really is a harm), but by leaving out judgments crucially important to any account of autonomy reflective of a world in which medically assisted death is always all things considered harmful, they defend an account of autonomy that is only acceptable to those who already agree that medically assisted death is at least sometimes permissible. The supposedly independent concept of autonomous agency instead begs the question.

The problem is a general one. We are trying to evaluate the decision-making ability of an agent by looking at his or her decisions and the deliberative processes from which they flow. Since the threshold for making any decisions at all is certainly very low, we can only describe certain patterns of decisions as autonomous by means of external criteria—and these criteria are precisely a series of judgments, with their corresponding values, about what goods matter most and to what extent.

That last paragraph leaves open one final strategy. Perhaps all we really need is the minimal criterion that someone has indeed made a decision. That decision, no matter how distasteful, must be respected (assuming it poses no harm to others). This is not a common way to use autonomy to defend medically assisted death, but it has been developed by Philip Nitschke, the founder of Exit International. In 2001 he was asked if he saw "any restrictions that should be placed on euthanasia generally." He responded by saying, "If we believe that there is a right to life, then we must accept that people have a right to dispose of that life whenever they want.... So all people qualify, not just those with the training, knowledge, or resources to find out how to 'give away' their life. And someone needs to provide this knowledge, training, or recourse necessary to anyone who wants it, including the depressed, the elderly bereaved, the troubled teen."[15] As long as you have made a choice, you have made an autonomous choice that should be respected.

But suppose you are confronted by someone who asks to be assisted in his or her suicide. Assuming you had no objections to assisting the suicides of others, your first reaction would never be merely straightforward compliance. Some requests are complied with immediately (when someone says, "Excuse me," we do not ask if the person really means it), but it is very difficult, if not impossible, to imagine a world in which the request for assistance to die would fall in this category. Our use of and responses to language contain unspoken assumptions about the relative importance of human goods. You are much more likely to say, "Are you having a bad day?" than "Just give me a moment to find a syringe." That is, your response will be an implicit examination of the autonomy of your interlocutor. These kinds of complications, involved in any response to a verbal request for assistance in dying, reflect the fact that we bring to such a request a set of prior judgments about what human goods are important, when they can be outweighed by other goods, and a conception of autonomy informed by these judgments. If this were not the case, we could give no coherent answer as to why you did not immediately go for the syringe. Nitschke, it seems unwittingly, gestures toward this when he adds that suicide pills should be readily available to all who are "old enough to understand death."[16] If this is right, then Nitschke's own position is in principle no different from the more common argument from autonomy that requires competent decision making, and we find ourselves in the same position as those who must determine what competence requires (and may leave to one side).

All this might suggest that it would never be permissible for opponents of medically assisted death to allow voluntary euthanasia or physician-assisted suicide in specific cases. But this conclusion does not follow. If you believe that medically assisted death is always immoral, no matter the circumstances, you might still permit me to kill myself or permit me to enlist the help of others in doing so. You might even tolerate a law permitting these things under special circumstances. But you could not appeal to autonomy as your justification; instead, you would need to argue that, while my actions in bringing about my death are of course wrong and I should not do them, in this case it is too difficult to stop me; or perhaps nothing much will be gained by trying; or since you must risk your life if you are to make the attempt, you are under no obligation to do so. But I cannot say that I should respect your autonomous decision to die simply because it is autonomous. Indeed, permitting your death is not an act of "respect" at all but instead a regrettable concession to the practical difficulties of the particular situation.[17]

Appeals to autonomy in the debate over medically assisted death cannot therefore protect us from having to make judgments about the goodness or badness of voluntary euthanasia or physician-assisted suicide; instead, appeals to autonomy presuppose these judgments, which in turn give to the argument from autonomy whatever final justificatory power it possesses.

Consider now the argument based on the best interest of the patient, succinctly stated by Mary Warnock: "If a patient is killed by his doctor or offered a lethal dose to take by himself, then that doctor is, in effect, saying 'your suffering is worse than death, and death alone can relieve it'. And this is indeed the message that the patient has himself accepted.... In the case of Diane Pretty, her desire to commit suicide was based on a perfectly rational preference for avoiding the inevitable and clearly foreseen horror of her death, if she allowed 'nature to take its course'. Suicide was in her best interest."[18] Some lives are so burdened by suffering that it can be better for a person to commit suicide or to be killed by others than to remain alive. Just as we put a suffering animal out of its misery, so too we should put a suffering person out of his or her misery—it is the humane, the compassionate, thing to do. Supporters of this claim can describe cases of truly horrific human suffering, in which the suffering patient is begging for death, and conclude that surely medically assisted death in such cases is good. And like the argument from autonomy, though it is less obvious in this case, the argument based on a patient's best interest is also at home in a variety of moral traditions. We might at first suppose that appealing to happiness or welfare is very different from appealing to Kantian notions of dignity. But this would be a mistake, since for any particular patient, that person's "best interest" can be construed either in terms of happiness and welfare or in terms of dignity. We will appeal to the same medical condition in both cases, and each construal can be translated into the opposing terms.[19] It might be in one's best interest to die either because one wishes to avoid unhappiness or because one's dignity as a rational person is threatened. But because the threat to one's dignity will consist in specific suffering, it makes no practical difference whether we appeal to dignity itself or to the suffering when we explain that it is in one's best interest to die.

According to Warnock and others, therefore, it is at least sometimes permissible, and even quite good, for a suffering patient to be killed intentionally; death is in the person's overall best interest. Opponents of this claim usually respond that the criteria used for determining the value of a patient's life are always arbitrarily chosen.[20] Why should we identify this particular amount of pain (or "disintegration of the self") as the critical one, and how can we rationally commensurate the goods and bads of a patient's life so that the decision to die is a rational one? My strategy here is different and depends on a deeper claim that will be true for the identification and application of any chosen set of criteria, even if the particular evaluations are themselves unproblematic. This deeper claim is that, if it is legitimate to conclude that a life is no longer worth living (assuming, again, that harm suffered by others is not involved), the judgment of the patient should be decisive.

To see this, suppose that you and I each experience the same kinds of objectively measurable physical, emotional, and psychological factors that in turn cause us severe suffering. We also share our particular evaluations of these different elements of our suffering; we agree that our physical pain causes much less suffering, for example, than the emotional distress we feel at being a burden on our loved ones. Given these circumstances, it is nevertheless perfectly possible that you see value in your life and therefore wish to remain alive, whereas I do not and wish to die. The judgments we make concerning the value of our lives are not determined by our identical underlying conditions. In general, any person's judgment regarding the value of his or her life is not determined by whatever underlying suffering might be present, since it is always possible that two patients could come to opposite judgments. This suggests that we cannot point to any underlying factors as a justification for medically assisted death, since no combination of factors will be sufficient justification. Only when the patient's own adverse judgment is included can we suppose that sufficient justification is present. And this is precisely what Mary Warnock suggests when she says that "it is the value of the life as it is lived by the person, not any value that it has in someone else's eyes, that is crucial in determining whether he should go on living."[21] Indeed, no particular level of suffering is ever sufficient in itself to make a human life not worth living, since no matter the suffering, it remains possible that two persons experiencing the same degree of suffering could reach opposite conclusions about the overall value of their lives.[22]

It likewise seems true that if we focus on you alone, who are suffering and nevertheless insist that your life is valuable and that you should not be killed, it is not possible for me to make your life no longer worth living merely by steadily increasing your suffering. (Indeed, I might make your life more valuable, say as an instance of courageous endurance under torture, by making your suffering ever greater.) Any particular person might well never conclude, on the basis of the suffering, that his or her life is no longer worth living, and so we have no way of showing that "just this much suffering" always entails that a life has lost its value in this way. The conclusion can only be that increasing a person's suffering is not what determines whether or not a life is worth living, nor does it determine the value of the life in question. If it is indeed legitimate to conclude that it is in the best interest of someone to die, the judgment of that patient regarding the value of his or her life must be decisive.

One way to escape this conclusion would be to claim that, given two patients in the same circumstances who nevertheless come to contradictory conclusions, one patient is simply mistaken. The set of underlying factors *does* determine life's value, and both our lives are not worth living, even though only one of us has come to this conclusion. But this is not an attractive strategy, since it means that, other things being equal, we will be justified in killing those who do not wish to die (since death is in their best interest, even though they do not recognize this). We could escape this conclusion by arguing that imposing death on you will make your (brief remaining) life even worse than before and certainly worse than my own (brief remaining) life, since I myself chose my death. But we would have to show that the extra suffering created by the forced death outweighs all the suffering that makes your life not worth living, and since this extra suffering could be arranged so that it is minimal or nonexistent (perhaps we plan a painless death for you of which you will be completely unaware), this is not a persuasive line of defense. And this is tacitly acknowledged by the strategies of Warnock and others who argue that your life is valuable and mine is not, not because of the difference in our underlying conditions, but because of the attitudes we take toward our conditions or other available goods.

Notice a curious implication of all this. On the one hand, the evaluation of a competent and aware person's life must be made by that particular person; we will not tolerate killing someone because we judge that this is in the person's best interest, whereas the person in question vigorously denies that death is best. But we must also recognize that there is something unpredictable, and perhaps even unstable, about the person's own judgment about his or her life; the particular judgment is not entailed by whatever conditions are present, and just as two individuals might come to opposite conclusions despite the same underlying conditions, so a single individual's judgment could be for death or for life or both at different times, and we cannot look to the suffering itself to see which it will be.

Before returning to the larger problem of the arguments from autonomy and a patient's best interest, notice a peculiar feature of our interpersonal deliberation about death and what is in one's best interest. If you wish to die because you believe that your life is not worth living, we do not instinctively criticize someone who tries to persuade you that, after all, your life is not worthless and it is not "in your best interest" that you be dead. But if you are suffering just as much as before, and instead wish to stay alive and believe that your life is valuable, we do not think well of the person who tries to persuade you that, after all, your life is not worth living and you are better off dead. Even if it is acceptable to encourage a person to consider the problem, we are not supposed to work at convincing someone that death is in the person's best interest over against the person's convictions, and this is particularly true of the doctor who plays, supposedly, a merely informational role. Yet while we are not permitted to argue someone into the conviction that his or her life is no longer worth living, it is acceptable to persuade people that their lives are valuable. But should it not be the case that it is either equally acceptable to persuade someone that he or she is better off dead or we should be critical of anyone who tries to change the way a person values his or her life?

This peculiar situation is a smaller version of the larger relationship between the arguments from autonomy and a patient's best interest, and I return now to these two arguments as a whole in order to defend my claim that while they are both necessary for defenders of medically assisted death, in the end their antagonistic relationship undermines their usefulness and leaves us without any independent justification of voluntary euthanasia and physician-assisted suicide.

The argument from autonomy begins by emphasizing the respect we must show to the free choices of individuals that do not involve harm to others. My autonomous choice for death, harming as it does (so we assume) only myself, should be respected, and I should be allowed to die and to engage the help of others in doing so. Nevertheless, it is only autonomous choices that should be respected, and even if all choices are ipso facto autonomous, the response of respect always involves at least an implicit evaluation of the autonomy of the chooser. While I might respect a free autonomous choice, the identification of a choice as autonomous involves the imposition of a conception of rational behavior that is decidedly not an attitude of "respect" but is instead an evaluation of the ability of an agent to be an independent reasoner (and chooser). We are unwilling, after all, to allow the irrational suicide of the heartbroken young adult. The argument from autonomy, therefore, rests eventually on the imposition of a particular conception of rational autonomy, which in turn entails a particular set of values (and so a conception of the good human life). It turns out, therefore, that the argument from autonomy ends up in exactly the place it ostensibly wished to avoid, and the deep danger is that once we speak of imposing a conception of the good on our interactions with a person, there is no reason for thinking that this imposition will involve only failing to help someone die who wants to; it could just as easily involve killing someone who does not wish to die. The formal structure is identical: if you are a free and rational person, I must respect your choices, but I identify whether or not you are rational and free by seeing whether or not your judgments and values properly reflect my own understanding of rationality and human goods. And if it turns out that you are not after all an autonomous agent, then how I treat you will be determined by other considerations and could lead to bringing about your death. The problem with the argument from autonomy is that, paradoxically, it cannot prevent us from killing those who manifestly do not wish to die.

The argument from a patient's best interest begins in a very different way. On its face, it suggests that we should help a patient die because circumstances are such that the person's life no longer has value; the suffering or loss of dignity is so severe that death is best. But it is immediately apparent that a set of objective criteria for one's "best interest" is problematic, since any particular patient might find value in continuing to live no matter how much suffering is present. We rightfully recoil at the possibility that I might be killed against my wishes through the imposition of some particular set of external criteria. Indeed, it is perfectly plausible to claim that the suffering experienced by a patient never entails a particular judgment about the value of that patient's life. If I decide that death is in my best interest, then it should be this account of my interest that should determine whether or not medically assisted death is appropriate. But once we move to the particular subjective judgment of the patient as determinative, we cannot prevent instances of medically assisted death that are manifestly irrational. The heartbroken youth, according to this argument, must be allowed to die, because his judgment that death is in his best interest is decisive. As with the argument from autonomy, the argument from a patient's best interest is unable to exclude exactly the thing it is trying to avoid. In this case, it is medically assisted deaths that are not grounded in the best interest of patients.

Each of these arguments depends on the other to avoid its particular unwanted implication. The argument from autonomy uses the considerations of the argument from a patient's best interest to avoid killing those who do not wish to die (I must defer to your judgment, instead of my own, regarding the connection between your suffering and the value of your life), and the argument from a patient's best interest uses the argument from autonomy to avoid allowing the deaths of those who make grossly irrational decisions (if you lack rational autonomy, then I should ignore your judgment regarding the connection between your suffering and the value of your life). And yet, whereas advocates of medically assisted death see these arguments as a jointly sufficient justification of medically assisted death[23] (if my decision for suicide is an autonomous choice to die and death is indeed in my best interest, then I should be allowed to die), each argument, when brought to bear on the other, directly opposes its core claims, and in doing so negates its force. The argument from autonomy implies that I must judge whether or not your own evaluation of your best interest is correct, and I can do so only according to some standard that is external to your own subjective judgment. The argument from a patient's best interest implies that, on the contrary, you yourself are the decisive judge of your own best interest, and therefore you cannot have another account of your best interest imposed upon you (and you likewise have the right to die in the light of your own judgment of your best interest). Instead of moderating one another, these two arguments are in direct contradiction. Neither argument is sufficient on its own, since we are unwilling to accept the unwanted implication of each, and together they evacuate the rational force of both.

In short, if our criteria are external to the patient's own conclusions, then our position is too strong, and we will have no way of preventing the killing of those who do not wish to die. If instead we follow the personal judgments of the patient, then our position is too weak, and we will have no way of preventing the suicides of those who wrongly see no value in living. In practice, we advocate one criterion and then the other, depending on the repugnant result we wish to avoid. Our way of covering some cases some of the time conflicts with how we cover other cases at other times. In this way, advocates of medically assisted death are without consistent rational principles, applying one principle at one time (deference to the patient's judgment that life is still worth living) and then the contrary principle at another (rejection of the patient's judgment in light of our own conception of rational judgment). Each principle is coherent in itself, but we are, quite rightly, unable to accept the full implications of each argumentative strategy, and so we depend on one and then the other without rational explanation, our practical lives exhibiting an incoherent stumbling from one principle to the other and back again. The conclusion can only be that the autonomy and best interest defenses fail, separately and jointly, to justify medically assisted death.

Bibliography

Ackerman, Felicia. "Assisted Suicide, Terminal Illness, Severe Disability, and the Double Standard." In *Physician Assisted Suicide: Expanding the Debate*, edited by Margaret P. Battin, Rosamond Rhodes, and Anita Silvers, 149–61. New York: Routledge, 1998.

Dworkin, Ronald, Thomas Nagel, Robert Nozick, John Rawls, Thomas Scanlon, and Judith Jarvis Thomson. "Assisted Suicide: The Philosophers' Brief." *New York Review of Books*, March 27, 1997.

Finnis, John. "Euthanasia and Justice." In *Collected Essays*, vol. 3, *Human Rights and Common Good*, 211–41. Oxford: Oxford University Press, 2011.

———. "Reflections and Responses." In *Reason, Morality, and Law: The Philosophy of John Finnis*, edited by John Keown and Robert P. George, 459–584. Oxford: Oxford University Press, 2013.

Foster, Charles. *Choosing Life, Choosing Death: The Tyranny of Autonomy in Medical Ethics and Law*. Oxford: Hart, 2009.

Gormally, Luke, ed. *Euthanasia, Clinical Practice and the Law*. London: Linacre Centre for Healthcare Ethics, 1994.

Keown, John. *The Law and Ethics of Medicine: Essays on the Inviolability of Human Life*. Oxford: Oxford University Press, 2012.

Lillehammer, Halvard. "Voluntary Euthanasia and the Logical Slippery Slope Argument." *Cambridge Law Journal* 61, no. 3 (2002): 545–50.

Lopez, K. J. "Euthanasia Sets Sail: An Interview with Philip Nitschke." *National Review Online*, June 5, 2001. https://www.nationalreview.com/2001/06/euthanasia-sets-sail-kathryn-jean-lopez/.

McCall Smith, Alexander. "Beyond Autonomy." *Journal of Contemporary Health Law and Policy* 14 (1997): 23–39.

Oderberg, David. *Applied Ethics: A Non-consequentialist Approach*. Oxford: Blackwell, 2000.

———. *Moral Theory: A Non-consequentialist Approach*. Oxford: Blackwell, 2000.

O'Neill, Onora. *Autonomy and Trust in Bioethics*. Cambridge: Cambridge University Press, 2002.

Rachels, James. "Active and Passive Euthanasia." *New England Journal of Medicine* 292 (1975): 78–80.

———. *The End of Life: Euthanasia and Morality*. Oxford: Oxford University Press, 1986.

Steinbock, Bonnie, and Alastair Norcross, eds. *Killing and Letting Die.* New York: Fordham University Press, 1994.

Velleman, J. David. "A Right of Self-Termination?," *Ethics* 109, no. 3 (1999): 606–28.

Warnock, Mary, and Elisabeth Macdonald. *Easeful Death: Is There a Case for Assisted Dying?* Oxford: Oxford University Press, 2008.

Young, Robert. *Medically Assisted Death.* Cambridge: Cambridge University Press, 2007.

11

SOME THOUGHTS ON SECULARIZATION

Alasdair MacIntyre

What I owe in gratitude to David Solomon for nearly forty years of intellectual exchange and friendship is much more than a chapter. Happily this chapter *is* more than a chapter. If its arguments were adequately spelled out, if its large generalizations were properly qualified and supported, the result would be a book, perhaps several books. Unhappily this means that it is also less than a chapter, not so much a chapter as a promissory note, and at my age these are plainly promises that are not going to be kept.

I

I begin at some considerable distance from recent discussions of secularization with a set of thirteenth-century controversies concerning the authority of positive law, controversies in which Aquinas found himself at odds not only with that enemy of the church, Emperor Frederick II, but also with that good friend of the church, Louis IX of France.[1] Both of the latter—and the councilors who advised them—understood the authority of positive law and their own authority as rulers and lawmakers in theological terms. Both took themselves to be the legitimate heirs of the Roman emperors, as such designated by God to exercise imperial and royal authority in making and administering laws. For the dubiously Christian Frederick II, this authority is unqualified. To question or to attempt to limit the exercise of his authority is not only to defy him; it is to defy God. For Louis IX what God calls him to be is a Christian monarch, someone who is to exercise his authority in accordance with God's will as revealed in Scripture. Just because, so far as possible, what the royal law prescribes and punishes is what the gospel teaches, the king's commands have the authority of God's revealed commands. For Aquinas, however, matters are quite otherwise. On his account laws can only be enacted by those with authority to enact them, those, that is, on whom authority to make laws for a particular people has been conferred.[2] But decrees uttered even by such rulers are only laws insofar as they conform to the precepts of the natural law,[3] and those who are ruled are required to respect them only because and insofar as they conform to those precepts. What then are the precepts of the natural law?

They are precepts of reason directed toward the achievement of common goods.[4] If we fail to act as they dictate, we fail as rational agents. If we fail to conform to them in our deliberations with others, whether in households or in political societies, about what has to be done here and now to achieve our common goods, we will fail to achieve those goods. Since the achievement of our individual goods (i.e., of our goods qua human beings) generally and characteristically depends on the achievement of such common goods (i.e., of our goods qua subject or citizen or great aunt), if we fail to achieve our common goods, we will also fail to achieve our individual goods. All such failures are failures of rational agents to act as reason dictates. The authority of the precepts of the natural law—that is to say, whatever authority positive law possesses—is no more and no less than the authority of reason.

The function of positive law is to educate subjects and citizens in and into respect for the precepts of the natural law so that they can develop those virtues that they need to achieve their common goods. But it does not follow that positive law should replicate the natural law. The natural law, for example, forbids untruthfulness, but a political society in which lying was prohibited and punished would not in fact become a more truthful society. (My example, not Aquinas': his example concerns the occasions when the brothels should not be closed down.) What justifies the making of a positive law is that the effects of enforcing it will be such as to increase regard for the natural law, a regard expressed in the development of the moral virtues. Those virtues find or fail to find expression throughout the life of a culture. So it would, for example, be a failure in respect both of the virtues and for the precepts of the natural law not to give due place in our lives to the comic and to the entertaining, something that Aquinas makes clear in his discussion of the activities of the *jongleurs*, those groups of traveling players who had a key place in the popular culture of the thirteenth century.[5] Here is a prime example of how significantly different Aquinas' view is from that of some modern Thomists. They agree with him in saying such things as "How vicious he is! He tells lies and fornicates." What we do not find them saying is "How vicious he is! He tells no jokes and never sings comic songs!"

As to how we ought to conduct ourselves then, not just in respect of obedience to positive law, but more generally, through the whole range of activities that constitute a culture, we are to be guided by the precepts of the natural law. Their authority is the authority of secular practical reason, reason that finds expression in a variety of subordinate precepts and rules and that authority may not be set aside by any other authority, including ecclesiastical authority. So, for example, the precepts of the natural law, on Aquinas' account, assign to fathers the responsibility for deciding and the right to decide in what religion their children should be brought up.[6] No appeal to revealed truth can provide a sufficient ground for violating this right. Indeed what revealed truth confirms is that God as the creator of human beings as rational agents is the author of the natural law, so that, if we act as God wills that we should act, we will treat the precepts of the natural law as authoritative, just because they are precepts of reason. Among such precepts, we should note, are those that enjoin us to worship God, no matter how known to us.

It is important that every rational agent is potentially able to identify those precepts. On this we may supplement what Aquinas himself says[7] with Suarez' discussion,[8] since in this area, unlike some others, there is no reason to doubt Suarez' Thomist credentials. Suarez distinguished first between those precepts whose binding force is evident without difficulty to all and those of which we become aware only by rational reflection and inference and then between those of the latter class where the truth is more easily discerned and those where it is more difficult to discern. What matters in all three cases is not only that we learn what is required of us by the exercise of our reasoning powers but that we are justified in denying any claim to practical authority that is inconsistent with what reason discloses. Aquinas was of course well aware that human beings may not know that they know what they know. Frederick II and Louis IX and the legal theorists who advised them were after all examples of such human beings. He was also aware that cultures could be such that knowledge of this or that aspect of the natural law could be, as it were, blotted out. His example was what he—mistakenly—took to be practical ignorance of the precept forbidding theft in the Germans of the first century. Our example might well be the practical ignorance of the precept forbidding mass murder exhibited by some Germans of the twentieth century. Yet on Aquinas' view, both of these will be exceptional cases, explicable only as deviations from the human norm as Aquinas characterized it.

We now need to note that Aquinas advances his view both as philosopher and as theologian. This is how human beings are to understand themselves, both when they acknowledge God's existence and the truths of his self-revelation and engage in appropriate religious practices, whether as Jews, Moslems, or Catholic Christians, and when they do not. What then would happen to that self-understanding if their society were to become secularized? When I speak of a secularized society, I follow Charles Taylor in meaning not only a cultural condition in which religion is excluded from the public square and in which there has been a large decline in religious observance but also one in which belief in God has become deeply problematic and for many impossible. It must seem obvious that the only way to answer my question is to ask what did happen when our own society did in fact become secularized, did in fact become what it is now. Yet if we examine two major accounts of what did happen and is still happening, those of Charles Taylor and Philip Rieff, we find that even when sympathetic to Aquinas' view, as Taylor is, they do not do anything like justice to that view. Why not?

II

Taylor treats the contrast between secular unbelief and religious and more particularly Christian belief as one between "alternative ways of living our moral/spiritual life."[9] To have a moral/spiritual life is to have a sense of what it would be to attain to a state in which whatever fullness or completeness one's life is capable of has been achieved. For believers, that sense directs us toward what lies beyond nature and human nature, toward God, since to achieve such fullness would be to stand in a certain relationship with God. For modern unbelievers by contrast, "the power to reach fullness is within,"[10] a power variously conceived. Some find it in our nature as rational agents, whether reason is understood in Kantian or more naturalistic terms. What does this movement that exalts reason at the expense of the transcendent amount to?

When Taylor develops his historical account of the stages through which the secularized mind emerged, he describes how in the early modern period, while God is still taken to be the initiator of the universe, what He had created was understood as an impersonal, immanent order, whose "workings can be understood in its own terms."[11] The law constituting this order can be grasped independently of any reference to God, and its prescriptions are expressed in such rational codes as those of "Natural Law, the Utilitarian Principle, the Categorical Imperative." Here Taylor is referring to not of course Aquinas but "the new theories of natural law" advanced by Grotius and other theorists in the seventeenth century,[12] theorists who, like their utilitarian and Kantian counterparts, suppose that in appealing to what reason discloses, they are excluding any appeal beyond the human order. It is presumably among their followers that there are to be found those who aspire to identify the source of fullness—in Taylor's special sense of that word—within their lives, within their own reason, rather than in God.

What should puzzle us here is that "rather than." For, if Aquinas is right, those who identify the source of fullness in their lives as God, at least if the God in question is the God of whom Aquinas speaks, do so as rational agents, albeit often imperfectly rational agents. Not only are they able to accept the authority of reason, but their recognition of that authority is presupposed by their everyday practical reasoning. So for them acknowledgment of God's authority and of reason's authority, far from being incompatible, are complementary, each requiring the other. That Taylor does not discuss this possibility is odd, since he comes so close to doing so when he describes the attitude to nature of Aquinas and other thirteenth-century Aristotelians. For them, Taylor allows, nature is to be understood in its own terms, and he speaks of an "autonomization of nature." But so to understand nature, writes Taylor, "doesn't turn us away from God. Nature offers another way of encountering God."[13] It is only later, as Taylor recounts it, when the dominant conception of nature has been radically transformed, that nature can be and is understood as that within which and in terms of which we may discover the source of that which gives meaning to our lives and so becomes an alternative to God. What therefore we might have expected from Taylor but do not receive is a closely related account of the radical transformation of the dominant conception of reason. Why might this omission matter? It would certainly matter, if such a transformation was in fact central to the development of the secularized mind, as I shall suggest.

What then is the contrast between reason as understood by Aquinas and the modern secularized understanding of reason? For both, reason is that in us that enables us to give rationally justified answers to the questions "How is nature to be understood?" "How is human nature to be understood?" and "How should we act?" But for Aquinas, the goals that reason sets itself can only be achieved by exhibiting the unity of nature and of human activity, and that unity is such that the contingencies of finite nature require in the end explanation in terms of what is neither finite nor contingent, while the activities of rational agents can only be construed as directed toward a final end that lies beyond finitude and contingency. It is not that Aquinas adds to a set of theses about nature and activity an additional set of theses about God, which, if they proved to be unjustified, could then be subtracted, leaving us with a coherent atheistic view of things. It is rather that everything in nature and human nature is understood in terms that point beyond contingency and finitude and, by so doing, to God.

By contrast, the modern secularized conception of reason from the outset excludes the possibility of God's existence, although it took some time for this to become clear. Reason can provide justifiable accounts only of objects that satisfy certain limiting conditions, conditions that may be specified either in empiricist or in Kantian terms. What lies beyond those limits perhaps cannot be coherently thought and certainly cannot be an object of rational inquiry. It does not follow that someone cannot consistently hold the modern view of reason *and* affirm divine existence, but only if he or she acknowledges, perhaps in Kierkegaardian, perhaps in some other style, that he or she is at odds with secular reason in so doing. So in secularized societies, there is a place for religion, understood as a set of beliefs and practices of private individuals that cannot be rationally justified in public terms. What had to happen for this latter conception of reason and the corresponding conception of religion to displace its predecessor? To answer this question, we need to return to Aquinas' view.

It is central to that view that a line can be drawn between the sacred and what is legitimately secular, a line that is crossed whenever someone insists that some issue that is resolvable and should be resolved by secular reason is instead to be resolved by appeal to divinely revealed truth or that some issue resolvable only by appeal to such revealed truth be settled by rational inquiry. It would be of notable historical interest to identify those areas of life in the European thirteenth century, where something like this line was respected. But we have only to remind ourselves of the rejection of Aquinas' view by Frederick II and Louis IX to recognize how widely that line was ignored or obliterated by those in church and state with the power and the will to do so. It was during the long history of insistence by medieval rulers and their sixteenth-century successors that their rule was divinely sanctioned and that this sanction extended to whatever area of life they chose to extend it to that it became plain that secular activity had to be protected from what had become at numerous points a tyranny of the sacred. That tyranny took different forms in different countries and within different institutions, as did resistance to it. What finally emerged from that resistance was the Enlightenment critique of the ancien régime, a critique with less and more radical versions. Enlightenment radicalism contended that only if the sacred is wholly excluded from secular life will reason's authority be sustained and that what reason requires therefore is an exhibition through education of the groundlessness of all claims made on behalf of the sacred. Secularization and rationality sustain each other in resistance to the sacred.

What I am contending then is that secularization and more especially the dominance of the secularized conception of reason has in key respects a political explanation and that the prime mover in generating the relevant political history was the systematic refusal of those with power in the later middle ages and the early modern period to respect the line between the sacred and the secular. It was the ancien régime and not the Enlightenment that was the prime mover of secularization and one of its effects was to tangle together the metaphysical question concerning God and the political question concerning the disestablishment of religion. This political history is of course far from the whole story. Economic change in the same period made it increasingly difficult for those engaged in market transactions to find application for the concept of common goods, a concept required for sound practical reasoning, as Aquinas understands it. The practitioners of a variety of arts and sciences found rich and powerful patrons who enabled their clients to pursue their avocations in fruitful independence, each of which negotiated its own relationship—or lack of it—to the sacred. So in each particular area—political, economic, and cultural—the large transformations that constitute the history of secularization can be broken down into a series of numerous small transactions, through which modernity liberated itself from the constraints of the ancien régime.

Two narratives are of particular importance for my present purposes: one is that of the extended debate between the moderate deistic Enlightenment and the predecessor culture that it aspired to displace, the other that of the extended debate between that same moderate Enlightenment and its more radical and atheistic successor. It is in the course of these debates that there emerges that distinctive secularized conception of reason whose canons of argument and inquiry exclude from the outset any possibility that God is, let alone that we might be addressed by Him. So the transition from secular reason, as understood by Aquinas, to secularized reason, as understood by Feuerbach, was completed. In emphasizing it, I may be thought to be merely supplementing Taylor's account rather than correcting it. But I put that issue on one side in order to note another aspect of Aquinas' view, one that can be brought out by considering how there is no place for it in another large and impressive narrative of secularization, that supplied by Philip Rieff.

III

Rieff's narrative can be best approached by first considering his successive treatments of Freud. In *Freud: The Mind of the Moralist* (1959), Freud was portrayed as an essentially conservative figure who had shown how badly needed repressive agencies were if our instinctual drives were to be transformed and controlled. In *The Triumph of the Therapeutic* (1966), he considered the impact of Freud understood very differently as the protagonist of liberation from those repressive agencies through psychotherapy, someone who had exposed what were taken to be the false claims to moral authority of any agency but our own. By the time that he wrote *Fellow Teachers* (1972/1973), he had become clear that this was among the key attitudes that, by undermining badly needed authority, had become destructive of cultural standards both within and without universities. Rieff had been convinced from the outset that culture needs repressive belief in the sacred and argued that, while theorists may criticize such belief, it itself is not founded on theory; "One cannot have a theoretical belief."[14] So sociological theorists of culture, inhabiting the culture about which they theorize, must nonetheless acknowledge sacred authority if they are not to subvert that culture. The history of cultures is a history of changing relationships to sacred authority.

Every culture is the translation of some attitude to sacred order into social forms whose embodiments in action constitute what Rieff calls a world. Such worlds are of three types. First-world cultures are pretheistic and polytheistic, notably those of ancient paganism. Second-world cultures are theistic, Jewish, Christian, or Islamic, acknowledging the inflexible authority of divine command, interdict, and remission. Third-world cultures are by contrast anticultures, denying the reality of sacred order and so subverting the principles required for there to be civility, let alone worthwhile cultural achievement. What we now inhabit is the closing period of a second-world culture, already largely defeated by the protagonists of a third-world culture, protagonists who turn out to be enemies of culture as such. If there is a key date in the transition from the second-world culture to the third, it is 1882, the year in which Nietzsche announced the death of God.

Rieff's own stance was complex. As a sociologist he drew upon Durkheim and Weber, inverting Durkheim's account of the relationship between sacred and social orders and relying at various points on Weber's theses about the need for and the nature of authority. As a Jew he appealed to rabbinic tradition and to that in Christianity, which he recognized as authentically Judaic. As both sociologist and Jew, he was not just theorist or observer but committed to ongoing conflict with the emissaries of the third order. Yet although the enemy of Christianity's enemies, he was wholly unsympathetic to Christianity itself as it had historically developed. "I have not the slightest affection for the dead church civilization of the West," he wrote in *Fellow Teachers*.[15] Yet interestingly and surprisingly, among those whom he lists as second-world sociologists, and therefore his predecessors, are not only the Plato of the *Republic* and the authors of the Pentateuch but also Josef de Maistre,[16] defender of the ancien régime, of just that church civilization that Rieff so disliked. Yet de Maistre had argued that hierarchical political and social order can only be sustained if those who are ruled over are persuaded without good reason that such an order is divinely ordained and so demands uncritical obedience, thus anticipating Rieff's sociology of the sacred.

What then is the conception of reason that Rieff's arguments presuppose? The key expression that he used in characterizing the frame of mind needed to inform intellectual inquiry was "feeling intellect."[17] Our objectivity is from within our cultural commitments and is not to be confused with value neutrality, with what he called the "indifferent reason of the secularized mind."[18] Knowledge of what sacred order and the culture that gives it expression require always presupposes some committed cultural standpoint, some faith. "Faith is not a sacrifice of the intellect . . . but the predicate of all decisive *life/knowledge*."[19] Life/knowledge, however, is distinguished not only from indifferent reason but also from what Rieff calls *prudence/intellect*. To act intelligently from prudence is not to act as obedient faith requires.[20] Rieff thus put himself at odds with secularized reason in a way that also and equally distanced him from anything like

Aquinas' conception of reason. Where Taylor merely ignored that conception, Rieff's conceptual and explanatory scheme excludes it. What is the source of this exclusion? It is to be found, I shall suggest, in Rieff's much too narrowly restricted notion of what it is to enter into relationship with the sacred, of what it is to be before God.

Command, interdict, transgression, remission: these are Rieff's key terms for the commanding sacred truths whose authority is recognized when a theistic culture is in good order. But those terms are too abstract and general and as such fail to capture one key aspect of the relationship to God of those who acknowledge Him, at least as it is understood in Scripture. Consider Abraham's conversation with God about God's proposal to destroy the entire city of Sodom because of the wickedness of so many of its inhabitants (Genesis 18:22–32). Abraham calls God to account, arguing that He is about to wrong those of the Sodomites who are not wicked. Abraham appeals to an independent standard of justice by which both he and God are bound. So too, when God proposes to destroy the people of Israel because they have become idolaters, Moses reminds God that He made a covenant with Israel that He will violate if He acts as He proposes (Exodus 32:11–14). He appeals to an independent standard of promise keeping by which both he and God are bound. In both cases God concedes the conclusion advanced against Him. Later, when Job in his suffering puts God to the moral and philosophical question with an early version of the problem of evil, God responds in a very different mode, but He shows no disapproval of Job's questioning. And it is not only in Scripture that we find those most engaged by their conversation with God on such good argumentative terms with Him.

The Hasidic rabbi, Levi Yitzchak (1740–1809), rabbi of Berditchev in the Ukraine, told of a tailor who after Yom Kippur, the Day of Atonement, reported that on that day, he had asked God for forgiveness for his sins but had then pointed out to God that God's sins—leaving widows and orphans without support—were much greater than his. But said the tailor, if you will forgive my small sins, I will forgive your great sins. And he asked the rabbi if, in so speaking, he had done wrong. The rabbinic response was, "Why did you let God off so easily? You might have forced Him to redeem all Israel!" Berditchev was a center of Enlightenment culture, and Rabbi Yitzchak was portrayed to and by the secularized Jews among whom he had chosen to live as an absurd figure, as he indeed was by the standards of secularized reason. But the standards to which he appealed in pleading to God for Israel are recognizable as standards of secular reason. He holds

God to independent standards of reciprocity and fairness, just as Abraham and Moses had held Him to standards of justice and promise keeping. So it is also with Catholic Christian friends of God, as when Teresa of Avila on a day of great difficulties remarked to God, "If this is how you treat your friends, small wonder that you have so few!" holding God to independent standards of friendship.

What Abraham, Moses, the Berditchev rabbi, and Teresa recognize is that, even in their dealings with what is most sacred, they can achieve whatever good is at stake only as rational agents—that is, only if their activities accord with those standards that find expression in the precepts of the natural law. In de Maistre's authoritarian conception of the relationship between sacred order and social order, which Rieff admired, there is no place for such a recognition and, as with de Maistre, so too with Rieff. What neither understood was the difference between a culture in which the shared judgments are those of secularized reason and a culture whose shared judgments are those of a legitimately secular reason sustained by allegiance to the standards of the natural law. Rieff therefore never enquired whether the absence of any explicit acknowledgment of the sacred in modern cultures might not on occasion be compatible with something quite other than a secularization that rejects the sacred. Hence the works of art of secular modernity were one and all classified by him as deathworks, as expressions of third-world anticulture. What modern secular works of art might have shown him to be mistaken?

IV

Henri Matisse (1869–1954), although baptized a Catholic, was throughout his thinking life an atheist. He disappointed his father by abandoning the study of law for that of painting but retained habits of work—and a dress code—more characteristic of a lawyer than a painter. He developed quite unusual skills both in drawing and in the use of color, at first following carefully the example of the painters taken seriously by his teachers. But when he was introduced by a friend to the impressionists, and more especially to Van Gogh, his response was extraordinary: an original and striking grasp of what could be achieved by the use of strong and dissonant colors. "Wild" was an adjective used by unsympathetic viewers who lacked a sense of what he was doing. Yet in such paintings as the wonderful and enjoyable *Woman with a Hat*—note what the colors of the hat contribute to the image of the woman—he opened up new possibilities for portrait painting. Matisse had become a problem solver, a painter who, as a productive and practical reasoner, recurrently advanced his craft in unpredictable ways. "Matisse's art," Apollinaire had said, "is eminently reasonable."

So confronted by the achievements of cubism at an early stage, he set himself to reckon with the formal aspects of his representations. So too he honed skills that enabled those who attended to his paintings not only to see in new ways but also to feel in new ways about what they saw. In 1935, while painting *Large Reclining Nude*, a portrait of Lydia Delectorskaya, he took twenty-two photographs of the painting at each stage of its development. Arthur Danto has suggested that "the sequence does more than document the stages of a painting," that it records a transformation of Matisse's feelings toward his model, and that "Matisse used painting as a way of discovering what his feelings were."[21] His relationship to a later model took quite another turn. In 1941, while recovering from surgery for cancer, Matisse advertised for a nurse. His chosen applicant was Monique Bourgeois, then twenty-one years old. Matisse became fond of her and she of him, and she posed as a model for him on several occasions. In 1942 she became a novice in the house of the Dominican Sisters of Monteil, Sister Jacques-Marie.

In 1947, on behalf of the sisters, she invited Matisse to design for them a new chapel on a site beside the high school where they taught at Vence. What resulted was extraordinary, by Matisse's own judgment the greatest work of his final period, the Chapelle du Rosaire de Vence. Matisse worked closely with Father Marie-Alain Couturier and Brother Louis-Bertrand Rayssiguier, who had some experience in designing and building churches, as well as with an architect, but all the significant decisions were Matisse's, and all the works of art are his, created while he was crippled in a wheelchair: the murals of St. Dominic and the Virgin and Child; the fourteen paintings of the stations of the cross; and the stained-glass windows portraying the Tree of Life, the altar, the crucifix, and the vestments. And these are not just a set of separate works. They are so placed in relation to each other and to the changing light that they compose a whole, a setting for the daily prayers of the Dominican nuns and, above all, for the action of the mass. As with his nude portrait, they express and elicit feelings that would otherwise go unexpressed.

Matisse, I have already said, was not a believer. He led an entirely secular life and one far from wholly admirable. Quentin Bell records the judgment of a family who knew him well that he "was the greatest living painter, the greatest living egotist, and the greatest living bore."[22] Yet in this light, the Chapelle du Rosaire is all the more remarkable as evidence of Matisse's openness to the sacred as an artist. Here we have a paradigmatic example of a mode of secular life and of peculiarly modern secular life that has not excluded the possibility of God. There are, I want to suggest, numerous examples of this type of life in the cultures of modernity, too often unrecognized as such.

One that, unlike that of Matisse, Rieff does discuss is that of Schoenberg. What is notable in Rieff's remarks about Schoenberg's opera *Moses und Aron*[23] is how misleadingly selective Rieff's attention is, focusing as he does on the scene that portrays the transgressive idolatry of the Israelites, an episode that, if read as libretto without the music, is indeed a dramatic failure, while saying nothing at all about the portrayal of Moses and Aaron in their relationship to God and, most strikingly, ignoring the music altogether. Moreover, Rieff's readers are given no sense of the place of *Moses und Aron* in Schoenberg's remarkable history as a composer,[24] a history throughout which Schoenberg remained open to the sacred. To understand that openness more fully, we would need to take note of Schoenberg's relationship to Bach, and that I cannot do here. What I can do is to remark upon the influence of *Moses und Aron* on Daniel Liebeskind's design of the Jewish Museum in Berlin, not a deathwork, but a great memorial to the dead. Liebeskind has said of his own work that "you have to put yourself in a state of mind that isn't just purely secular to do something good."[25]

Both Matisse then, obviously, and Schoenberg, rightly understood, provide decisive counterexamples to Rieff's generalizations. Just as Rieff's sociology of culture has too limited a notion of the authority of the sacred, so correspondingly it has too limited a notion of what the secular can be and of its range of possible relationships to the sacred. We need then to reject Rieff's narrative of cultural secularization and to do so just because it cannot accommodate those aspects of human nature and activity that are central to Aquinas' account. What then would a narrative of secularization that took that account seriously look like?

It would have a very different starting point from either Taylor's narrative or Rieff's. Or rather it would have a set of very different starting points in a variety of religious cultures. It would distinguish those cultures in which the authority of the sacred is or was, at least to some significant extent, understood very much as Aquinas understood it, an authority exercised over rational and questioning agents, from those at the other extreme in which the authority of the sacred requires, at least to some significant extent, some superstitious capitulation of secular reason. From those different starting points, secularization has developed very differently. Where the starting point was of the latter kind, secularization has been apt to develop so that the secular became in various ways the enemy of the sacred, not only circumscribing or denying its authority, but reconceiving reason in terms well designed to exclude the possibility of a rational acknowledgment of the existence of the God of theism. Where the authority of the sacred continues up to the present to be invoked as a ground for denying secular truths that should be acknowledged by any rational agent, then secularized reason tends to become correspondingly hostile to the possibility of theological truth. So the modes of secular reason in the United States are in part at least a response to the fact that about 40 percent of Americans reject scientific findings about the age of the earth.

Where the starting point was of the former kind, the first question is, Why did secularization occur at all? The answer is, as I already suggested, through the development of an increasing range of secular practices, modes of work, modes of trade, arts, sciences, theater, about each of which there is a story to be told concerning how older and traditional acknowledgments of the sacred became increasingly incidental, then marginal, then irrelevant. Those who became first engaged in and then engrossed by such practices were apt to find meaning for their lives in achieving the ends set before them within those practices but were often not able to learn how to relate that meaning to the ends proposed by an established theistic religion that was content to leave the unthreatening secular to its own devices. Such religion may then become in time just one more practice among others, perhaps attractive in its own terms to those who feel a need for it, as in the United States; perhaps understood as something to be supported for its moral and social utility but not practiced, as in parts of Germany and Scandinavia; and perhaps treated as irrelevant, as in much of the United Kingdom. Those thus secularized are no longer believers, but they are not unbelievers either, from time to time lapsing back into belief. Their lack of militant unbelief is often found deeply irritating by those who have been secularized into hostility toward the sacred.

The differences between any narrative structured in this way and Rieff's narrative are obvious. It will, however, be compatible with much in Taylor's account, although differing from his in being primarily sociological. Fifty years ago in my Riddell Memorial Lectures of 1964,[26] I argued in some detail that secularization in England had been the result of types of social, economic, and moral change that had made the churches in various ways irrelevant, change that preceded the rise of unbelief, let alone of militant unbelief. The challenges presented by the rise of the natural sciences in the nineteenth century were, so I argued, a secondary phenomenon. Doubtless, were I to revisit that history now, I would need to make corrections on some matters of detail and to rethink some of what is said or implied about the relationship between practices and institutions. But the central thesis, I believe, stands, and what I then argued in the particular case of England finds its place within the more general account of secularization that I am now able to advance.

V

What then are we to say about openness as a characteristic that differentiates some secular cultures from others, some secular thinkers from others? Here we can learn from two very different twentieth-century characterizations of philosophy, from Gadamer's hermeneutics and from John Paul II's phenomenology. I have argued elsewhere[27] that a central lesson to be learned from Gadamer is that in interpretative inquiry and more generally in philosophical inquiry, no one can ever justifiably claim to have said the last word. There always may be more to be said, new as yet unimagined questions to be asked. The history of Platonic interpretation, for example, is a narrative in which the reading of Plato's texts recurrently discloses new possibilities of understanding what is at stake in Plato's arguments and can be expected to do so indefinitely. To the further discovery of such possibilities, we always have to remain open.

In *Fides et Ratio*, John Paul II argued that the secular activity of philosophical inquiry develops through the reformulation of a set of questions posed in every culture about human existence and meaning and through debate as to how they are to be answered. He then asked whether this activity of questioning had been or should have been brought to an end by biblical revelation of the truths that are the decisive answers to those questions. John Paul's reply is "No." It is to human beings as questioning and self-questioning agents that God addresses his revelation of Himself, and our responses to God cannot but be questioning responses. The time for questioning is never over. Inquiry will never be finally closed.

To think other than as Gadamer and John Paul thought on these issues would be to fail in the exercise of the secular virtue of *phronēsis, prudentia*. Yet the possession of that virtue is not at all incompatible with having arrived at some conclusion about whether or not God exists, perhaps in agreement with Aquinas that there are compelling arguments for holding that God exists, perhaps in agreement with Sartre in holding that there are compelling arguments for holding that God does not exist, perhaps in agreement with Anthony Kenny that neither set of arguments are compelling. What differentiates the open philosophical mind from the closed philosophical mind is not the presence or absence of firmly held conclusions but the willingness on appropriate occasions to question one's own conclusions by considering and, whenever necessary, reconsidering the full range of objections to them in their strongest form. It was of course Aquinas who made of this a method of inquiry in theology and in so doing upheld secular standards of inquiry against Frederick II and Louis IX.

Openness of mind of this kind is not just a philosophical or a theological virtue but a quality necessary for cultural flourishing. It is the lack of this openness that, so I have been arguing, is the vice of the secularized mind when it becomes closed to the possibility of God's existence. At the moment, only one-fifth of Americans avow no religious allegiance, but among Americans under the age of thirty, the proportion rises to one-third. So secularization is still proceeding in this country. If the overall argument of this chapter is sound, the crucial question is, What kind of secularization is it going to be? Some relevant evidence is provided by the growing and unfamiliar presence of Islam and the responses to it both of secularized unbelievers and of Christians. Where they take no trouble to distinguish between very different Islamic traditions or to ask what is to be learned from Islam's most impressive teachers, as Aquinas most notably did, we have evidence of minds that are closed not only to Islam but thereby to a good deal more than Islam. By contrast, it is where constructive conversation begins to open up between both the unbelieving and the Christian inhabitants of the secularized world and those Muslims who have been encountering that world for the first time that we find signs of cultural openness and hope. When those signs are lacking, when the closed mind prevails, the result is likely to be a secularization that misunderstands itself as the self-congratulatory outcome of a history of growing enlightenment. That misunderstanding, like Rieff's, will be one more obstacle to recognizing that one effect of the checkered history of secularization from the thirteenth century to our own has been to deprive us of anything like an adequate account of how the sacred and the secular are related. This chapter is a much too brief attempt to make a new beginning.

Bibliography

Bell, Quentin. "Meeting Matisse." In *Encounters*, edited by K. Erikson, 44. New Haven: Yale University Press, 1989.

Danto, Arthur. *Unnatural Wonders: Essays from the Gap between Art and Life*. New York: Columbia University Press, 2007.

Harnack, Adolph. *Outlines of the History of Dogma*. Boston: Beacon, 1957.

MacIntyre, Alasdair. "On Not Having the Last Word." In *Gadamer's Century: Essays in Honor of Hans Georg Gadamer*. Cambridge, Mass.: MIT Press, 2002.

———. *Secularization and Moral Change*. London: Oxford University Press, 1967.

———. *Selected Essays*. Vol. 2, *Ethics and Politics*. Cambridge: Cambridge University Press, 2006.

Rieff, Philip. *Fellow Teachers*. Chicago: University of Chicago Press, 1985.

———. *Freud: The Mind of the Moralist*. New York: Viking, 1959.

———. "Fellow Teachers." *Psychological Man: Approaches to an Emergent Social Type* 20 (Summer-Fall 1972): 5–85.

———. *My Life among the Deathworks*. Charlottesville: University of Virginia Press, 2006.

———. *The Triumph of the Therapeutic: Uses of Faith after Freud*. Chicago: University of Chicago Press, 1966.

Rosen, Charles. *Schoenberg*. New York: Viking, 1975.

Suarez, Francisco. *On Law and God the Lawgiver*. Translated by G. Williams, A. Brown, and J. Waldron. Oxford: Oxford University Press, 1966.

Taylor, Charles. *A Secular Age*. Cambridge, Mass.: Harvard University Press, 2007.

ELIZABETH ANSCOMBE AND THE LATE TWENTIETH-CENTURY REVIVAL OF VIRTUE ETHICS

W. David Solomon

Elizabeth Anscombe's devastating critique of twentieth-century Anglophone academic moral philosophy in her seminal 1958 article "Modern Moral Philosophy" is frequently cited as marking the beginning of the revival of virtue ethics. Although it is not until the 1980s, after the publication of another seminal work in moral philosophy, Alasdair MacIntyre's *After Virtue*, that the flood of work on the virtues began, many see the foreshadowing of these developments in Anscombe's influential earlier discussion. At the time Anscombe wrote "Modern Moral Philosophy," however, there was little interest in Aristotelian virtue ethics among Anglophone moral philosophers and, indeed, little interest in any style of normative ethical theory. Moral philosophers in the half century after Moore published *Principia Ethica* largely confined their work to the toolsharpening tasks that constituted metaethical theory. With the publication in 1971 of John Rawls' *A Theory of Justice* and the social dislocations of the 1960s, however, the interest of moral philosophers returned to foundational questions in normative ethics. There were spirited rebirths of neo-Kantian normative theories (as in Rawls) as well as consequentialist theories (as in Derek Parfit) and finally Aristotelian virtue theories (as in MacIntyre, McDowell, Nussbaum, and, indeed, Anscombe herself). In the decades after "Modern Moral Philosophy" appeared, virtue ethics has been enthusiastically pursued by moral philosophers and prominently discussed in the social sciences, in literary theory, and in critiques of popular culture.

In this chapter, I want to look more closely at the claim that Anscombe's alternative account of moral philosophy, as it was practiced in 1958, foreshadows the revival of virtue ethics in Anglophone academic moral philosophy. I begin first with a brief discussion of the famous three theses that are at the heart of Anscombe's paper. My goal here is simply to remove some puzzling features concerning these claims. Second, I turn to a discussion of the particular forms virtue ethics has taken in its recent revival. I suggest that contemporary virtue ethics is extraordinarily diverse, with different virtue theorists claiming different historical pedigrees for their accounts (some Aristotle, some Hume, some Nietzsche) and also disagreeing about how their theories might relate to the characteristic questions and problems of modern moral philosophy. I claim that there is a particularly important distinction between what I call "radical" (or revolutionary) virtue theories, those that radically reject the standard problematic of modern moral philosophy, and the merely "routine" virtue theories, those that work more conventionally within the problematic of modern moral philosophy. I explore the differences between these two conceptions of virtue ethics, paying special attention to how moral philosophers have attempted in different ways to incorporate virtue into modern accounts of ethics. I finally conclude that Elizabeth Anscombe would have felt her rightful heirs to be the radical virtue theorists and that she would have felt that the ambitions she expressed in "Modern Moral Philosophy" have not yet been realized. Hence the agenda set out in "Modern Moral Philosophy" has not yet, in an important sense, been carried through.

I presented the first version of this chapter, "Elizabeth Anscombe and the Late Twentieth Century Revival of Virtue Ethics," almost a decade ago as the keynote address at a conference on the occasion celebrating the fiftieth anniversary of the publication of "Modern Moral Philosophy" in 2008 at Santa Croce University just down the street from the Piazza Navona in Rome. Among those present on the occasion were Anscombe's husband, Peter Geach, her daughter, Mary Geach, and such other notable Anscombians as Father Kevin Flannery, S.J.; Professor Candace Vogler; and other students and scholars associated with the celebration. Although I have discussed many of the ideas in this chapter and my particular take on

Anscombe's approach to contemporary moral philosophy on many occasions, this particular attempt at a larger synthesis, and the details of the defense of the historical thesis at the center of it, are new. The ideas in this chapter found their way into a number of my other philosophical essays and, I hope, will eventually be part of a monograph on the history of contemporary virtue ethics.[1] What follows is an attempt to weave together a coherent narrative of the distinctive features of the development of virtue ethics in which I have been most interested. The reader can look at the particular articles referenced in the previous endnote for more detailed and focused discussions of particular themes.

It seemed particularly appropriate, on the occasion of the publication of this volume of essays by a number of my friends and students who share my deep and long-standing interest in Anscombe's work and its significance for the history of twentieth-century Anglophone academic moral philosophy, to present it as a gift to the thirty-nine Ph.D. students with whom I have worked throughout my career. I first taught my graduate seminar on the History of Twentieth Century Ethics at the University of Notre Dame in the summer of 1970 and taught it annually (with an occasional hiatus) until my retirement from Notre Dame in 2016. Elizabeth Anscombe's contributions to ethics have been at the heart of that course from its inception, including of course the ideas central to "Modern Moral Philosophy." I am grateful for the opportunity I have had to work with this marvelous group of students over such a long period who have shared with me the pleasure of the philosophical challenge of unraveling some of the deepest puzzles in the history of twentieth-century Anglophone moral philosophy. I am especially honored that Raymond Hain organized first a conference in the spring of 2014 and now this collection of essays focused on my years of teaching ethics at the University of Notre Dame. I have incurred debts in this regard I can never repay.

I

With Elizabeth Anscombe's death in January 2001, a remarkable life was brought to an end. It was a life that combined (1) philosophical work of the very highest scholarly distinction, (2) a courageous countercultural engagement with moral and political issues of the first importance in the second half of the twentieth century, (3) a kind of integrity in the pursuit of truth that allowed her to serve as a model for many others in these difficult years, and (4) a simple and consistent practice of her Catholic faith at a time of great turmoil in the Church.

Elizabeth Anscombe did not have a career just in philosophy; she had a life, and a life many of the episodes of which made her impossible not to notice. While still a student in the late 1930s, she, together with a friend, published a pamphlet that called into question the justice of the coming war with Germany. It earned her her first public notoriety and a rebuke from a bishop.[2] She had a special relation with Wittgenstein, and she was chosen by him from all his students to translate his masterwork, the *Philosophical Investigations*. She came to public notice once again in the mid-1950s, when she organized a motion to deny Harry Truman an honorary degree from Oxford University on the ground that the university should not honor a man who had been the prime mover in the dropping of atomic bombs on the civilian populations of Hiroshima and Nagasaki. Although it is hardly credible today that a British academic audience, given an opportunity to shame an American president, let the opportunity slip through their fingers, that is what happened. Anscombe's motion got only four votes—her own vote, her husband Peter Geach's vote, her best friend Phillipa Foot's vote, and Phillipa's husband's vote. If it hadn't been for the support of her friends and family, she would have been shut out. It was the disillusionment she suffered from garnering so little support for this motion, especially from the moral philosophers at Oxford, that led her to turn her attention to ethics and to write "Modern Moral Philosophy."

The year 2018 marked the sixtieth anniversary of Elizabeth's Anscombe's remarkable article "Modern Moral Philosophy." It appeared in 1958 in the journal *Philosophy* and was based on a set of lectures she gave the previous year in Sommerville College at Oxford on moral philosophy. Her daughter, Mary Geach, describes the occasion on which this article was written in the introduction to a collection of Miss Anscombe's papers on ethics edited by Mary Geach and her husband, Luke Gormally:

> Anscombe came to write "Modern Moral Philosophy" when Philippa Foot, who ordinarily taught ethics in Somerville, asked her to do it while she (Foot) was away in America. My mother settled down to read the standard modern ethicists and was appalled. The thing these people had in common, which had made Truman drop the bomb and the dons defend him, was a belief which Anscombe labeled "consequentialism." I believe she invented the term [she did]; it has come to mean much the same as "act utilitarianism", but without the view that the good is to be equated with pleasure and evil with pain. As Anscombe first

explained it, however, consequentialism is the view that there is no kind of act so bad but it might on occasion be justified by its consequences, or by the likely consequences of not performing it.[3]

I have long thought, as have others, that this paper is the most important paper in ethics written in the last half of the twentieth century, if not the most important paper in academic ethics written in the entire century. It is important in a number of different ways. First, it contains more ideas per page than almost any piece of philosophy I know. Its philosophical density is staggering. Second, most of these ideas are utterly original or presented in a way that is original. Third, virtually all of them are brilliant. Fourth, the paper was enormously influential. Here are a few of its influences: (1) It anticipates, and lays the groundwork for, the revival of virtue ethics a couple of decades in the future. (2) Along with Anscombe's *Intention*, one of the classics of midcentury philosophy, published at approximately the same time, it inaugurates a new discussion of practical reason and largely invents the philosophical specialty of action theory. (3) It introduces the term—as well as the idea—of consequentialism into contemporary ethics. (4) It takes seriously the history of moral philosophy as well as the historical and cultural influence on ethical ideas in a dramatically new way and in a way that reinvigorates a serious interest in the history of moral philosophy among moral philosophers. In an important sense, Anscombe reintroduces moral philosophy to its history. (5) It argues in a way that will be picked up by a number of later thinkers—especially Alasdair MacIntyre—that the important differences in the history of moral philosophy are those between the modern and the classical, not the differences between modern traditions like Kantian rationalism and Benthamite utilitarianism that are merely minor variations on modern themes. (6) It raises serious questions about the coherence of the modern notion of "morality" as a distinctive and autonomous sphere of human life and evaluation. (7) It allows the voice of the moral philosopher to have a kind of moral content even when it is speaking from the perspective of the philosophical. (Consider, for example, her remark near the end of "Modern Moral Philosophy" in which she says of those who will seriously consider judicially executing an innocent man that she will not speak to them because they exhibit "a corrupt mind".[4] Her comment marks a sharp break with the style of tame and largely unengaged Oxbridge moral philosophy that had gone before.)

What are the central claims of this article and why have they led so many to regard it so highly? Although Mary Geach highlights Anscombe's introduction of the term *consequentialism* as the most remarkable feature of this article, this sweeping rejection of consequentialism is not identified by Anscombe herself as one of the main points of the paper. She suggests instead that the three main concerns of the paper are to establish that

1. it is unprofitable presently (i.e., in 1958) to do moral philosophy,
2. the moral "ought" should be jettisoned,
3. there is no significant difference among all the main English moral philosophers since Sidgwick.

These three points taken together constituted a frontal assault on moral philosophy as it was practiced in the leading philosophy departments in England and America at that time. The heart of the charge was that moral philosophy as it was practiced in the academic world was utterly impotent in achieving its alleged object—which was presumably to guide the actions of its audience in the direction of the good. The impotence charge came at three different levels: first, moral philosophy lacked the tools to do what it claimed to do (hence, it was unprofitable to do moral philosophy); second, its record, at least in the twentieth century, was miserable, since, in spite of what appeared to be significant disagreement in the ranks of moral philosophers, vigorous debate, and claims of progress of various sorts, there was no real difference in the views of all the contending parties in these debates; and finally, the investigations were bound to fail, since the object of these investigations—the moral "ought"—was itself a mere survival of earlier conceptions of ethics that had disappeared. Anscombe's charge then was that Anglophone academic moral philosophy was inadequately prepared to do real ethics, that its history was one of simple acquiescence in the ethical trends of the time, and that its conception of its object was shot through with a lack of historical awareness and a deep self-deception. It was a severe indictment.

The first point is put in terms of the unprofitability of doing moral philosophy in our present condition. The present condition, as Anscombe is quick to explain in this article, is the condition of having an inadequate philosophical psychology. It was the inadequate understanding of notions like intention, willing, desiring, pleasure, and foreseeing taken together with the utter failure to develop a well-founded account of practical reason that made ethics utterly unprofitable for Anscombe. Her suggestion is that we should turn our attention away from ethics proper to these conceptual questions as a kind of prolegomena to future ethics. Anscombe herself, of course, was contributing at this very moment to the tool-sharpening tasks she was recommending. In 1957, the year before she published "Modern Moral Philosophy," her book *Intention*, regarded by many as her best work (and called by Donald Davidson "the best treatment of practical reason since Aristotle"), had appeared.[5] In this book, inspired as was "Modern Moral Philosophy" by the frustration she felt in the vapid arguments put forward by leading moral philosophers against her crusade to deny Truman his honorary degree, she lays the groundwork for a sophisticated and comprehensive treatment of these issues in philosophical psychology. Although many of the particular claims in *Intention* were deeply controversial and are still subjects of dispute, there can be no doubt that this book changed the face of philosophy. In this slim, tightly argued, and tersely expressed monograph, Anscombe, among other things, invents the field of action theory, a field that comes to attract some of the most talented philosophers of the next half century and a field that will in large measure do the conceptual work in philosophical psychology that she calls for in "Modern Moral Philosophy."

The second point claims that there is no significant disagreement among all the main English moral philosophers from Sidgwick to the present day. We must, of course, take account of the usual insularity of those writing from the perspective of British universities, especially Oxford and Cambridge, and understand that when Anscombe talks about *all English philosophers*, she means those who went to schools that she attended and those with whom she, perhaps, would have had a glass of sherry in the senior common room of one of the colleges at Oxford or Cambridge. She does not mean that there is no significant disagreement between Thomists and Marxists or between pragmatists and idealists or between the Frankfurt school and the English Dominicans. Her claim is meant to encompass the tradition of broadly English moral philosophy that stretched from Sidgwick to Hare and that would have included the range of views that would have been encountered at Oxford and Cambridge (and the schools colonized by Oxbridge philosophy in the United States—e.g., Princeton, Michigan, Harvard, and Chicago—whose practitioners of ethics had been socialized into Oxbridge ethics). We are all familiar with the main lines of this tradition—Sidgwick himself, followed by the English intuitionists, most prominently Moore, Prichard, and Ross; the various strands of noncognitivism represented by Ayer and Stevenson; and the more sophisticated prescriptivist forms of noncognitivism represented by Richard Hare, Anscombe's contemporary at Oxford and the main object of her criticism here. Even if we restrict our attention to the Oxbridge crowd, though, Anscombe's charge must surely initially appear simply false. Even among this restricted group of moral philosophers, there seems to be abundant evidence of deep disagreement—disagreement between cognitivists and noncognitivists, between cognitivists who were naturalists and those, like Moore, who were nonnaturalist intuitionists, intuitionists like Prichard, who had a deeply Kantian orientation in ethics, and other intuitionists like Ross, who seemed much more Aristotelian. There was also ample evidence that even among those philosophers who were in her special circle of philosophical friends, especially Iris Murdoch and Phillipa Foot, many deeply disagreed, as Anscombe did, with most of this tradition.

So how are we to understand her claim so that it is not just obviously false? The answer here is to note that Anscombe is not denying that *there is any disagreement* but rather that *there is significant disagreement*. It is her criterion of significance that will save her point if it can be saved. What leads her to claim that there is no difference is the fact that all the figures in this tradition espouse some form of consequentialism—that is, they all hold that any action can be justified under any description if it is productive of appropriate outcomes. As Anscombe notes in explaining the lack of significant difference,

> The overall similarity is made clear if you consider that every one of the best known English academic moral philosophers has put out a philosophy according to which, e.g., it is not possible to hold that it cannot be right to kill the innocent as a means to any end whatsoever and that someone who thinks otherwise is in error.... Now this is a significant thing: for it means that all these philosophies are quite incompatible with the Hebrew-Christian ethic. For it has been characteristic of that ethic to teach that there are certain things forbidden whatever *consequences* threaten, such as: choosing to kill the innocent for any purpose however good; vicarious punishment; treachery...; idolatry; sodomy; adultery; making a false profession of faith. The prohibition of certain things simply in virtue of their description as such-and-such identifiable kinds of action, regardless of any further consequences, is certainly not the whole of the Hebrew-Christian ethic; but it is a noteworthy feature of it; and, if every academic philosopher since Sidgwick has written in such a way as to exclude this ethic, it would argue a certain provinciality of mind not to see this incompatibility as the

most important fact about these philosophers, and the differences between them as somewhat trifling by comparison.[6]

So Anscombe's claim is not that there is no disagreement among these academic moral philosophers but rather that any disagreement is swamped, as it were, by their massive agreement in rejecting the Hebrew-Christian ethic.

The third point claims that we should jettison the moral "ought." Or as Anscombe puts it at somewhat greater length, "The concepts of obligation, and duty—moral obligation and moral duty, that is to say—and of what is morally right and wrong, and of the moral sense of 'ought,' ought to be jettisoned if this is psychologically possible; because they are survivals, or derivatives from survivals, from an earlier conception of ethics which no longer generally survives, and are only harmful without it."[7] This third point may seem somewhat surprising after the emphasis in the second point on Anscombe's loyalty to the Hebrew-Christian ethic. Some might express that ethic by saying something like this: it holds that there are some actions—say, sodomy or directly killing the innocent—that are always morally wrong, or that we always have a moral obligation to avoid. The Hebrew-Christian ethic itself embodies a strong sense of moral obligation. Anscombe is in what may seem like the puzzling position of suggesting that the most important feature of twentieth-century ethics is that it rejects the Hebrew-Christian ethic and then claiming that this same tradition of twentieth-century ethics goes wrong in taking as central the very notion of moral obligation, which some might think is essential for expressing the Hebrew-Christian ethic.

But Anscombe's view, of course, is more subtle than that. Her reason, as she says earlier, for wanting to jettison the moral "ought" is that she sees it as part of the cultural residue (or remainder) of the traditional divine command theory of ethics. As she puts it (and I am here stringing together a number of different passages),

> Between Aristotle and us came Christianity, with its *law* conception of ethics.... To have a *law* conception of ethics is to hold that what is needed for conformity with the virtues failure in which is the mark of being bad *qua* man ... is required by Divine law. Naturally it is not possible to have such a conception unless you believe in God as a law-giver; like Jews, Stoics and Christians. But if such a conception is dominant for many centuries, and then is

> given up, it is a natural result that the concepts of "obligation," of being bound or required as by a law, should remain though they had lost their root; and if the word "ought" has become invested in certain contexts with the sense of "obligation," it too will remain to be spoken with a special emphasis and a special feeling in these contexts.[8]

And developing her point further in a famous analogy, Anscombe says,

> It is as if the notion "criminal" were to remain when criminal law and criminal courts had been abolished and forgotten. A Hume discovering this situation might conclude that there was a special sentiment, expressed by "criminal," which alone gave the word its sense. So Hume discovered the situation in which the notion "obligation" survived, and the word "ought" was invested with that peculiar force having which it is said to be used in a "moral" sense, but in which the belief in divine law had long since been abandoned: for it was substantially given up among Protestants at the time of the Reformation. The situation, if I am right, was the interesting one of the survival of a concept outside the framework of thought that made it a really intelligible one.[9]

Some have read Anscombe's position here—mistakenly, I believe—to be a defense of a divine command theory of ethics, as if she were arguing as follows:

1. Our deepest moral commitments can be expressed only by using the language of categorical moral obligation.
2. Such language is coherent only if one believes in God as a lawgiver.
3. Therefore, moral commitment requires that one believe in God.

Rather, I think she is arguing as follows:

1. Most people since the seventeenth century haven't believed in God as a divine lawgiver.
2. The language of moral obligation is coherent only in language communities sustained by persons who believe in God as a divine lawgiver.
3. Therefore, the language of moral obligation has lost its coherence in modern culture and should be jettisoned.

It is important to see that she is not suggesting that we abandon ethical reflection but rather that we abandon that form of ethical reflection that makes the concept of moral obligation central. She argues elsewhere in the paper that Aristotle did ethics perfectly well without using the concept of moral obligation, so why shouldn't we be able to do so as well (especially if we straighten out our philosophical psychology)? She takes not the Dostoyevskian position—"If God doesn't exist, everything is permitted"—but rather the far more subtle Nietzschean position, expressed in his response to Dostoyevsky as "If God doesn't exist, nothing is permitted," meaning that the notion of permission simply loses its sense.

II

At roughly the same time in the late 1950s that Anscombe was developing her devastating critique of modern moral philosophy, many moral philosophers turned their attention once again toward reopening many of the deepest questions in traditional normative ethics that had been largely neglected in the opening decades of the twentieth century. After taking their lead from certain strands in G. E. Moore's thought and focusing their attention on tool-sharpening metaethical questions for most of this century, moral philosophers have in recent decades been influenced more by the model of John Rawls' *A Theory of Justice*. It is not, of course, that they have all agreed with Rawls' broadly Kantian conclusions about normative theory but that they have followed him in reopening the great questions of traditional normative theory and eschewing the normative minimalism that characterized most academic English-speaking ethics from the collapse of Sidgwick's consequentialism, Spencer's evolutionary naturalism and Bradley's idealism under the critical fire of Moore and others. Since Rawls reopened these questions in the 1960s and 1970s by attempting to rehabilitate in *A Theory of Justice* the neo-Kantian moral perspective, a number of other philosophers have entered the discussion by exploring and defending alternative normative theories. There have been especially ambitious attempts to do for consequentialism and for neo-Aristotelian virtue theories what Rawls had done for neo-Kantianism, and there are now on offer in contemporary ethics a number of philosophically sophisticated and comprehensive reconstructions of traditional normative theories.[10] In this regard, the contemporary student of moral philosophy is confronted with an embarrassment of riches. And the main narrative of the history of Anglophone academic moral philosophy has become a much more complicated story.

Current discussions in moral philosophy are dominated by the lively debates among these three competing normative theories.[11] Frequently, these latter debates—among consequentialists, for example, about how consequentialism is best formulated—involve disagreements that are as deep, and sometimes as divisive, as those that arise across normative theories. The disagreements among proponents of an ethics of virtue are particularly complicated, involving disagreements along a number of different axes. Some virtue theorists see themselves in the Aristotelian tradition, others in the Humean tradition, and others yet feel more affinity with Nietzsche. Some virtue theorists regard their theories as essentially critical of central features of late modernity; others feel comfortable regarding their theories as just another instance of a modern ethical theory. These deep and crisscrossing disagreements among virtue theorists have made some despair of giving a general characterization of virtue ethics. Others characterize it in a way that is hardly informative. Alasdair MacIntyre, for example, is reduced to this quite uninformative characterization of virtue ethics in an encyclopedia entry he wrote on virtue ethics: "Contemporary virtue ethics is in part a revival of some Greek preoccupations, transformed by the need to address the problems of modern moral philosophy."[12]

One place to begin thinking seriously about the revival of virtue ethics of the sort Anscombe explored in "Modern Moral Philosophy" is to ask whether her view of a genuine ethics of virtue might be radically different from most modern conceptions of a normative theory offered in her day and earlier. One could compare her conception of ethics that placed virtue at the center of ethical thinking to a conception of ethics that kept a focus on rules and the maximization of good states of affairs, as do Kantian deontologists like Rawls and consequentialists like Sidgwick. There is no question that she was prepared to accept such a virtue approach to ethics as radical indeed. After all, she had placed at the center of her critique of modern ethics the rejection of the concept of the "moral ought" and the deontological concepts associated with a Kantian approach to ethics as well as the rejection of consequentialism and the concepts associated with classical utilitarianism. But has the turn to virtue in ethics involved a *genuine revolution in ethics,* or have we simply been undergoing *a slight course correction* in ethical theory? Instead of attempting a simple history of the rise of virtue—and of providing yet another taxonomy of the different kinds of virtue ethics—I would like to focus on that question.

The phrase "revolutionary ethics" may sound a little overwrought when applied to something as sedate and as irrelevant (for the most part) to larger cultural concerns as twentieth-century Anglophone ethics. But it seems to me that we can speak, if we are careful, about some of the changes in the academic study of ethics with which we are familiar even in the twentieth century as, in important respects, revolutionary.

These revolutions are typically marked by a piece of philosophy that divides prerevolutionary moral philosophy from post. Although there might be some disagreement among contemporary moral philosophers on the exact number of these radical changes, there would surely be a broad consensus that Moore's *Principia Ethica*,[13] Ayer's famous chapter 5 of *Language, Truth and Logic*,[14] Rawls' *A Theory of Justice*,[15] and MacIntyre's *After Virtue*[16] mark such revolutionary developments. It is not the case that these works are themselves the first expression of new revolutionary thoughts. Indeed, in the case of each of these works, it is more likely to be a culminating event in a kind of buildup to change. Moore's work could be regarded, for example, as a natural response to the theoretical despair into which his teacher, Sidgwick, fell after the collapse of his project of generalized commitment to universal benevolence; Ayer brings his big idea back from Vienna, while Rawls builds on the work of an already developing revival of traditional normative theory; and MacIntyre's work draws heavily on a renewed tradition of neo-Aristotelian thought that received its initial impetus almost twenty-five years before the publication of *After Virtue* in Anscombe's "Modern Moral Philosophy."

Nor is it the case that these changes in direction are unrelated to the views that they aim to overturn. Moore's intuitionism prepares the way for emotivism (recall, for example, Stevenson's claim that "non-natural properties are the shadows cast by emotive meaning"[17]), just as Hare's subtle elaboration of noncognitivism in *Freedom and Reason* prepares the way for the full-blooded normative theorizing of Rawls. Indeed, it is not uncommon for those philosophers who come before the revolutionary change to interpret the change not as a radical change but rather as an extension of what has come before. In this way, noncognitivism was seen by some as just another possible metaethical position alongside intuitionism, and Rawls' neo-Kantian views were taken by some of those he displaced as yet another metaethical theory. (This is surely the best way to understand Hare's remarkable review of *A Theory of Justice* in which he claims that Rawls is just another intuitionist—and not a very good one at that.[18]) There is always an attempt to draw revolutionaries back into the theoretical contexts from which they are attempting to escape.

Although I will not attempt to give definitive criteria for determining when a change in ethics is revolutionary, it seems clear that these works I have suggested as revolutionary have in common an attempt to change the set of theoretical aims appropriate to moral philosophy. This can best be seen by looking briefly, and very inadequately, at some of the particular features of the changes these works introduced. The particular issues around which this putative revolutionary activity in twentieth-century ethics takes place (I will take it as understood from now on that I restrict myself to Anglophone, broadly analytic, ethics—no Sartre, no Maritain, no Dewey) are complex. The three revolutions associated, roughly, with Moore, Ayer, and Rawls, however, seem best characterized as follows:

Moore's revolution focused on the rejection of the broad-scale normative theorizing characteristic of his nineteenth-century predecessors. There is a transition from moral philosophy dominated by Spencer, Bradley, and Sidgwick to moral philosophy dominated by Moore, Prichard, and Ross. The changes in the approach to ethics are almost palpable, although many of the arguments used by Moore would certainly have been familiar to Sidgwick and many other nineteenth-century figures. The ambitions of moral philosophy are curtailed in a number of different ways, and the cultural position of moral philosophy and its degree of cultural engagement changes dramatically. Sidgwick caught the train to London regularly to discuss the affairs of the day with the prime minister—and it was part of the job of a moral philosopher at that time to catch that train. It is unthinkable that Moore would catch that train.[19]

Ayer's revolution centrally involved the semantic turn as applied to ethics. There was a transition from a set of issues in ethics dominated by Moore, Prichard, and Ross to a set of issues dominated by Ayer, Stevenson, and Hare. Not only is large-scale theorizing about normative issues given up (as in the first revolutionary turn), but the normative is altogether expunged from moral philosophy. With the advent of Ayer's noncognitivism, moral neutrality reigns within normative ethics. A sharp distinction is drawn between metaethics and normative ethics, and moral philosophers are forbidden to trespass in the realm of the normative. Moral philosophers, qua moral philosophers, are not even allowed with due Rossian sincerity to remind us that we ought to return our library books on time. That is the task of those who actually use moral language (the familiar litany in books of the period: preachers, novelists, and ordinary people), and moral philosophers, qua moral philosophers, aren't allowed that privilege.

Rawls' revolution welcomes back a chastened but still robust normative theory. Moral philosophers are allowed to use their more sophisticated twentieth-century tools in pursuing once again the project of constructing large-scale normative theories. For the most part, this Rawlsian revolution does not attack those whose privileged positions within moral philosophy it usurps—it simply marches in and takes possession. Rawls barely mentions in *A Theory of Justice* his classical metaethical predecessors whose conception of the task of moral philosophy he utterly rejects.[20] Hare's work, which had dominated discussion among moral philosophers for two decades, was dispatched by Rawls in a very brief section of *A Theory of Justice* titled "Some Remarks on Moral Theory." The easy victory, no doubt, is partly to be explained by both the theoretical and practical exhaustion of classical metaethics.[21]

The Rawls revolution though was not just a revolution in favor of Rawls' favored neo-Kantian style of normative ethical theory but a revolution that opened the door, once again, to the construction of comprehensive normative theories of a variety of sorts. Moral philosophers could once again catch the train to London—or at least to Washington, D.C.[22] And they did. Rawls spawned an entire generation of students who pursued the elaboration of his favorite style of normative theory. The work of Rawls and his students, in turn, was confronted by ambitious theoretical work in defense of the consequentialist theories that Rawls had criticized in *A Theory of Justice*.

In addition to the neo-Kantian and consequentialist efforts to revive traditional normative theory, there is a third effort exemplified by the work of MacIntyre and others—the revival of neo-Aristotelian virtue theories. And this gives a kind of symmetry to our story of revolutionary activity in twentieth-century analytic ethics. Spencer, Bradley, and Sidgwick give way to Moore, Ross, and Prichard, who in turn give way to Ayer, Stevenson, and Hare, who, finally, give way to Rawls, Parfit, and MacIntyre. The pursuit of this kind of trinitarian neatness has been known to mislead philosophers, however, and I think we do well to avoid it in this case also.

One might regard the emphasis on virtue exemplified in the work of MacIntyre and other neo-Aristotelians, including, of course, Anscombe herself, as itself revolutionary and not as a set of arguments responding to the same theoretical demands as their Kantian and consequentialist opponents. Or one might see the revival of virtue ethics as structurally similar to the revival of neo-Kantian and consequentialist normative theories in that it is a return to the kinds of questions to which the comprehensive nineteenth-century normative theories were responding. It would then be operating on the same theoretical stage, as it were, with these other normative theories—asking the same questions but giving different answers.

That is, it would be, relative to other normative theorizing, merely "routine." It would be driven by the same theoretical demands but would be responding to these demands in different ways. Alternatively, one could see the turn to virtue as harking back to the kind of classical approach to moral philosophy that characterized the aims of that enterprise in a quite different way from the way in which they are characterized typically within modern moral philosophy. This would make the turn to virtue "radical" indeed.

I believe that some of the work now being done in moral philosophy that is labeled "virtue ethics" is merely routine, some is revolutionary, and perhaps some cannot make up its mind. I will not attempt here to name names (or at least not many names), but a brief preliminary survey of some of what is labeled virtue ethics will be useful in fixing our ideas.

There is no doubt that Elizabeth Anscombe thought that the return to virtue she advocated in "Modern Moral Philosophy" would be anything but routine. Her thundering indictment of twentieth-century analytic ethics as well as her claim that there were no substantial differences among all the "main" moral philosophers following Sidgwick should assure her of a comfortable place among the revolutionaries. Alasdair MacIntyre, also, has made his attempt to revive what he has called the "tradition of the virtues," an integral part of a much broader attack on central features of modernity—and especially modern conceptions of practical rationality—that undergird much of the theory and practice of contemporary analytic normative theory. Among the many ways in which MacIntyre and Anscombe are similar is their tendency to downplay the differences, from the point of view of an Aristotelian approach to ethics, between deontological and consequentialist normative theories. The suggestion that deontological theories and consequentialist theories are simply minor variations on a style of modern moral theorizing to which an ethics of virtue is radically opposed is a common feature of those virtue theories that I would regard as radical.

If Anscombe and MacIntyre, as well as some others,[23] have promoted a return to virtue as a radical move within contemporary ethics, others have emphasized talk about the virtues while working comfortably within the conventions of contemporary ethical theory. Here there are two kinds of cases. There are those like Michael Slote who claim to be doing virtue ethics but who do it in such a way that their work fits neatly within the conventions of contemporary analytic normative theory.[24] Others—here I would include consequentialists like Shelly Kagan and neo-Kantians like Barbara Herman—are not doing virtue ethics explicitly but struggle mightily and, in some cases, I think, brilliantly to find a place for virtue and the concerns of those who have pushed virtue within their own theories.[25] While rejecting virtue ethics, they have tried to assimilate virtue. There are then three broadly different kinds of ways to take virtue seriously in contemporary ethics, I think—a radical way, a routine way, and a way that merely accommodates it within a normative structure that doesn't give it a privileged place.[26]

III

I will conclude by attempting to give a bit more substance to the distinction between what I am calling routine and radical (or revolutionary) virtue ethics. I have described the competing normative theories—Kantian, consequentialist, and virtue ethics—and now wish to delve more deeply into the nature of the disagreements among them. Consider first which notion plays the primary role within the overall structure of each of the three styles of normative theory.

This question of a central role gets its sense from a certain picture of how the three main kinds of competing normative theories—deontological, consequentialist, and virtue theory—relate to one another. The picture suggests that each theory is specified by its relation to a key notion—deontological theories to rules, consequentialist theories to good states of affairs, and virtue theories to virtues. On this view, then, the central dispute among these theories is a dispute about which of these key notions—the notion of a rule, an intrinsically good state of affairs, or a virtue—plays a primary structural role in the overall theory. A deontological theory will (in some sense to be specified) make rules the fundamental notion in the theory, while consequentialist theories will make intrinsically good states of affairs fundamental, and virtue theories will make virtues fundamental. The basic disputes among these theories then will be over this question of which notion has the privileged place.

Notice however that, in thus characterizing the nature of the *differences* among competing normative theories, they are also treated as remarkably similar. Each theory will place some notion in the privileged place and presumably will have a structure similar to the other theories. There is certainly the suggestion that the fundamental notion in each theory will have to serve the same function—essentially of motivating and justifying particular actions.[27] While there will certainly be differences among these different theories when characterized in this way, the differences do not seem to go very deep. They can be made to seem like matters of mere theoretical convenience, as if we were choosing among alternative axiom sets for a formal system.

Now contrast this way of characterizing the differences between virtue ethics and its opponents with a second way that involves differences of much greater variety and depth. Many advocates of virtue ethics—including Alasdair MacIntyre and Elizabeth Anscombe—have drawn the contrast between virtue ethics and its opponents in a much more complicated way. Here are just some of the themes that run through much of contemporary virtue ethics and that are seen by many of its advocates as central to their advocacy of virtue in preference to the Kantian and consequentialist alternatives:

1. A suspicion of rules and principles as adequate to guiding human action in the complex and variegated situations in which human agents find themselves.
2. A rejection of conscientiousness as the appropriate motivational state in the best human action.
3. A turn for an understanding of the ethical life to concrete evaluative terms like the virtue terms in preference to more abstract terms like *good*, *right*, and *ought*.
4. A critique of modernity and especially the models of practical rationality that underlie such enlightenment theories as Kantian deontology and Benthamite consequentialism. This critique frequently extends to the bureaucratic and impersonal features of many central modern social practices.
5. An emphasis on the importance of community, especially local communities, both in introducing human beings to the ethical life and sustaining their practice of central features of that life. This emphasis is typically contrasted with the individualism that seems to many advocates of virtue ethics to permeate Kantian and consequentialist approaches to ethics.
6. A focus on the importance of the whole life as the primary object of ethical evaluation, in contrast to the tendency of Kantian and consequentialist theorists to give primacy to the evaluation of actions or more fragmented features of human lives.
7. An emphasis on the narrative structure of human life as opposed to the more episodic picture of human life found in Kantian and consequentialist approaches to ethics. This narrative structure is

especially important in understanding the special nature of human projects and human goods that can be understood only within the context of the story of a whole life.
8. An emphasis on the centrality of contingently based special relationships, especially with friends and family, for the ethical life in contrast to the tendency within Kantian and consequentialist theories to downplay such relationships in favor of alienating ideals of universality.
9. A suspicion of morality understood as an abstract and distinctive grid of obligations and rights cut off from the more concrete features of human practical life.
10. A special emphasis on thick moral education understood as involving training in the virtues, as opposed to models of moral education frequently associated with Kantian and consequentialist moral theories that tend to emphasize growth in autonomy or in detached instrumental rationality.

I do not intend, of course, this laundry list of issues associated with contemporary virtue ethics to be in any way definitive of an ethics of virtue. Nor do I intend my brief characterization of each item to constitute anything like an argument for it. I do intend this list, however, to be a reminder of how diverse and rich are the differences between many contemporary advocates of the virtues and their Kantian and consequentialist opponents. The attempt to reduce the difference between an ethics of virtue and its contemporary alternatives to a single, crucial issue—the place of the notion of virtue in the overall justificatory structure of a theory—is surely one of the marks of thinking of virtue ethics as routine.

One might try to argue, of course, that the diverse and complex set of disagreements contained in this list all derive from a more basic ur-disagreement over which of the favored notions—rule, virtue, or intrinsically good state of affairs—is to be taken as fundamental within a normative theory. But this really doesn't seem very convincing—not least because this complex set of overlapping and intertwining disputes seems to involve a disagreement rather about the very idea of a normative theory within which something might be basic.

IV

Anscombe's three theses did indeed attack the very core of Anglophone moral philosophy as it was practiced in 1958. Her insistence that the moral "ought" be jettisoned contains both a power and a subtlety that philosophers have sought to understand and challenge ever since. There is also no question that the arguments central to "Modern Moral Philosophy" transformed the history of Anglophone academic philosophy in the half century since they appeared. In this regard, her revival of virtue ethics embodied many radical elements. In contrast, the responses to Anscombe by many more conventional competing normative theories have been, as she suggested, shallow and tending toward the conventional. In this regard, like MacIntyre's later work, her work contains a distinctiveness, variety, and complexity not seen in later virtue ethics.

Of course, these are bold claims and need to be supported by much more careful studies on the history of twentieth-century Anglophone academic ethics. Even though we are now well into the twenty-first century, we do not yet have a comprehensive history of twentieth-century Anglophone academic ethics that could deal with these historical questions with the subtlety they demand—especially in their cultural and social dimensions as well as their epistemological and metaphysical ones. It is certainly one of my fondest hopes that the remarkable young moral philosophers who have worked on the essays in this volume will turn to this task with energy and insight.

Bibliography

Anscombe, Elizabeth. *Intention*. Oxford: Basil Blackwell, 1959.

———. "Modern Moral Philosophy." In *Ethics, Religion and Politics*, edited by G. E. M. Anscombe, 26–42. Oxford: Basil Blackwell, 1981.

———. "Mr. Truman's Degree." In *Ethics, Religion and Politics*, 51–61. Oxford: Basil Blackwell, 1981.

Anscombe, Elizabeth, and Daniel Norman. "The Justice of the Present War Examined." In *Ethics, Religion and Politics*, 72–81. Oxford: Basil Blackwell, 1981.

Ayer, A. J. *Language, Truth and Logic*. London: Gollancz, 1936.

Foot, Philippa. "Moral Beliefs." *Proceedings of the Aristotelian Society* 59 (1958): 83–104.

Geach, Mary. "Introduction." In *Human Life, Action and Ethics: Essays by G. E. M. Anscombe*, edited by Mary Geach and Luke Gormally, xiii–xxi. Essex: Imprint Academic, 2005.

Hampshire, Stuart. "Liberalism: The New Twist." Review of *A Theory of Justice*, by John Rawls. *New York Review of Books*, August 12, 1993.

Hare, R. M. *Freedom and Reason*. Oxford: Oxford University Press, 1973.
———. "Review: Rawls' Theory of Justice—I." *Philosophical Quarterly* 23, no. 91 (1973): 144–55.
———. "Review: Rawls' Theory of Justice—II." *Philosophical Quarterly* 23, no. 92 (1973): 241–52.
Herman, Barbara. *Moral Literacy*. Cambridge, Mass.: Harvard University Press, 2008.
Kagan, Shelly. *The Geometry of Desert*. Oxford: Oxford University Press, 2012.
MacIntyre, Alasdair. *After Virtue*. Notre Dame: University of Notre Dame Press, 1981.
———. "Virtue Ethics." In *The Encyclopedia of Ethics*, vol. 3, edited by Charlotte B. Becker and Lawrence C. Becker, 1757–63. New York: Routledge, 2001.
Moore, G. E. *Principia Ethica*. Cambridge: Cambridge University Press, 1903.
Murdoch, Iris. *The Sovereignty of Good over Other Concepts*. Cambridge: Cambridge University Press, 1967.
Parfit, Derek. *Reasons and Persons*. Oxford: Oxford University Press, 1984.
Prichard, H. A. "Does Moral Philosophy Rest on a Mistake?" *Mind* 21, no. 1 (1912): 21–37.
Rawls, John. *A Theory of Justice*. Cambridge, Mass.: Harvard University Press, 1972.
Ross, W. D. *The Right and the Good*. Oxford: Oxford University Press, 1930.
Slote, Michael. *From Morality to Virtue*. Oxford: Oxford University Press, 1992.
Solomon, David. "Domestic Disarray and Imperial Ambition: Contemporary Applied Ethics and the Prospects for Global Bioethics." In *Global Bioethics: The Collapse of Consensus*, edited by H. Tristram Engelhardt. Salem, Mass.: Scrivener, 2006.
———. "Early Virtue Ethics." In *The Oxford Handbook of Virtue*, edited by Nancy Snow. Oxford: Oxford University Press, 2017.
———. "Internal Objections to Virtue Ethics." In *Ethical Theory: Character and Virtue, Midwest Studies in Philosophy, XIII*, edited by Peter French, Theodore Uehling, and Howard Wettstein, 429–41. Notre Dame: University of Notre Dame Press, 1986.
———. "Keeping Virtue in Its Place: A Critique of Subordinating Strategies." In *Recovering Nature: Essays in Natural Philosophy, Ethics, and*

Metaphysics in Honor of Ralph McInerny, 83–104. Notre Dame: University of Notre Dame Press, 1999.

——. "Virtue Ethics: Radical or Routine?," In *Intellectual Virtue: Perspectives from Ethics and Epistemology*, edited by Michael DePaul and Linda Zagzebski, 57–80. Oxford: Oxford University Press, 2003.

Stevenson, Charles. *Ethics and Language*. New Haven: Yale University Press, 1944.

Williams, Bernard. *Ethics and the Limits of Philosophy*. Cambridge, Mass.: Harvard University Press, 1985.

NOTES

Introduction

1. G. E. M. Anscombe, "Modern Moral Philosophy," *Philosophy* 33, no. 124 (1958): 1–19.
2. G. E. M. Anscombe, *Intention* (Oxford: Basil Blackwell, 1957).

1: Toner

1. *Nicomachean Ethics* (*NE*) 1.8.1099a29.
2. *NE* 1.9.1100a9.
3. *De finibus* 5.18.
4. Daniel Russell, *Happiness for Humans* (Oxford: Oxford University Press, 2012), 91.
5. Russell, *Happiness for Humans*, 109.
6. Russell, *Happiness for Humans*, 109.
7. Russell, *Happiness for Humans*, 121.
8. Russell, *Happiness for Humans*, 118.
9. Russell, *Happiness for Humans*, 120; quoting Cicero, *Cicero: Tusculan Disputations*, trans. J. E. King (Cambridge, Mass.: Harvard University Press, 1927), 5.51.
10. Russell, *Happiness for Humans*, 129.
11. Russell, *Happiness for Humans*, 124.

12 Russell, *Happiness for Humans*, 126. Julia Annas raises a similar objection to what she calls the "internal-use" view of the relation of external goods to happiness, discussed in this chapter. I should note that she reads Arius Didymus differently, holding that he accords to external goods, in addition to their value in contributing to virtuous activity, a value independent of this contribution—a version of what she calls the "external-use" view (also discussed in this chapter). See Julia Annas, *The Morality of Happiness* (Oxford: Oxford University Press, 1993), 378–84, 415–18. For our purposes, we need not decide which has Arius right.

13 It seems to me that this is Aristotle's position—he holds that "activities in accord with virtue control happiness, and the contrary activities control its contrary" (*NE* 1.10.1100b10–11) and that the good man may be deprived of happiness but not made miserable, for "what is fine shines through" (1.10.1100b31). To be sure, stating a position and defending it persuasively are two different things.

14 Annas, *Morality of Happiness*, 378.

15 Annas, *Morality of Happiness*, 379.

16 Annas, *Morality of Happiness*, 380.

17 Annas, *Morality of Happiness*, 381.

18 Annas, *Morality of Happiness*, 381. It seems to me that the floor and ceiling may have to be one and the same—due to the criterion of self-sufficiency, must not the amount of external goods that is "enough" also be that amount beyond which more will not add to eudaimonia?

19 Annas, *Morality of Happiness*, 381. I should mention here Robert Heinaman's interpretation of Aristotle; see Robert Heinaman, "Eudaimonia and Self-Sufficiency in the *Nicomachean Ethics*," *Phronesis* 33 (1988): 31–53. Heinaman intends his article as a contribution to the debate between inclusive (or comprehensive) end theorists and exclusive (or dominant) end theorists and not as a response to the kind of argument Annas is making. Still, if his interpretation of Aristotle is correct (which I will not attempt to decide here), it might seem to help get Aristotle off Annas' hook. Heinaman maintains that, once necessary distinctions are made, we can see that one can consistently say that the life of a eudaimon person can be made still better by the addition of other goods. As Heinaman argues, Aristotle uses "life" in many ways, and in a sense, each person lives many lives: a nutritive life, a perceptual life, an emotional life, an active and/or contemplative rational life; the sum of all these "lives" may be called the person's "total life" (32). Aristotle further holds, Heinaman contends, that eudaimonia is to be identified with the rational life (lived virtuously) and not with a person's total life. We must not, Heinaman warns, conflate eudaimonia with "the best total life" (33)—note that both Annas and Russell do seem to conflate them. The *total life* of a person who is already eudaimon (living a self-sufficient *rational life*) can be made better by the addition of goods of the soul, such as pleasure from amusements, goods of the body such as a restoration to health, or external goods such as a raise or the miraculous return of a war-time friend long thought dead: "Aristotle's position is that contemplation [or, for a noncontemplative person, morally virtuous activity] is the best part of the total life of a person. But that does not mean that there are no other valuable elements in the total life of a person" (51). These other elements can wax or wane and

contribute to or take away from the goodness of the total life in a way at least to some degree independent of their bearing on the virtuous activity that constitutes eudaimonia. Yet even if this is right, it seems as though Annas could grant Heinaman his understanding of the term *eudaimonia* and rerun her argument in terms of the best total life—what is it that makes a total life "choiceworthy and lacking nothing," to use Aristotle's phrase (NE 1.7.1097b16)? For surely, even if one were eudaimon in the granted sense and yet lacked something that would make her total life better, she would continue to seek for that which fills the lack. Whether we call it "eudaimonia" or not, and indeed whether it is humanly attainable or not, the best total life will be our final end. Annas can then ask about the place of external goods in that life, whether it is best understood along the lines of an internal- or external-use view, and how the problems she raises for each view are to be addressed. Aristotle is still on the hook.

20 Russell, *Happiness for Humans*, 5–7.
21 Russell, *Happiness for Humans*, 95.
22 Russell, *Happiness for Humans*, 96.
23 Russell, *Happiness for Humans*, 98.
24 Russell, *Happiness for Humans*, 98.
25 Russell, *Happiness for Humans*, 98.
26 Russell, *Happiness for Humans*, 99.
27 Russell, *Happiness for Humans*, 98.
28 Russell, *Happiness for Humans*, 101.
29 See Russell, *Happiness for Humans*, chap. 7.
30 Russell, *Happiness for Humans*, 102.
31 Russell, *Happiness for Humans*, 103, 113–15.
32 Annas, *Morality of Happiness*, 378.
33 Russell, *Happiness for Humans*, chap. 9.
34 Annas, *Morality of Happiness*, 380.
35 Annas, *Morality of Happiness*, 381.
36 Thomas Merton, *The Seven Storey Mountain* (San Diego: Harcourt Brace Jovanovich, 1948), 56. My point is that accepting the embodied conception of the self allows one to include external goods in eudaimonia while still denying that adding more external goods always increases the goodness of one's life, so that we are not required, in order to avoid making such a "deeply mysterious" denial, to deny instead that eudaimonia is a complete and self-sufficient good. I am not arguing that accepting the embodied conception gives us a way to show that a complete and self-sufficient good is attainable in this life—if anything, the correctness of the conception, with its attendant vulnerability, would suggest (prove?) that it is not, for reasons familiar from Augustine and Aquinas.
37 Russell, *Happiness for Humans*, 256.
38 Russell, *Happiness for Humans*, 257.
39 Russell, *Happiness for Humans*, 256.
40 Russell, *Happiness for Humans*, 257.
41 Russell, *Happiness for Humans*, 6.
42 Russell, *Happiness for Humans*, 195.
43 Russell, *Happiness for Humans*, 2.
44 Russell, *Happiness for Humans*, 2.

45 See Christopher Toner, "Virtue Ethics and Egoism," in *The Routledge Companion to Virtue Ethics*, ed. Lorraine Besser-Jones and Michael Slote (New York: Routledge, 2015), 345–57. Much has been written on virtue ethics and its relation to egoism, but any investigation of the matter should begin by taking up David Solomon's "Internal Objections to Virtue Ethics," in *Midwest Studies in Philosophy XIII: Ethical Theory: Character and Virtue*, ed. P. French, T. Uehling, and H. Wettstein (Notre Dame: University of Notre Dame Press, 1988), 428–41.

46 One of the philosophically interesting features of the AMC show *The Walking Dead* is that we see the characters wrestling with just this problem and resolving it in different ways.

47 I should make it clear that the objection I am pressing against the formalized conception here is *not* the objection that someone taking this view will not exercise care toward others (toward one's daughter, say); like the Stoics, such a one would use such indifferents virtuously. The objection is instead just to the very fact that such a one would regard his daughter as an indifferent, preferred or otherwise, in the first place.

48 Annas, *Morality of Happiness*, 9.

49 This is one of the problems, or supposed problems, of eudaimonism that Scotus is attempting to solve by introducing the *affectio iustitiae* to act as a rein on the *affectio commodi* (and in doing so, he is of course intentionally abandoning eudaimonism).

50 Annas, *Morality of Happiness*, 378.

51 An intrinsically good thing may also make a demand on an agent that is short term so that the good does not demand to become part of the agent's embodied self. For example, a drowning child presented to a strong swimmer—there is a demand here, a requirement of virtue, but unlike the demand presented by, say, the existence of a daughter, it is one that can be quickly discharged. We may distinguish, then, between fleetingly and stably demanding goods; I use, in this chapter, the term *intrinsically demanding* to refer only to goods of the second sort, which require an investment of self (mutatis mutandis, similar distinctions could be drawn with respect to what I will call inviting goods).

52 Is the view I am espousing really a eudaimonist one? Surely, it might be claimed, on any eudaimonist view, the agent's final end must be her own well-being. Perhaps, but we must recognize that "well-being" has many senses, including those corresponding to welfare (or what is good *for the agent*) and to being and living well (living the most choice-worthy life available); see Toner, "Virtue Ethics and Egoism," for further discussion of these senses. I do not accept that eudaimonism must conceive the agent's final end to be well-being in the sense of welfare. Anne Baril ("The Role of Welfare in Eudaimonism," *Southern Journal of Philosophy* 51 [2013]: 520–21) helpfully distinguishes between "welfare-prior" eudaimonism (which espouses good-for dependence: "A human being ought to live her life in a way that is good for her") and "excellence-prior" eudaimonism (which espouses excellence dependence: "A human being ought to live her life excellently [or in the way that is good *as* a human being]"). I am rejecting welfare-prior eudaimonism, but the view I am espousing *is* a eudaimonist one; it is just of the excellence-prior variety (and as Baril notes [519, n. 21], other eudaimonists in good standing—Foot, McDowell, Annas—also hold this sort of view).

53 I would like to thank an anonymous reviewer of this chapter, as well as the audience, and in particular Karen Chan, for helpful comments on an earlier version that was presented at the conference from which this festschrift grew. I would also like to take this opportunity to thank David Solomon for his teaching, mentoring, and friendship over many years.

2: FLANNERY

1 John Finnis, *Aquinas: Moral, Political and Legal Theory* (Oxford: Oxford University Press, 1998), 188. On pp. 215–17 of the same work, Finnis includes a long note in explanation of the thesis that Thomas' classifications of justice are "unstable."
2 Finnis, *Aquinas*, 187.
3 In this chapter, *NE* abbreviates *Nicomachean Ethics*. There are two systems of dividing the chapters on *NE*; I follow the system employed by the *Revised Oxford Translation* (Jonathan Barnes, ed., *The Complete Works of Aristotle: The Revised Oxford Translation* [Princeton: Princeton University Press, 1984]). The Greek text followed in this chapter is by Franciscus Susemihl and Otto Apelt, eds., *Aristotelis Ethica Nicomachea* (Teubner: Leipzig, 1912).
4 Thomas Aquinas, *Summa Theologiae*, cura et studio Instituti Studiorum Medievalium Ottaviensis (Ottawa: Garden City Press, 1941); Thomas Aquinas, *Sententia libri Ethicorum*, vol. 47, *Opera Omnia* (Rome: Commissio Leonina, 1969). I abbreviate the latter as *in EN*, followed by the paragraph divisions in Thomas Aquinas, *In decem ethicorum Aristotelis ad Nicomachum expositio*, ed. A. M. Pirotta (Turin: Marietti, 1964).
5 NE 5.7.1134b18–19.
6 In fact, as indicated, Aristotle uses slightly different Greek expressions for the two types of legal justice.
7 NE 5.1.1129b25–27.
8 NE 5.1.1129b31–1130a3. Bias of Priene was one of the "Seven Sages" of ancient Greece; he lived during the sixth century B.C.E. Thomas cites a piece of this quotation in the *sed contra* of *ST* 2-2.58.6, discussed in note 9.
9 See *in EN* §§904–912 and *ST* 2-2.58.6c: "Just as, therefore, charity, which looks toward divine good as its proper object, is a certain special virtue according to its essence, so also legal justice is a special virtue according to its essence, according as it looks toward the common good as its proper object. And thus it is in the ruler principally and as if architectonically, in his subordinates secondarily and as if being ministered to" ("Sicut ergo caritas, quae respicit bonum divinum ut proprium obiectum, est quaedam specialis virtus secundum suam essentiam; ita etiam iustitia legalis est specialis virtus secundum suam essentiam, secundum quod respicit commune bonum ut proprium obiectum. Et sic est in principe principaliter, et quasi architectonice; in subditis autem secundario et quasi ministrative"). Thomas goes on here in *ST* 2-2.58.6 to say, however, that any virtue can be referred to general justice (which is essentially a special virtue, only general because of such referrals) and therefore called legal justice ("dici iustitia legalis"; see also ad 3). It is only in *this* sense that "legal justice is the same in essence with every virtue; it differs, however, in its account" ("Et hoc modo loquendi

iustitia legalis est idem in essentia cum omni virtute, differt autem ratione"). It differs in account because it has the common good as its proper object but the other virtues do not. "And thus there must be one superior virtue which orders all the virtues toward the common good. This is legal virtue, which is in essence different from every virtue" ("Et sic oportet esse unam virtutem superiorem quae ordinet omnes virtutes in bonum commune, quae est iustitia legalis, et est alia per essentiam ab omni virtute"; *ST* 2-2.58.6 ad 4).

10 *NE* 1.2.1094a27–b6.
11 *Pol.* 7.16.1335b19–26.
12 *NE* 9.10.1170b31–32.
13 See *ST* 2-2.58.7.
14 *NE* 5.1.1130a9.
15 *NE* 5.2.1130a14; see also 1130a22–23.
16 *NE* 5.2.1130a33–b1.
17 *NE* 5.2.1130b5.
18 *ST* 2-2.58.7; see also *in EN* §§916–917.
19 *NE* 3.6–9.
20 *NE* 4.7.
21 Thomas excludes from consideration this type of generic relationship in the first section of *ST* 2-2.58.6c.
22 *Pol.* 1.1.
23 *Pol.* 3.6.1278b38.
24 *Pol.* 2.2.1261a16–18. This quotation is taken from the *Revised Oxford Translation* (Barnes, *Complete Works of Aristotle*).
25 See note 9.
26 *ST* 2-2.58.6c.
27 *NE* 5.1.1129b14–17. Note that I follow the Susemihl-Apelt text here and not Bywater's (Ingram Bywater, ed., *Aristotelis Ethica Nicomachea*, Oxford Classical Texts [Oxford: Clarendon, 1894]). See also 1129b10,18–19; 1130a2, 4–5. The Latin that Thomas was probably reading had "Leges autem dicunt de omnibus coniectantes, vel communiter conferente omnibus, vel optimis, vel dominis, vel secundum virtutem, vel secundum alium aliquem modum talium." See also *in EN* §912: "Verum, quia ubi est specialis ratio obiecti etiam in materia generali, oportet esse specialem habitum, inde est, quod ipsa iustitia legalis est determinata virtus habens speciem ex hoc quod intendit ad bonum commune."
28 *ST* 2-2.58.7 ad 1; 2-2.58.8.
29 *ST* 2-2.58.7 ad 2; Thomas is referring to *Pol.* 1.1.1252a7–23. The complete (and even more explicit) text of *ST* 2-2.58.7 ad 2 runs as follows: "Ad secundum dicendum quod bonum commune civitatis et bonum singulare unius personae non differunt solum secundum multum et paucum, sed secundum formalem differentiam, alia enim est ratio boni communis et boni singularis, sicut et alia est ratio totius et partis. Et ideo Philosophus, in *Pol.* i, dicit quod non bene dicunt qui dicunt civitatem et domum et alia huiusmodi differre solum multitudine et paucitate, et non specie." No doubt both Thomas and Aristotle have in mind Plato's *Republic*.
30 *NE* 3.1.1110a15–16.
31 See *NE* 5.7.1135a.6–8; see also *in EN* §1031.

32 On commensuration, see NE 5.5.1133a16–22; see also chap. 4 of Kevin L. Flannery, *Acts amid Precepts: The Aristotelian Logical Structure of Thomas Aquinas' Moral Theory* (Washington, D.C.: Catholic University of America Press, 2001).
33 On geometrical proportionality as used in distributive justice, see Henry Jackson, ed., *The Fifth Book of the* Nicomachean Ethics *of Aristotle* (Cambridge: Cambridge University Press, 1879), 88–89.
34 NE 5.4.1132a24–27.
35 "Manifestum est autem quod omnes qui sub communitate aliqua continentur comparantur ad communitatem sicut partes ad totum. Pars autem id quod est totius est, unde et quodlibet bonum partis est ordinabile in bonum totius" (*ST* 2-2.58.5c). The emphasis is (obviously) added, but it helps to bring out the sense of the remark.
36 *ST* 2-2.58.5c (my emphasis); see also note 9.
37 *ST* 2-2.61.1 ad 3.
38 "Ad tertium dicendum quod actus distributionis quae est communium bonorum pertinet solum ad praesidentem communibus bonis, sed tamen iustitia distributiva est et in subditis, quibus distribuitur, inquantum scilicet sunt contenti iusta distributione" (*ST* 2-2.61.1 ad 3). I cannot accept, therefore, the interpretation of Paul-Dominique Dognin, O.P., who says that Thomas is here identifying the active and passive sides of distributive justice, the former existing in him who has charge of the common goods, the latter existing in those who receive their share from him (Paul-Dominique Dognin, "Justice particulière comporte-t-elle deux espèces?," *Revue Thomiste* 65 [1965]: 406). See also note 9. In adding the point about being contented, Thomas is not saying that the justice of a distribution depends on our consenting to it. He presupposes that the distribution is just.
39 NE 5.9.1136b25–31; Barnes, *Complete Works of Aristotle*.
40 ὥστ' ἔσται τι ἄδικον μὲν ἀδίκημα δ' οὔπω, ἐὰν μὴ τὸ ἑκούσιον προσῇ (5.8.1135a22–23). The same distinction comes into Thomas' characterization of particular justice: "cum iustitia ordinetur ad alterum, non est circa totam materiam virtutis moralis, sed solum circa exteriores actiones *et res secundum quandam rationem obiecti specialem*, prout scilicet secundum eas unus homo alteri coordinatur" (*ST* 2-2.58.8c).
41 "Quamvis etiam distributio quandoque fiat bonorum communium non quidem civitati, sed uni familiae, quorum distributio fieri potest auctoritate alicuius privatae personae" (*ST* 2-2.61.1 ad 3).
42 καὶ ἡ μὲν δικαιοσύνη ἐστὶ καθ' ἣν ὁ δίκαιος λέγεται πρακτικὸς κατὰ προαίρεσιν τοῦ δικαίου, καὶ διανεμητικὸς καὶ αὑτῷ πρὸς ἄλλον καὶ ἑτέρῳ πρὸς ἕτερον οὐχ οὕτως ὥστε τοῦ μὲν αἱρετοῦ πλέον αὑτῷ ἔλαττον δὲ τῷ πλησίον, τοῦ βλαβεροῦ δ' ἀνάπαλιν, ἀλλὰ τοῦ ἴσου τοῦ κατ' ἀναλογίαν, ὁμοίως δὲ καὶ ἄλλῳ πρὸς ἄλλον (NE 5.6.1134a1–6). Thomas connects this remark with both commutative and distributive justice (*in EN* §§994–995).
43 *ST* 2-2.58.7 ad 3; NE 5.6.1134b9–17; see also *in EN* §1004.
44 On general justice "writ small," see Plato, *Republic* 2.368c8–369a4.
45 *ST* 2-2.61.1 ad 2.
46 Doubtless, Thomas has in mind Aristotle's remark in the first book of the *Nicomachean Ethics* that the end of the individual and of the city are the same,

"although the good of the city appears to be a greater and more perfect thing both to attain and to maintain, for it is lovable also with respect to the individual himself, but it is more beautiful and more divine with respect to a people and to cities" (1.2.1094b7–10). My guess would be that this remark is the source of Thomas' own remark in *ST* 2-2.61.1 ad 3 about the contentment of the receivers of the common goods. The Latin that Thomas would have been reading is as follows: "Si enim et idem est uni et civitati, maiusque et perfectius quod civitatis videtur et suscipere et salvare. Amabile quidem enim et uni soli, melius vero et divinius genti et civitatibus." Aristotle's remark comes immediately after his remark about the lawmaker legislating about "what one must do and what refrain from doing" (*NE* 1.2.1094b5–7). This would establish the connection between general (legal) justice and distributive justice (at least, as exercised at the level of the city's government).

47   The fuller quotation runs as follows: "There are three species of justice, as there are three types of relationships in any 'whole': the relations of the parts amongst themselves, the relations of the whole to the parts, and the relations of the parts to the whole. And likewise there are three justices: legal, distributive and commutative." And then comes the sentence to which is attached this note. This is Finnis' translation (John Finnis, *Natural Law and Natural Rights* [Oxford: Oxford University Press, 2011], 185). The original is at Thomas Aquinas and Thomas de Vio Cajetan, *Summa theologiae cum commentariis Thomae de Vio Caietani Ordinis Praedicatorum*, vols. 4–12, *Opera omnia* (Rome: Typographia polyglotta S. C. de Propaganda Fide [Commissio Leonina], 1888–1906), vol. 9, 35 (ad *ST* 2-2.61.1). In blaming Cajetan, Finnis is following Dognin (Dognin, "Justice particulière comporte-t-elle deux espèces?," 415).

48   Finnis, *Natural Law and Natural Rights*, 186.

49   Finnis, *Natural Law and Natural Rights*, 186. These are Finnis' words; he cites Robert Nozick, *Anarchy, State, and Utopia* (New York: Basic Books, 1974), x, 167–74.

50   See *NE* 5.3.1131a24–29.

51   *NE* 5.2.1130b31–32.

52   In his commentary on *ST* 2-2.61.1, Cajetan calls attention to an important difference between commutative and distributive justice. He makes this point in the continuation of the very comment that Finnis quotes in part when tracing back to him the regrettable restriction of the responsibility for distributive justice to the state ("the whole"). Cajetan is discussing Thomas' replies to the second and the fifth objection of that article. The second objection (which is the more interesting) argues that "the act of justice consists in rendering to each that which is his own. Now in a distribution one does not render to each that which is his own but each receives as new what was held in common. This, therefore [that is, distribution], does not pertain to justice." Thomas' reply to this objection we have already in part seen. He says, "Part and whole are in a certain sense [*quodammodo*] the same thing, so that that which is of the whole is in a certain sense [*quodammodo*] of the part; and so, when from the common goods something is distributed to individuals, each in some sense [*aliquo modo*] receives what is his own." Thus distributing that portion to him is a type of justice.

Cajetan calls special attention to the qualifying phrases used by Thomas: "in a certain sense" (see Thomas Aquinas and Thomas de Vio Cajetan, *Summa Theologiae*, vol. 9, 35 [ad *ST* 2-2.61.1]). To paraphrase his argument, in commutative justice, a person receives that which is his own simply speaking ("simpliciter"); in distributive justice, there is, so to speak, more "wiggle room"—room, that is, for deliberation and choice. This is because in commutative justice, things are—or are rendered—commensurable, while in distributive justice, this is not possible. It is not possible because distributive justice involves not just things but also persons: see *NE* 5.3.1131b15–16 and René-Antoine Gauthier and Jean Yves Jolif, *L'Éthique a Nicomaque: Introduction, traduction et commentaire* (Louvain-la-neuve, Belgium: Éditions Peeters, 2002), 2.1, 377. See also my discussion of the relationship between distributive and commutative justice in *NE* 5.5.

Dognin regards this interpretation of Cajetan's as the source of the erroneous position that distributive is not really justice at all ("Cajetan semble être à la source de tout le mal"; Dognin, "Justice particulière?," 411). But Cajetan does not deny that distributive justice is justice. In commenting upon *ST* 2-2.61.3, for instance, he says, "Est ergo iustitia commutativa una species specialissima. Et similiter distributiva una alia species specialissima, propter eandem rationem: quia scilicet suam unicam adaequationis formam operatur, diversam formaliter ab aequalitate commutativae, ut patet ex supradictis." (The latter reference is to his comment on *ST* 2-2.61.2, which speaks about the formal difference between commutative and distributive justice. The difference is that the latter considers directly the persons involved—it considers them, that is, qua persons.)

53 See, for instance, Jackson, *Fifth Book*, xx. See also Gauthier and Jolif, *L'Éthique a Nicomaque*, 2.1, 369–72.

54 Cf. Finnis, *Natural Law and Natural Rights*, 179: "So it was that Thomas Aquinas, purporting to interpret Aristotle faithfully, silently shifted the meaning of Aristotle's second class of particular justice, and invented a new term for it: 'commutative justice.'"

55 See *NE* 5.2.1131a1; 5.4.1131b25; 5.5.1132b24–25. The word *directivum* was also used to translate the word ἐπανορθωτικόν in *NE* 5.4.1132a18. The two words are, in any case, very close in meaning. See René-Antoine Gauthier, *Aristoteles Latinus. 26, 1–3, Ethica Nicomachea. Fasc. 5, Indices verborum*, Corpus Philosophorum Medii Aevi (Leiden: Brill, 1973), 703, 707. Thomas never uses the word *correctivus* (or derivatives), although it does appear in Albert the Great: Albert the Great, *Commentarii in octo libros Politicorum Aristotelis*, vol. 8, *Opera Omnia* (Paris: Vivés, 1891), 418b. There the word *correctiva* is used of a type of law-court; the Greek word is εὐθυντικόν (*Pol.* 4.16.1300b19–20).

56 This first appearance of the word occurs in *NE* 5.2.1131a1. See Gauthier, *Aristoteles Latinus*, 231, 233–34, 236, 457, 459–60, 462.

57 The phrase occurs at *in EN* §994; see also §947.

58 Having in *NE* 5.4.1131b25 introduced διορθωτικόν δίκαιον, Aristotle himself within a few lines (i.e., at 5.4.1131b32–33) speaks instead of τὸ ἐν τοῖς συναλλάγμασι δίκαιον, which would be the positive justice that any correction seeks to achieve.

59 "The term 'corrective justice' (τὸ διορθωτικόν, or, as it is afterwards [1132a18] called, τὸ ἐπανορθωτικόν δίκαιον) is itself an unfortunate name, because it appears only to lay down principles for restitution, and therefore implies wrong. Thus it has a tendency to confine the view to 'involuntary transactions,' instead of stating what must be the principle of the just in all the dealings between man and man" (Alexander Grant, *The Ethics of Aristotle: Illustrated with Notes and Essays* [London: Longmans, Green, 1885], vol. 2, 112). Grant is alluding to Aristotle's statement at the beginning of NE 5.4 (1131b25–26) that the justice to be discussed there concerns both voluntary and involuntary transactions.

60 τὸ δ' ἀντιπεπονθὸς οὐκ ἐφαρμόττει οὔτ' ἐπὶ τὸ νεμητικὸν δίκαιον οὔτ' ἐπὶ τὸ διορθωτικόν (NE 5.5.1132b23–25). For the moment, I refrain from translating διορθωτικόν (δίκαιον), since, of course, the issue here is whether the translators were right to render it "iustum directivum" rather than "iustum correctivum."

61 NE 5.5.1132b31–34.
62 See Jackson, *Fifth Book*, 90–91. Jackson refers to this type of proportion ("reciprocal proportion") as geometrical.
63 NE 5.5.1133a10–12.
64 NE 5.5.1132b33–34.
65 In EN §972.
66 NE 5.5.1133a27, 1133b6.
67 NE 5.5.1133a18.
68 NE 5.5.1133b7.
69 NE 5.5.1132b24–25.

3: O'Callaghan

1 Martha Nussbaum, "Tragedy and Self-Sufficiency: Plato and Aristotle on Fear and Pity," *Oxford Studies in Ancient Philosophy* 10 (1992): 108–59; Nussbaum, "Equity and Mercy," *Philosophy and Public Affairs* 22 (1993): 83–125; Nussbaum, "Pity and Mercy: Nietzsche's Stoicism," in *Nietzsche, Genealogy, Morality: Essays on Nietzsche's Genealogy of Morals*, ed. Richard Schacht (Berkeley: University of California Press, 1994), 139–67. In subsequent work she switches to the term *compassion*. See Nussbaum, "Compassion: The Basic Social Emotion," *Social Philosophy and Policy* 13, no. 1 (1996): 27–58; Nussbaum, "Compassion: Human and Animal," in *Ethics and Humanity: Themes from the Philosophy of Jonathan Glover*, ed. N. Ann David, Richard Keshen, and Jeff McMahan (Oxford: Oxford University Press, 2010), 202–26; Nussbaum, *Upheavals of Thought* (Cambridge: Cambridge University Press, 2001), especially part 2, "Compassion," 295–454.

2 In contemporary contexts the Greek is familiar from the Christian liturgical petition "Κύριε, ελέησον," typically translated into English as "Lord, have mercy." So it is not extraordinary for ἔλεος to be translated with "mercy." Nussbaum, however, thinks it is better to translate ἔλεος with "pity" because the latter is the term in contemporary philosophical discussions regularly used to translate both the Greek ἔλεος and the French *pitié*. The French is important because of the role Rousseau plays in her account of the pity tradition. Acknowledging, however, that the term *pity* in contemporary discussions suggests an offensive

condescension of the superior to the inferior, she also uses "compassion" when trying to avoid that association; however, she treats the terms as strictly interchangeable. See Nussbaum, "Compassion: Basic Social Emotion," 29. See also Nussbaum, "Pity and Mercy," 140–41; and Nussbaum, *Upheavals of Thought*, 239, 301. But that synonymy should be challenged. It is questionable whether Aristotle's analysis of ἔλεος allows for it to be understood as what compassion means in contemporary English, as compassion involves suffering with another as opposed to suffering upon the occasion of another's suffering; the latter is closer to Aristotle's ἔλεος. In addition, Nussbaum is clear that pity as a translation of ἔλεος does not extend to those who suffer deservedly. See Nussbaum, *Upheavals of Thought*, 239, 301. And yet it is not at all awkward to speak in English of having compassion for those who are being punished deservedly. See my "*Misericordia* in Aquinas: A Test Case for Theological and Natural Virtues," in *Jaarboek 2013, Thomas Instituut te Utrecht*, ed. Henk J. M. Schoot (Utrecht: Thomas Instituut te Utrecht, 2014), 25, and the discussion in the chapter.

3   See Nussbaum, "Pity and Mercy," 144–49. See also Nussbaum, "Tragedy and Self Sufficiency," 123–28; and Nussbaum, "Compassion: Basic Social Emotion," 41–44; but see especially the very rich discussion in Nussbaum, *Upheavals of Thought*, parts 1–3, 295–400 passim. For Nussbaum's discussion of Rousseau and Smith, see "Compassion," passim. On Rousseau specifically, see Nussbaum, "Pity and Mercy," 143–44; Nussbaum, "Tragedy and Self-Sufficiency," 122–23; and note 32.

4   Nussbaum, "Pity and Mercy," 160–61.

5   See Nussbaum, *Upheavals of Thought*, 365, and 364–86 passim. Under the pressure of analyzing Augustine's criticism of Stoicism in *Upheavals of Thought*, Nussbaum mitigates the charge of Stoicism against Christianity; still, the charges of "otherworldliness" and "denigration" remain fundamentally in place.

6   There is another difficulty of translation here. Nussbaum treats "pity" (concerning undeserved suffering) as distinct from and opposed to "mercy" (concerning forgiveness or mitigation of deserved punishment). And she suggests that *misericordia* be translated as "pity" (*Upheavals of Thought*, 303). But the common translation of *misericordia* is in fact "mercy" and not "pity"; translations of Aquinas almost uniformly translate it as "mercy," perhaps because of the theological and religious context. Consider the translation of the Greek prayer "Κύριε, ἐλέησον" in the Roman Catholic Mass, which is translated as "Lord, have mercy," not "Lord, have pity"; from the Mass there is also the translation of "*Angus Dei, qui tollis peccata mundi, miserere nobis*" as "Lamb of God, who takes away the sins of the world, have mercy on us"—not "pity us." Also the prayer "*Salve Regina, Mater Misericoriae*" is standardly translated "Hail Queen, Mother of Mercy," not "Hail Queen, Mother of Pity." Common ordinary spoken English does not hold strictly to a clear dichotomy between the senses of the two terms; one might hear such pleas as "have pity on me" in contexts in which one could equally well hear "have mercy on me." So in general, the reader will have to keep in mind that in the context of the discussion of Aquinas, *misericordia* is related to the Greek ἔλεος as well as to what Nussbaum means by "pity." When Aquinas discusses what Nussbaum means by "mercy," his Latin is *clementia*, which is best translated as "clemency" or "forgiveness," or he uses *remittere*, translated as "to remit."

7. *Summa Theologiae (ST)* 1.21.3 ad 2.
8. See John Rawls, *A Theory of Justice* (Cambridge, Mass.: Harvard University Press, 1971); and John Rawls, "Justice as Fairness," *Philosophical Review* 67, no. 2 (1958): 164–94.
9. Nussbaum, "Compassion: Basic Social Emotion," 37.
10. Nussbaum, *Upheavals of Thought*, 340–42.
11. See Nussbaum, *Upheavals of Thought*, 24–30, 354–56, 368–70; and Nussbaum, "Compassion: Basic Social Emotion," 29–30.
12. Nussbaum acknowledges but does not emphasize the element of the passion of fear as such; more important for her is the general self-interest in establishing a society in which the effects of tragedies befalling others are mitigated by the recognition that such tragedies may also happen to oneself. See Nussbaum, *Upheavals of Thought*, 306, and especially pp. 315–27, where she argues that the judgment of similar possibilities and fear for oneself are epistemologically useful to pity but not logically necessary to it; rather a "eudaimonistic judgment" that the good of the other is part of "my scheme of goals and projects, an end whose good is to be promoted" takes the place of φόβος as necessary to pity. Nonetheless, while acknowledging her point about strictly logical necessity and her stress upon the fellow feeling character of ἔλεος to enrich the account of justice, one might wonder if it really is not rather this φόβος for oneself informing the rational calculation that is doing the heavy lifting in the account. Indeed, while no longer using the word *fear* in the relevant passages in which she argues that "the judgment of similar possibilities is part of a construct that bridges the gap between prudential concern and altruism," fear for oneself haunts the discussion; because of that element of fear driving the concern for justice, one might argue that in her account, altruism amounts to a fear-driven prudential concern for oneself (see Nussbaum, "Compassion: Basic Social Emotion," 36).
13. Thus Nussbaum writes little about the *Nicomachean Ethics* (NE) in discussing Aristotle's place in the pity tradition, not even in order to explain why ἔλεος seems so unimportant in NE. There are but two explicit references to NE in Nussbaum's most extensive and developed discussion of pity (compassion), *Upheavals of Thought*. The first is to Aristotle's arguments against attributing inappropriate importance to such things as pleasure, status, and wealth in the flourishing life (Nussbaum, *Upheavals of Thought*, 373, esp. n. 37). The second is to his remarks on mildness opposed to vengeance (p. 393). This latter is odd, since with it Nussbaum intends to find a role for compassion in the discussion of virtue in NE. It concerns the passion of anger and not strictly compassion, but Nussbaum translates Aristotle as saying that the mild person has "sympathetic understanding" and then concludes "the sympathetic understanding characteristic of compassion offers an antidote to revenge." To be fair, she makes general remarks about Aristotle on moral virtues throughout. Still, see the discussion of the absence of the discussion of ἔλεος in NE in my "*Misericordia* in Aquinas," 18–27.
14. See Nussbaum, *Upheavals of Thought*, 425–35; and Nussbaum, "Compassion: Basic Social Emotion," 50–51.
15. For the similarity to Rawls, see Nussbaum, "Pity and Mercy," 142, but especially Nussbaum, "Compassion: Basic Social Emotion," 36–37; and Nussbaum, *Upheavals of Thought*, 340–42.

16 Aquinas' discussion of the distinction between philosophy and theology, or rather, what he calls the philosophical disciplines and *sacra doctrina* in *ST* 1.1, is important here for understanding why a discussion found in his theological works can nonetheless count as philosophical in the generally accepted sense of contemporary thought. Briefly, there he holds that some things that are of a generally philosophical character and subject to philosophical analysis are nonetheless revealed in Scripture and sacred tradition because they are necessary for human flourishing and thus salvation.

17 For the distinction between theological virtues and moral virtues, see *ST* 1-2.62.2.

18 For the distinction between infused and acquired virtues, see *ST* 1-2.55.4.

19 See my "*Misericordia* in Aquinas," 37–38.

20 Most importantly, when Aristotle lists ἔλεος among the passions at *NE* 1105b21–22, the Latin translation that Thomas used has "*misericordia*." Thomas Aquinas, *Sententia Libri Ethicorum* (Rome: Leonine, 1969).

21 Perhaps he will rejoice having first experienced *nemesis*, pain at another's undeserved good fortune.

22 This scene from the *Iliad* plays a particularly significant role in Nussbaum's development of the pity tradition. See Nussbaum, *Upheavals of Thought*, 315; and Nussbaum, "Tragedy and Self-Sufficiency," 120–21.

23 Or perhaps long-dead heroic figures of history or myth.

24 *ST* 2-2.30.1 *respondeo*.

25 Compare how Socrates explicitly refused to play upon the emotions of his jury by trotting out his wife and children to weep and wail in front of them as others do in similar situations. Socrates refuses the rhetorical appeal to ἔλεος as unworthy of a philosopher. Again it is clear that friendship plays no part in the court, as one would not expect the accused to be friends with the jury, at least that part of the Athenian jury looking to convict the accused. Indeed, as with Socrates' trial, many of the accused's enemies may make up a majority of the jury. Had Socrates attempted to prompt ἔλεος in the jury, it would not have been directed at his friends but rather his enemies, attempting to get them to see a likeness in him to themselves. So in rhetorical contexts, it seems ἔλεος has its application in contexts in which one is confronted by others who are not well disposed by friendship toward one but rather enmity.

26 For Cicero, see "On Behalf of Ligarius," in *The Speeches with an English Translation*, trans. N. H. Watts (London: William Heinemann, 1931). For Seneca, see "De Clementia," in *Seneca: Moral Essays with an English Translation*, trans. John W. Basore (London: William Heinemann, 1985).

27 Nussbaum's later identification of pity and compassion begs the question about the proper interpretation of ἔλεος in the Greeks and Aristotle, particularly if one emphasizes ἔλεος arising within the viewing audience and, as I do, the fictional or historically distant and perhaps mythical character of its object. Just how does an audience member actually suffer *with* Hector or Oedipus? One might respond, "Well obviously one 'suffers with' Oedipus imaginatively." But how would one respond to the assertion that "my anguish at the fate of Hector was as significant for me as was the anguish I felt when my lieutenant died on Omaha Beach"? "But ultimately what is this compassion (*misericordia*) for

fictional and theatrical characters like? For the listener is not provoked to act on behalf of them, but simply invited to grieve.... if he grieves, he remains intent and full of joy." Augustine, *Confessions* 3.2.

28 *ST* 2-2.30.1 *respondeo*.
29 And yet consider the altar in Athens devoted to the goddess Ἔλεος. See my "Misericordia in Aquinas," 12–13; W. H. S. Jones, *Pausanias Description of Greece with an English Translation*, 6 vols. (London: William Heinemann, 1931), books 1–2, 1.17.1; Statius, *Thebaid with an English Translation by J. H. Mozley*, 2 vols. (Cambridge, Mass.: Harvard University Press, 1989), books 5–12, 12.481–496. There is no mention of this deity in Nussbaum's account of the pity tradition. One difficulty acknowledging it as part of the pity tradition would be that the goddess concerns herself in part with those who may suffer justly, which is forbidden in the pity tradition described by Nussbaum. For a general discussion of divinity in respect to pity, see Nussbaum, "Tragedy and Self Sufficiency," 120; and Nussbaum, "Pity and Mercy," 142–43. But then contrast that discussion with her discussion in *Upheavals of Thought* (318–25), in which, having denied the necessity of the Aristotelian judgment of similar possibilities, she considers the possibility that an "invulnerable" god could have compassion. David Konstan agrees with Nussbaum as far as the implications of Aristotle's thoughts on pity go but argues that it is not generally the case in other Greek sources that the gods do not pity human beings. See his *Pity Transformed* (London: Gerald Duckworth, 2001).
30 Although Nussbaum employs the story of Achilles and Priam in her construction of the pity tradition, there is at least one significant problem with doing so. The likenesses do not line up. It is not Priam's sufferings as such and recognition of a likeness to himself that prompt ἔλεος in Achilles but the mediation of the thought of his father Peleus' sufferings. If anything it appears that Achilles, by identifying Priam with Peleus, ought to identify himself with dead Hector, whom he has conquered and whose body he has desecrated; perhaps his ἔλεος is better understood as directed to dead Hector, and his act of aiding Priam is to honor Hector in whom Achilles sees a likeness of himself. Although not pursued in the *Iliad*, this would also allow for the possibility of φόβος to occur in Achilles in anticipation that he too will die bested by an opponent—namely, Paris.
31 I am indebted to Innocent Smith, O.P., for confirming this fact about the medieval practice of Compline.
32 See Aquinas' analysis of predicative statements and identity statements in divine naming in *ST* 1.13.1 ad 2.
33 *ST* 2-2.30.4 *respondeo*.
34 See *ST* 1.21.3 ad 2. Aquinas maintains that even the damned in Hell experience God's *misericordia*, for they are not punished as much as their sins warrant. See *ST* 1.21.4 ad 1.
35 *NE* 1166a7–8.
36 Instead of grieving with his friend Marrulus at the loss of his son, the stoic Seneca chastises him for his grief. "You expect solace? Receive abuse." See Seneca, *Seneca Ad Lucilium Epistulae Morales*, trans. Richard M. Gummere (London: William Heinemann, 1925), ep. 99.2.

37 NE 9.11.1171b6–12.
38 "Contingit secundum unionem realem, utpote cum malum aliquorum propinquum est ut ab eis ad nos transeat." *ST* 2-2.30.2 *respondeo*.
39 *ST* 2-2.30.2 *respondeo*.
40 "Uno modo, secundum unionem affectus, quod fit per amorem. Quia enim amans reputat amicum tanquam seipsum, malum ipsius reputat tanquam suum malum, et ideo dolet de malo amici sicut de suo." *ST* 2-2.30.2 *respondeo*. Notice the use of the verb *dolere*, the root term in *condolere*, in *dolet de malo*.
41 *ST* 2-2.30.2 *respondeo*.
42 See *ST* 2-2.30.1 ad 1 and the discussion of Aquinas on the three ways of suffering in my "*Misericordia* in Aquinas," 44–46.
43 Friedrich Nietzsche, *Daybreak: Thoughts on the Prejudices of Morality*, trans. R. J. Hollingdale, ed. Maudemarie Clark and Brian Leiter (Cambridge: Cambridge University Press, 1997), 137, 138.
44 *ST* 2-2.32.5 *respondeo* and 6 *respondeo*. Also Ia.20.1 ad 3: "Insofar as someone loves another, he wills him good. And so he treats the friend as himself, rendering a good to him as if to himself."
45 Here I agree with David Gallagher's excellent discussion of Aquinas on making the good of another one's own in "Thomas Aquinas on Self-Love as the Basis for Love of Others," *Acta Philosophica* 8 (1999): 31.
46 *ST* 2-2.28.1 *respondeo*.
47 Notice that Aquinas does not hesitate to say of God that He is distressed without at the same time suffering a passion.
48 It does not follow that addressing the suffering of those who deserve punishment must violate justice. But pursuing this line of discussion would require a separate discussion of both judicial remission of punishment for the sake of the common good and the virtue of *clementia* in Aquinas, which is a part of temperance, as well as ways in which one might mitigate contingent contextually determined features of a justly imposed punishment that cause additional suffering among those who deserve punishment.
49 I am indebted to Gary Anderson for the Hebrew here.
50 See Gary A. Anderson, *Charity* (New Haven: Yale University Press, 2013). Anderson is careful to point out, however, that in Jewish and Christian theological reflection upon this biblical theme of heavenly investment, it should not be taken in a simplistic utilitarian fashion but rather for the insight it provides to the normative metaphysical structure of the world and thus the more important insight into the character of God who created it.
51 It is worth remarking that the etymological root of the English term *mercy* is the Latin *merces*, meaning pay, recompense, salary, reward, but also bribe. The etymological root of "market" is the related Latin term *merx*, meaning commodity, merchandise, goods. It is no doubt these economic associations that allow for some of the wordplay concerning mercy in *The Merchant of Venice*.
52 Thus Nussbaum's subordination of ἔλεος to justice may not be as far afield of certain aspects of revealed religion as her account of the pity tradition might otherwise suggest. The ideally just society appears to be a Godless and earthly but still biblical Heaven.
53 *ST* 2-2.30.1 *respondeo*.

54 Augustine, *Concerning the City of God against the Pagans*, trans. Henry Bettenson (London: Penguin Books, 2003), 9.5, 349.

55 Consider Portia's praise of mercy as befitting the power of kings in act 4, scene 1 of *The Merchant of Venice*: "'Tis mightiest in the mightiest: it becomes the throned monarch better than his crown."

56 Cicero, *Tusculan Disputations*, trans. J. E. King (London: William Heinemann, 1927), 4.26, 57–61. Of course, Augustine knew Cicero well, including the *Tusculan Disputations*. See, for example, *City of God* 8.5, 305. And in general on Augustine and Cicero, see Augustine Curley, "Cicero, Marcus Tullius," in *Augustine through the Ages: An Encyclopedia*, ed. Allan Fitzgerald et al. (Grand Rapids: Eerdmans, 1999), 190–93. See also the various essays in Mark Vessey, ed., with the assistance of Shelly Reid, *A Companion to Augustine* (West Sussex: John Wiley, 2012).

57 "Idest, aliis dimittite, si vultis ut dimittatur vobis." *Sancti Thomae de Aquino Super Evangelium S. Matthaei lectura a capite VI versiculo XIX ad caput XII Reportatio Leodegarii Bissuntini*, chap. 7, 1.1 (http://www.corpusthomisticum.org/cml0619.html#87343).

58 Again, see Anderson, *Charity*, passim.

59 Luke 6:36: "Estote ergo misericordes sicut et Pater vester misericors est."

60 "Unde qui debet facere misericordiam nobis, vel nos ipsi, sub nomine 'proximi' continetur. Sed non est aliqua rationalis creatura, cui non debeamus misereri, et e converso: et ideo sub nomine 'proximi' continetur homo et angelus." *Super Evangelium S. Matthaei lectura*, chap. 22, lect. 4 (http://www.corpusthomisticum.org/cml21.html#87391). Notice Aquinas includes among one's neighbors the angels because they are rational creatures. But presumably that is not because we are to show *misericordia* to the angels but rather because they are to show it to us. But then in context, Aquinas is making the extraordinary interpretation of Scripture that the two great commandments are commandments directed to the angels as much as to human beings.

61 At least for the case of the priest, see Richard Bauckham, "The Scrupulous Priest and the Good Samaritan: Jesus' Parabolic Interpretation of the Law of Moses," *New Testament Studies* 44 (1998): 475–89.

62 The Latin of the Vulgate that Aquinas read has "misericordia motus est." Despite many English translations translating *misericordia* in that passage with "compassion," I have chosen deliberately to translate it etymologically, first because the Latin for "compassion" is *compassio*, which is not in the text of Scripture, and second because Aquinas had given that etymology, "a distressed heart," for *miserum cor*, when first analyzing *misericordia* in *ST* 2-2.30.1.

63 Aristotle mentions in *NE* 1155a20–21 that one observes in traveling how every human being is dear to every other human being. Aquinas is aware of this text of Aristotle's; indeed, in his commentary on it, he shifts its meaning somewhat into giving assistance to strangers who are lost on the road, helping them avoid making the wrong turn, reminiscent of course of the parable of the Good Samaritan: "Et ideo laudamus philanthropos, idest amatores hominum, quasi implentes id quod est homini naturale, ut manifeste apparet in erroribus viarum." *Sancti Thomae de Aquino Sententia libri Ethicorum a libro VIII ad librum IX*, book 8, 11, n. 4

(http://www.corpusthomisticum.org/ctc08.html). And yet Aquinas does not cite Aristotle in this instance.

64 ST 2-2.114.1 ad 2. It might be tempting to reduce what Aquinas says here to Aristotle's reflections in NE 9.5 on the goodwill that human beings express toward one another that, without being friendship, is like friendship and may be the beginning of friendship. But such a reductive reading of Aquinas will not work, since as Aquinas understands Aristotle, in that discussion those with goodwill wish others well, "nevertheless neither doing anything for them nor being distressed for them by their misfortunes." See *Sententia Libri* Ethicorum, book 9, l.5, n. 6. In addition, throughout NE 9, the stranger is not seen as a friend; the stranger functions precisely as not a friend, as if by definition, in order to bring out the qualities of friendship by contrast. But Aquinas' discussion of friendship for the stranger is precisely one in which one is distressed by the misfortune of the stranger and one in which one does something for him or her, particularly when we consider the background of Luke 10:27. Those facts are why Aquinas' claim seems so startling against the limited scope of friendship in Aristotle.

65 Recall Luke 6:36.

66 Aquinas treats of the love of oneself and the love of neighbor according to God as end earlier in ST 2-2.2–5. The gist of the discussion is that since the love of God as end is a kind of friendship, one loves what belongs to God as well as loving God. And so loving God as end, one loves oneself as belonging to God by a love of friendship, and one loves one's neighbor as also belonging to God by a love of friendship.

67 See my "Imago Dei: A Test Case for St. Thomas' Augustinianism," invited contribution to *Aquinas the Augustinian*, ed. Michael Dauphnais, Barry David, and Matthew Levering (Washington, D.C.: Catholic University of America Press, 2007), 100–144.

68 See ST 2-2 *prooemium* and q. 1–3.

69 See note 36.

70 "Gaudere cum gaudentibus, flere cum flentibus." ST 2-2.30.2 *respondeo*. See also Sirach 7:34.

71 Consider Augustine's concern in the *Confessions* with the way in which he wept excessively in his youth for the loss of his young friend as for the loss of a possession, tears in which the mature Augustine understands himself to have been in fact weeping for himself (*Confessions* 3.4–9), a kind of weeping he later struggles against at the death of his mother (9.12). Compare that type of weeping for oneself by contrast with the weeping he later approves of (9.13), where one weeps for the dead person, here his mother, that he or she must suffer death due to sin.

72 See ST 1.9 passim, 19.11 *respondeo*, 20.1 ad 1–2; and 3.46.12. Nussbaum misses this crucial point about divine impassibility when she tacitly identifies "the Christian God" solely with the person of the Father and parallels the Father with Zeus with respect to "vulnerability" and "feel[ing] compassion" (Nussbaum, *Upheavals of Thought*, 318).

73 See ST 3.48.6 *respondeo* and 49.1 passim.

74 Aquinas argues that the original effect of divine *misericordia* is creation itself, in which case the incarnation follows as the second great effect of divine

misericordia. See my discussion of this point in "The Quality of Mercy: *Misericordia* and Three Forms of Forgiveness in Aquinas," in *The Virtuous Life: Thomas Aquinas on the Theological Nature of Moral Virtues*, ed. Henk Schoot and Harm Goris (Peeters: Louvain, 2015).

75 In particular, Christ does not weep before the tomb of Lazarus because he fears his own death. By contrast, in the Synoptic Gospels at the Garden of Gethsemane, Christ is presented as experiencing with us in his humanity anguish and sorrow in his soul over his impending death but not fear. "If this cup may pass me by . . ." And yet he does not weep for himself. The only other instance apart from the death of Lazarus in which Christ is presented as weeping is in Luke 19:41-44, when he weeps over Jerusalem and prophesies its downfall.

76 Compare this order with the opposite in Marjolein Oele's very interesting analysis of the scene between Priam and Achilles. Although I am not finally convinced by her conclusion, she argues strongly that the experience shared between the two men leads toward friendship and a kind of "almost divine, shared, admiration" for one another. See her "Suffering, Pity and Friendship: An Aristotelian Reading of Book 24 of Homer's *Iliad*," *Electronic Antiquity* 14, no. 1 (2010): 63.

77 Thomas Aquinas, *Super Evangelium S. Ioannis: Lectura* (Turin: Marietti, 1952), chap. 7, lect. 5.

78 *ST* 1.21.4 *respondeo*: "And so *misericordia* is shown in every work of God considered as its primary root. [Indeed] the power of it is preserved in everything that follows from it; and works within them even more powerfully, just as the power of a primary cause is more powerful than a secondary. And according to this those things which are due to creatures, God, from an abundance of his goodness, dispenses [to them] in a greater proportion than is required. For less would suffice to preserve the order of justice than divine goodness confers." And *ST* 21.3 ad 2: "It is clear that *misericordia* does not take away from justice, but is in a way the fullness of justice. So it is said in 2 James that *misericordia* exalts itself beyond justice."

79 The *Catena Aurea* is a vast and remarkable work consisting of texts from the Church Fathers (more Greek Fathers than Latin) commenting passage by passage upon the Gospels. It is remarkable because, more than a mere collection of texts of commentary, by the choice of texts and their arrangement, read as a whole, it forms a kind of second order commentary by Aquinas upon the Gospels employing the voices of others as his own. See Jean-Pierre Torrell, *Saint Thomas Aquinas*, vol. 1, *The Person and His Work*, rev. ed., trans. Robert Royal (Washington, D.C.: Catholic University of America Press, 2005), 136–41 and 338.

80 So Nietzsche might prove to be a better reader of the history of philosophy since the advent of Christianity than Nussbaum gives him credit for, despite his criticism of Christianity, which Nussbaum does not think goes far enough.

81 *NE* 8.1a26–28.

4: Hibbs

1 Charles Taylor, "Diversity of Goods," in *Philosophical Papers*, vol. 2, *Philosophy and the Human Sciences* (Cambridge: Cambridge University Press, 1985), 230–47.

2 Elizabeth Anscombe, "Modern Moral Philosophy," in *Virtue Ethics*, ed. Roger Crisp and Michael Slote (Oxford: Oxford University Press, 1997).
3 David Solomon, "Virtue Ethics: Radical or Routine?," in *Intellectual Virtue: Perspectives from Ethics and Epistemology*, ed. Michael DePaul and Linda Zagzebski (Oxford: Oxford University Press, 2003), 57–80. Solomon observes that "Kurt Baier's attack on her paper—delivered a quarter of a century after it was written—characterized her views as an instance of 'Radical Virtue Ethics.'"
4 In addition to "Virtue Ethics: Radical or Routine?," see also David Solomon, "Internal Objections to Virtue Ethics," *Midwest Studies in Philosophy* 13 (1988): 428–41; Solomon, "Keeping Virtue in Its Place: A Critique of Subordinating Strategies," in *Recovering Nature: Essays in Natural Philosophy, Ethics, and Metaphysics in Honor of Ralph McInerny*, ed. John P. O'Callaghan and Thomas S. Hibbs (Notre Dame: University of Notre Dame Press, 1999), 83–104; and Solomon, "MacIntyre and Contemporary Moral Philosophy," in *Alasdair MacIntyre: Contemporary Philosophy in Focus*, ed. Mark Murphy (Cambridge: Cambridge University Press, 2003), 114–52.
5 Candace Vogler, "Aristotle, Aquinas, Anscombe, and the New Virtue Ethics," in *Aquinas and the Nicomachean Ethics*, ed. Tobias Hoffmann, Jörn Müller, and Matthias Perkams (Cambridge: Cambridge University Press, 2013), 239–57.
6 Taylor, "Diversity of Goods," 234.
7 Taylor, "Diversity of Goods," 231.
8 Taylor, "Diversity of Goods," 232.
9 Taylor, "Diversity of Goods," 234.
10 Taylor, "Diversity of Goods," 244.
11 Taylor, "Diversity of Goods," 244.
12 Solomon, "Virtue Ethics," 65.
13 Taylor, "Diversity of Goods," 244.
14 Taylor, "Diversity of Goods," 236.
15 Taylor, "Diversity of Goods," 246.
16 Anscombe, "Modern Moral Philosophy," 22.
17 Solomon, "Virtue Ethics," 60.
18 John Finnis, *Natural Law and Natural Rights* (Oxford: Oxford University Press, 1980), 51.
19 Yves Simon, *The Tradition of Natural Law* (New York: Fordham University Press, 1999), 83 and 85.
20 Solomon's entire list with descriptions runs thus:

   1. A *suspicion of rules and principles* as adequate to guiding human action in the complex and variegated situations in which human agents find themselves.
   2. A *rejection of conscientiousness* as the appropriate motivational state in the best human action.
   3. A turn for an understanding of the ethical life to *concrete terms* like the virtue terms in preference to more abstract terms like "good," "right," and "ought."
   4. A *critique of modernity* and especially the models of practical rationality that underlie such Enlightenment theories as Kantian deontology

and Benthamite consequentialism. This critique frequently extends to the bureaucratic and impersonal features of many central modern social practices.
5. An emphasis on the *importance of community*, especially local communities, both in introducing human beings to the ethical life and sustaining their practice of central features of that life. This emphasis is typically contrasted with the individualism that seems to many advocates of virtue ethics to permeate Kantian and consequentialist approaches to ethics.
6. A focus on the importance of *the whole life* as the primary object of ethical evaluation in contrast to the tendency of Kantian and consequentialist theorists to give primacy to the evaluation of actions or more fragmented features of human lives.
7. An emphasis on *the narrative structure of human life* as opposed to the more episodic picture of human life found in neo-Kantian and consequentialist approaches to ethics. This narrative structure is especially important in understanding the special nature of human projects and human goods that can only be understood within the context of the story of a whole life.
8. An emphasis on *the centrality of contingently based special relationships*, especially with friends and family, for the ethical life in contrast to the tendency within neo-Kantian and consequentialist theories to downplay such relationships in favor of alienating ideals of universality.
9. *A suspicion of morality* understood as an abstract and distinctive grid of obligations and rights cut off from the more concrete features of human practical life.
10. A special emphasis on *thick moral education* understood as involving training in the virtues as opposed to models of moral education frequently associated with neo-Kantian and consequentialist moral theories that tend to emphasize growth in autonomy or in detached instrumental rationality.

See Solomon, "Virtue Ethics," 68–69.
21 *Summa Theologiae (ST)* 2-2.16 ad 2.
22 *ST* 1-2.64.1 ad 2.
23 *ST* 1-2.7.3.
24 *ST* 1-2.61.2.
25 Jerome Schneewind, "The Misfortunes of Virtue," in *Virtue Ethics*, ed. Roger Crisp and Michael Slote (Oxford: Oxford University Press, 1997), 199–200.
26 Set aside for the moment the question of how agents can have the habit of acting in accord with right reason without the development of character or some attention being given to inculcating appropriate intentions in the character of individuals. Set aside also the astonishing naïveté in supposing that a healthy society could rest upon mere external obedience to a set of rules. Schneewind's account ignores a host of communitarian and feminist critiques of modern legalism. It also ignores the sort of critique that gave rise to the revival of virtue ethics in the first place.

27   Schneewind, "Misfortunes of Virtue," 183.
28   Schneewind, "Misfortunes of Virtue," 186.
29   Alasdair MacIntyre's work on justice, anything but routine, is an exception.
30   Larry Louden, "Vices of Virtue Ethics," in *Virtue Ethics*, ed. Roger Crisp and Michael Slote (Oxford: Oxford University Press, 1997), 207.
31   Louden, "Vices of Virtue Ethics," 207.
32   He does cite as an exception MacIntyre's discussion in *After Virtue* of the ways in which rules complement virtues.
33   Louden, "Vices of Virtue Ethics," 204.
34   Solomon, "Internal Objections to Virtue Ethics," 428–41. Solomon describes three standard types of objection: (1) The action-guiding objection that claims that a virtue theory fails to give adequate guidance in situations of practical perplexity. The rules and principles characteristic of deontological and consequentialist theories are alleged to guide action more effectively and more determinately. (2) The self-centeredness objection that claims that an ethics of virtue is insufficiently other-regarding. It alleges that virtue theories in their classical form ground the need for virtue on the part of agents in the desire of agents for their own fulfillment or satisfaction and that this seems to turn ethics upside down. Instead of my needing to be good in order to benefit others, I am required to be the sort of person who benefits others in order to be fulfilled myself. Virtue seems to be itself compromised by a kind of vanity or prissiness. And (3) the conscientiousness objection that claims that an ethics of virtue fails to do justice to the special kind of motivation peculiar to the moral. Genuine goodness, according to this objection, must involve acting under a certain kind of constraint. The perfectly virtuous person apparently finds it easy to do what he or she ought, but this seems to fly in the face of any realistic moral phenomenology.
35   Solomon, "Internal Objections to Virtue Ethics," 432, 434.
36   *ST* 2-2.58.10.
37   *ST* 2-2.53.3.
38   *ST* 1-2.60.3.
39   *ST* 2-2.58.1.
40   *ST* 2-2.17.1.
41   Ralph McInerny, *Aquinas on Human Action* (Washington, D.C.: Catholic University of America Press, 1992), 122.
42   *ST* 2-2.122.1.
43   *ST* 2-2.122.2.
44   *ST* 2-2.122.3.
45   *ST* 2-2.122.6 ad 2.
46   Solomon, "Keeping Virtue in Its Place," 88.
47   Solomon, "Keeping Virtue in Its Place," 98.
48   Solomon, "Internal Objections to Virtue Ethics," 439.
49   Solomon, "Keeping Virtue in Its Place," 89.
50   Solomon, "Keeping Virtue in Its Place," 89.
51   Vogler, "Aristotle, Aquinas, Anscombe," 248. See especially John McDowell, "Virtue and Reason," 50–73; "Values and Secondary Qualities," 131–50; and "Non-cognitivism and Rule-Following," 198–218, in *Mind, Value, and Reality* (Cambridge, Mass.: Harvard University Press, 1998).

52 The same concern, according to Vogler, motivated Peter Geach to question the adequacy of virtue ethics in the absence of a theological ground: "[Somebody] might very well admit that not only is there something bad about certain acts, but also it is desirable to become the sort of person who needs to act in the contrary way; and yet *not* admit that such acts are to be avoided in all circumstances and at any price. To be sure, a virtuous person cannot be ready in advance to do such acts; and if he does do them they will damage his virtuous habits and perhaps irreparably wreck his hard-won integrity of soul. But at this point someone may protest, 'Are you the only person to be considered? Suppose the price of your precious integrity is a most fearful disaster! Haven't you got a hand to burn for your country (or mankind) and your friends?' This sort of appeal has not, I think, been adequately answered on Aristotelian lines, either by Aristotle or by Mrs. Foot." Peter Geach, *God and the Soul* (London: Routledge and Kegan Paul, 1978), 123.
53 Anscombe, "Modern Moral Philosophy," 38.
54 Anscombe, "Modern Moral Philosophy," 41.
55 Anscombe, "Modern Moral Philosophy," 10.
56 Vogler, "Aristotle, Aquinas, Anscombe," 246.
57 Vogler, "Aristotle, Aquinas, Anscombe," 253.
58 Alasdair MacIntyre, "Plain Persons and Moral Philosophy: Rules, Virtues, and Goods," *American Catholic Philosophical Quarterly* 66 (1992): 3–19.
59 Alasdair MacIntyre, *After Virtue*, 3rd ed. (Notre Dame: University of Notre Dame Press, 2007), 151.
60 MacIntyre, *After Virtue*, 152.
61 MacIntyre, "Plain Persons and Moral Philosophy," 9–10.
62 David Solomon, "Filling the Void: Secular Bioethics and Academic Moral Philosophy," in *Secularism: Russian and Western Perspectives*, ed. David Bradshaw (Council for Research in Values and Philosophy, 2013), reprinted as the lead article in the *Russian Yearbook for Philosophy*. See also David Solomon, "Christian Bioethics, Secular Bioethics, and the Claim to Cultural Authority," *Christian Bioethics: Non-ecumenical Studies in Medical Ethics* 11, no. 3 (2005): 349–59; and David Solomon, "Domestic Disarray and Imperial Ambition: Contemporary Applied Ethics and the Prospects for Global Bioethics," in *Global Bioethics: The Collapse of Consensus*, ed. H. T. Engelhardt (Salem, Mass.: Scrivener, 2006), 335–61.
63 This quotation is drawn from private notes distributed by David Solomon for the thirty-first lecture of his long-running Medical Ethics course at the University of Notre Dame.

5: Haldane

1 H. A. Prichard, "Does Moral Philosophy Rest on a Mistake?," *Mind* 21, no. 1 (1912): 21.
2 G. E. Moore, "A Defence of Common Sense," in *Contemporary British Philosophy*, 2nd ser., ed. J. H. Muirhead (London: George Allen and Unwin, 1925).
3 Bernard Williams, *Ethics and the Limits of Philosophy* (London: Fontana, 1985), 93. In writing "but it would be unlikely to yield an ethical theory," Williams is

not taking that consideration to be an objection to this kind of moral philosophy. On the contrary, he thinks that much of what is wrong with the subject is that it is driven by the presumption that the forming of a general theory is necessary and hence possible. He thought it is neither. Although he does not mention him, I suspect that this passage shows the influence on Williams of the Hungarian philosopher Aurel Kolnai, who had been a colleague of Williams at Bedford College, London, and whose collection of essays Williams coauthored (with David Wiggins) an introduction. See F. Dunlop and B. Klug, eds., *Ethics, Value, and Reality: Selected Papers of Aurel Kolnai* (London: Athlone, 1977).

4 From "Annus Mirabilis," in *Philip Larkin Collected Poems*, ed. Anthony Thwaite (London: Faber & Faber, 2003). The Beatles' first LP was *Please Please Me*—itself a somewhat Larkinian title. With verse and irony in mind, and in the context of honoring David Solomon, whose mode of being a philosopher is in sharp contrast to that here parodied, I include, in the hope of his appreciation of it, an adaptation of W. S. Gilbert's lyrics for the patter song "I Am the Very Model of a Modern Major-General" from *The Pirates of Penzance*:

> I am the very model of a modern philosophical
> My research is specialised, sectorial, and technical
> I know the leading journals and departments hyperlogical
> From *PPR* and NYU in orders periodical.
>
> I'm very well acquainted, too, with matters academical,
> I understand peer-rankings, both the simple and Leiterial
> About the latest hirings I'm teeming with hot news
> and my web-site, blogs and twitters offer copious reviews.
>
> I excel in footnotes lengthy and parentheses ambiguous;
> I know the current names of theories quite ridiculous
> In short, in matters professional and sectional,
> I am the very model of a modern academical.
>
> Yet my knowledge, though I'm plucky and adventury,
> Barely reaches past the beginnings of this century;
> But still, in matters formalised and theoretical,
> I am the very model of a modern philosophical.

5 See G. E. M. Anscombe, "On Brute Facts," *Analysis* 18, no. 3 (1958); P. Geach, "Ascriptivism," *Philosophical Review* 69, no. 2 (1960); and P. Geach, "Good and Evil," *Analysis* 17, no. 2 (1956).
6 Both of these papers appear in B. Williams, *Moral Luck: Philosophical Papers 1973–1980* (Cambridge: Cambridge University Press, 1981), as chaps. 10 and 8, respectively.
7 David Solomon, "Ethical Theory," in *Synoptic Vision: Essays on the Philosophy of Wilfrid Sellars*, ed. S. F. Delaney, Michael J. Loux, Gary Gutting, and W. David Solomon (Notre Dame: University of Notre Dame Press, 1977).
8 Letter from Wilfred Sellars to David Solomon, June 28, 1976. For the text, see http://www.ditext.com/sellars/css.html#*.

9. David Hume, *Treatise of Human Nature*, book 3, part 1, sect. 1.
10. David Hume, *Enquiries*, appendix 1, "Concerning Moral Sentiment," section 2, paragraph 240.
11. G. E. M. Anscombe, "On Brute Facts," *Philosophy* 33, no. 124 (1958): 1–19.
12. Immanuel Kant, *The Critique of Judgment*, trans. Werner S. Pluhar (1790; repr., Indianapolis: Hackett, 1987), §4.2.
13. See K. Mulligan, "Promisings and Other Social Acts: Their Constituents and Structure," in *Speech Act and Sachverhalt: Reinach and the Foundations of Realist Phenomenology*, ed. K. Mulligan (Dordrecht: Nijhoff, 1987), 29–90.
14. Thomas Aquinas, *Summa Theologiae*, trans. Fathers of the English Dominican Province, 2nd and rev. ed. (London: Burns, Oates and Washbourne, 1920–1922).

6: Beaty

1. Elizabeth Anscombe clearly deserves mention in this group, but this chapter focuses on Foot and Murdoch. Anscombe was a friend and intellectual peer of Foot and Murdoch. Her contributions in metaphysics, especially on the nature of causation, in action theory (on intention), and in ethics (one among several influences is her work on double effect) have influenced subsequent work up to the present moment. Her book on *Intention* and her essay "Modern Moral Philosophy" have been especially influential.
2. Philippa Foot, *Natural Goodness* (Oxford: Clarendon, 2001), 5.
3. Iris Murdoch, "The Idea of Perfection," in *The Sovereignty of Good* (London: Ark Paperbacks, 1986), 44.
4. By noncognitivism, I mean a family of views about the nature of evaluative statements in contrast to descriptive statements. According to noncognitivism, evaluative statements, of which moral statements are a subset, are neither true nor false. Their purpose is to express emotions, attitudes, and desires or to influence their audience to agree and to share their noncognitive attitudes and behaviors. In ethics, cognitivism is the view that moral statements express moral beliefs that are either true or false. Moral realism is a form of cognitivism that contends that some moral statements are true. John Mackie accepts a form of moral irrealism because he embraces cognitivism about moral statements but claims that all moral statements are false.
5. Clearly, Foot and Murdoch were intellectual opponents of versions of both emotivism as proposed by A. J. Ayer and C. L. Stevenson and also the prescriptivism advocated by R. M. Hare. Two of the most prominent and formidable contemporary advocates of noncognitivism include Simon Blackburn and Allan Gibbard.
6. Foot, *Natural Goodness*, 5.
7. Foot, *Natural Goodness*, 5. Also see G. E. Moore, *Principia Ethica* (Cambridge: Cambridge University Press, 1993).
8. Foot, *Natural Goodness*, 2.
9. Foot, *Natural Goodness*, 3.
10. Nicholas Sturgeon, "Ethical Naturalism," in *The Oxford Handbook of Ethical Theory*, ed. David Copp (Oxford: Oxford University Press, 2006), 94.

11 G. E. Moore, "The Subject Matter of Ethics," in *20th Century Ethical Theory*, ed. Steven M. Cahn and Joram G. Haber (Upper Saddle River, N.J.: Prentice Hall, 1995), 15.
12 Of course, there is a scientific definition of "red": the longest wavelength of visible light. But most people don't have that in mind when they think of "red." While scientists have developed a quantifiable method of detecting the color red, the nonscientific way to detect red is to see it and to point to it. Similarly, Moore understands "good" as something we cannot define but we can "see" and "point" to.
13 Foot, *Natural Goodness*, 2.
14 Foot, *Natural Goodness*, 2.
15 Foot, *Natural Goodness*, 2.
16 Peter Geach, "Good and Evil," *Analysis* 17 (1956): 33–42. Reprinted in *Theories of Ethics*, ed. Philippa Foot (Oxford: Oxford University Press, 1967), 64–73.
17 Noncognitivists insisted that "good" did not entail an objective description but rather had other functions. Clearly, however, a good carving knife entails "being sharp" and being a good parent entails "intending the welfare of one's children." Thus "good" has descriptive meaning just as "large" does.
18 Foot, *Natural Goodness*, 5.
19 Foot, *Natural Goodness*, 28–29.
20 Foot, *Natural Goodness*, 31.
21 Foot, *Natural Goodness*, 15.
22 Foot, *Natural Goodness*, 15.
23 Foot, *Natural Goodness*, 44, 46.
24 Foot, *Natural Goodness*, 43. Foot hesitates to call the end of human aspiration "human flourishing" and does not identify it with a good human life.
25 Foot, *Natural Goodness*, 43, 92.
26 Foot, *Natural Goodness*, 43.
27 Foot, *Natural Goodness*, 44.
28 Foot, *Natural Goodness*, 44.
29 Foot, *Natural Goodness*, 44–45.
30 Foot, *Natural Goodness*, 51.
31 Foot, *Natural Goodness*, 51.
32 Foot, *Natural Goodness*, 69.
33 Foot, *Natural Goodness*, 81.
34 Foot is hesitant to endorse "human flourishing" as our natural end, arguing that while Wittgenstein was right to call his life a good life for a human being, it was not a flourishing life because "flourishing" suggests an untroubled life, and his was not that kind of life. It is clear that his life was troubled, while admirable in many ways, especially with respect to his contributions to philosophy. I am more inclined to see his life as lacking in some of the features of a good life for human beings. See pages 92–93 of Foot, *Natural Goodness*.
35 Foot, *Natural Goodness*, 97.
36 Foot, *Natural Goodness*, 93.
37 Iris Murdoch, "The Sovereignty of Good over Other Concepts," in *The Sovereignty of Good* (London: Ark Paperbacks, 1986), 93.
38 Foot, *Natural Goodness*, 93.

39 Murdoch, "Idea of Perfection," 44.
40 Murdoch, "Sovereignty of Good over Other Concepts," 78. See also page 79, where she says, "That human life has no external point or telos is a view as difficult to argue as its opposite, and I shall simply assert it."
41 Foot, *Natural Goodness*, 79.
42 By theism, I mean that there is but one God, a being that is omnipotent, omniscient, and perfectly morally good, a nonmaterial and personal being, who is creator and sustainer of the universe.
43 Murdoch, "Idea of Perfection," 3.
44 See Michael Smith, "Moral Realism," in *The Blackwell Guide to Ethical Theory*, ed. Hugh LaFollette (Oxford: Blackwell, 2000), 15–37, esp. 23–24.
45 Murdoch, "On 'God' and 'Good,'" in *The Sovereignty of Good* (London: Ark Paperbacks, 1986), 78.
46 Murdoch, "On 'God' and 'Good,'" 99.
47 Murdoch, "On 'God' and 'Good,'" 52.
48 Murdoch, "On 'God' and 'Good,'" 79.
49 Murdoch, "On 'God' and 'Good,'" 54.
50 Murdoch, "On 'God' and 'Good,'" 54.
51 Friedrich Nietzsche, *On the Genealogy of Morality*, ed. Keith Ansell-Person, trans. Carol Diethe (Cambridge: Cambridge University Press, 1994), 3.
52 Murdoch, "On 'God' and 'Good,'" 53.
53 Murdoch, "On 'God' and 'Good,'" 52.
54 Murdoch, "On 'God' and 'Good,'" 53.
55 Murdoch, "On 'God' and 'Good,'" 52.
56 Murdoch, "On 'God' and 'Good,'" 54.
57 Murdoch, "On 'God' and 'Good,'" 70.
58 Murdoch, "Idea of Perfection," 34.
59 Murdoch, "On 'God' and 'Good,'" 56.
60 Murdoch, "Idea of Perfection," 31.
61 Aristotle, *Nicomachean Ethics*, ed. Roger Crisp (Cambridge: Cambridge University Press, 2000), 27–28.
62 Murdoch, "Sovereignty of Good over Other Concepts," 94; Murdoch, "On 'God' and 'Good,'" 55.
63 Murdoch, "On 'God' and 'Good,'" 57.
64 Murdoch, "Idea of Perfection," 31.
65 Murdoch, "On 'God' and 'Good,'" 60.
66 Murdoch, "On 'God' and 'Good,'" 58–60.
67 By "authority" I presume that she means its "truthfulness" and its relenting, nonhypothetical demand on us. A sovereign commands unconditionally, absolutely. See Murdoch, "Sovereignty of Good over Other Concepts," 90.
68 Murdoch, "Sovereignty of Good over Other Concepts," 100.
69 Murdoch, "Sovereignty of Good over Other Concepts," 92–94.
70 Murdoch, "Sovereignty of Good over Other Concepts," 100.
71 Murdoch, "Sovereignty of Good over Other Concepts," 99; Murdoch, "On 'God' and 'Good,'" 62.
72 Murdoch, "Sovereignty of Good over Other Concepts," 101. By pointlessness of human virtue, I presume she means its nonconsequential, nonteleological character.

73 Murdoch, "Sovereignty of Good over Other Concepts," 99.
74 Philip Cafaro, "Virtue Ethics (Not Too) Simplified," *Auslegung* 22, no. 1 (1997): 52.
75 Tony Milligan, "Iris Murdoch and the Virtue of Courage" (paper presented at Sixth International Iris Murdoch Conference, University of Kingston, U.K., September 2012).
76 Douglas V. Henry, "Iris Murdoch's This-Worldly Eudaimonism" (paper presented at Conference on *Iris Murdoch and Virtue Ethics: Philosophy and the Novel*, Universita degli Studi Roma Tre, Rome, Italy, February 20–22, 2014).
77 Foot, *Natural Goodness*, 33.
78 Clearly, this claim is a matter of degree. One simple point is this: Murdoch devotes much more attention to human selfishness and the difficulties overcoming it than does Foot. But Foot does address these issues, though not extensively, in her chapter called "Immoralism." See Foot, *Natural Goodness*, 99–115.
79 Foot, *Natural Goodness*, 114–15.
80 Murdoch, "On 'God' and 'Good,'" 58.
81 My thanks to John Rosenbaum for suggesting this helpful example.
82 Dennis Whitcomb, Heather Battaly, Jason Baehr, and Daniel Howard-Snyder, "Intellectual Humility: Owning Our Limitations," *Philosophy and Phenomenological Research* 94, no. 3 (2017): 509–39.
83 Perhaps there are intrinsic excellences that cannot be accounted for by an appeal to the attributive nature of "good" and natural normativity. Robert M. Adams insists that there are. For a full defense of this claims, see his *Finite and Infinite Goods: A Framework for Ethics* (Oxford: Oxford University Press, 1999).
84 Murdoch, "Sovereignty of Good over Other Concepts," 93, 100.
85 Murdoch, "Sovereignty of Good over Other Concepts," 101–2.
86 Murdoch, "Sovereignty of Good over Other Concepts," 94–95.

7: KHAWAJA

1 David Solomon, "Internal Objections to Virtue Ethics," *Midwest Studies in Philosophy* 13 (1988): 428–41.
2 Solomon actually refers to "utilitarianism," but I think he uses this term to range across the broader category of consequentialist theories, so in what follows, I'll (somewhat misleadingly but harmlessly) regard the two terms as interchangeable.
3 Solomon, "Internal Objections," 428–29 (my emphasis).
4 Solomon, "Internal Objections," 429 (my emphasis).
5 Solomon, "Internal Objections," 429.
6 Solomon, "Internal Objections," 430 (my emphasis).
7 Solomon, "Internal Objections," 430.
8 Solomon, "Internal Objections," 431.
9 Of course, the disciplinary boundaries are themselves parasitic on distinctions between types of propositional content—ethical, nonethical, and so on.
10 Solomon, "Internal Objections," 431–32, footnotes 6 and 7 omitted (my emphasis).
11 Solomon, "Internal Objections," 436.

12 Solomon, "Internal Objections," 435.
13 Solomon, "Internal Objections," 434.
14 Solomon seems to downplay this in a brief remark about Plato and Aristotle (p. 432), but I think it's too obvious to be denied. The contrast between Solomon's view and that of two (then) contemporary accounts is instructive. See Bernard Williams' discussion of Aristotle's ethics in *Ethics and the Limits of Philosophy* (Cambridge, Mass.: Harvard University Press, 1985), 30–53, and Thomas Nagel's discussion of Plato's and Aristotle's ethics in *The View from Nowhere* (Oxford: Oxford University Press, 1986), 195–200.
15 Elizabeth Anscombe, "Modern Moral Philosophy," *Philosophy* 33, no. 124 (1958): 1.
16 Anscombe, "Modern Moral Philosophy," 14.
17 Thanks to Jeff Brenzel for his insightful written commentary on this chapter and to Kate Herrick, Patrick Kain, and Daniel Sportiello for some challenging questions and objections. I'm grateful to Raymond Hain for organizing the conference at Notre Dame at which an earlier version of this chapter was presented; I profited immensely from discussion with the audience there. Above all, thanks to David Solomon for teaching me what I know about ethics and for putting up with me for this long.

8: Vogler

1 I have given parts of this chapter as talks at Columbia University and the University of Sydney and had the tremendous benefit of audience discussion at both places. Jay Schleusener and Hank Vogler have worked through earlier drafts of the chapter with me in great detail, and Matthias Haase has provided very useful feedback.
2 Leonard Linsky, the philosopher who invented the title "philosophy of language" to name what he was working on in his doctoral dissertation at the University of California at Berkeley in the late 1940s and canonized the field by collecting its seminal essays in the 1952 anthology *Semantics and the Philosophy of Language* (Chicago: University of Illinois Press, 1952), once remarked in conversation that he thought that ethics should have become more interesting because it swerved in 1975 when John Rawls' *A Theory of Justice* made a decisive break from analytic philosophy. I explained that I regarded the change as a fall from discipline rather than a liberation from stultifying constraint.
3 *The Mikado* or *The Town of Titipu*, act 1, William S. Gilbert, music by Sir Arthur Sullivan.
4 For an excellent account of the rational structure of moral conduct, see Michael Thompson, "What Is It to Wrong Someone? A Puzzle about Justice," in *Reason and Value: Themes from the Moral Philosophy of Joseph Raz*, ed. R. Jay Wallace, Philip Pettit, Samuel Scheffler, and Michael Smith (Oxford: Oxford University Press, 2004), 333–84.
5 This sketch of morality sets up at least four requirements for philosophical work on the topic:

> There is the need to account for the identical practical precepts in the hearts and minds of the strangers.

There is the need to ensure that the strangers act from and for the sake of those very practical considerations.

There is the need to account for the normative authority of the moral precepts they share.

There is the need to say how and why a party to the exchange sides with morality, having crossed paths with a stranger who stands prepared to act well.

6 Tim Scanlon, however, suggests that what we owe each other is very much like what other theorists claim that I owe to myself. By Scanlon's lights, if I understand him, what I owe *anyone* is, *in the first instance*, an *explanation* showing that my conduct is or was reasonable on the grounds that I expect others to accept (where my expectation is based in my thought, hope, or conviction that the grounds do not admit of reasonable rejection). See T. M. Scanlon, *What We Owe to Each Other* (Cambridge, Mass.: Harvard University Press, 1998).

7 J. David Velleman, "A Brief Introduction to Kantian Ethics," in *Self to Self: Selected Essays* (Cambridge: Cambridge University Press, 2006), 20.

8 See J. David Velleman, "The Guise of the Good," *Noûs* 26, no. 1 (1992): 3–26.

9 Velleman, "Guise of the Good," 21.

10 Velleman, "Brief Introduction," 44.

11 Velleman, "Brief Introduction," 44.

12 Velleman, "Brief Introduction," 44. By Velleman's lights, all practically reasoning beings as such recognize that they can be asked to provide reasons for their actions and no practical consideration can *count* as a reason unless it is universally shared common knowledge among members of the community of persons.

In acting well, persons act from and for the sake of such reasons.

The normative authority of the reasons from and for the sake of which they act comes from the recognition of those reasons by the larger community of persons who are persons because they are members of that community.

The individual sides with morality first because the demand that he or she act for reasons is inescapable and second because personhood requires acting for reasons that are universally shared common knowledge among members of the community of practically reasoning beings.

Velleman likens the normative authority of moral precepts to the authority of arithmetical precepts (Velleman, "Brief Introduction," 25–27).

Is a shared framework for practical reasoning like a body of custom that informs conscience? If so, then some people—fellow members of my community—will share my framework for practical reason. Other people will not. Complaining about Hume on this account, Michael Thompson writes:

> Hume no doubt thought that it was enough that our relation to outsiders is governed by benevolence or natural sympathy. It simply did not occur to him, as a naive eighteenth-century writer, that apart from justice one might, out of natural sympathy, kill one person to remedy the plight of several others, or for any number of other beautiful purposes. A theory like Hume's can of course explain why *you* would not kill *Sylvia* even in order to save five others, where you and Sylvia are bearers of a single ... practice; it need only be that the practice constitutes a directed duty not to kill and a claim not to be killed among its

bearers. But he forgot that you might kill several recalcitrant practice-outsiders in order, from the deepest sympathy, to introduce your more exalted system of practices to their numerous backward compatriots. (Thompson, "What Is It to Wrong Someone?," 375–76)

But suppose that any such community, independently and for reasons of its own, accepts a practical precept forbidding the killing of other reasonable beings. This will make for more peaceable relations between communities and, if I plan to go abroad, and know that *those* people will not kill practically reasoning foreigners, I will have one less thing to worry about in planning my trip, and, provided that they know that I won't kill strangers, the locals I meet can rest assured that they will not face homicidal intent on my part. As Thompson argues, this coincidence in practical precepts does not suffice to bring my people into moral relations with theirs: "A manifold of 'persons' must together come under a genuinely common, and not merely similar or parallel, form of deonticity" (Thompson, "What Is It to Wrong Someone?," 372). By hypothesis, the fact that separate communities have come to settle on provisions forbidding the killing of practically reasoning outsiders is an accident. Morality is not supposed to be, in this sense, an accident. It is supposed to be non-accidentally developed and non-accidentally deployed by persons in their dealings one with another, and Velleman stresses this very aspect of morality. He insists that it is only as a practically reasoning person among other persons whose reasons for acting are the *same* as mine that I engage in moral conduct, and it cannot be the case that it is left to each of us to conjure up the force of moral reasons all on her own. We are not the source of the authority attaching to the reasons that we share. Velleman writes:

> Why can't reasons owe their authority to us? The answer is that endowing reasons with authority would entail making their validity common knowledge among all reasoners. And if we could promote reasons to the status of common knowledge among all reasoners, then we should equally be able to demote them from that status—in which case, the status wouldn't amount to rational authority. The point of a reason's being common knowledge among all reasoners ... is that there is then no way of evading it, no matter how we shift our point-of-view. No amount of rethinking will make such a reason irrelevant, because its validity as a reason is evident from every perspective. But if we could decide what is to be common knowledge among all thinkers, then a reason's being common knowledge would not entail its being inescapable, since we could also decide that it wasn't to be common knowledge, after all. Our power to construct a universally accessible framework of reasons would therefore undermine the whole point of having one. (Velleman, "Brief Introduction," 32–33)

And now a question arises: if we are after the inescapability and universality of morality, if our thought is that morality catches up and rightly constrains every person who has her wits about her, just in virtue of the fact that she has her wits about her, why the stress on *community*? Why mention a community *at all*?

If I understand him, the mention of community is an allusion to Kant's suggestion that practically reasoning beings as such are fellow legislators in a Kingdom of Ends. The Kingdom of Ends has no special geo-political coordinates. It is anywhere and everywhere there are practically reasoning beings. But Velleman rejects Kant's insistence that such beings give themselves the law that they obey. If we give ourselves a law, what's to prevent us from repealing it? Instead, Velleman gives us a picture of ourselves as fellow autonomous subjects in a community where reason rules.

13 Of course, even people with good intentions lose track and engage in unethical conduct now and then. Velleman points out that the reasonable response to my own failure to live up to my own standards in practice will likely occasion remorse or regret and that these can spur self-improvement programs on my part. See Velleman, "Brief Introduction," 38–40.
14 Velleman, "Brief Introduction," 16–19.
15 Velleman, "Brief Introduction," 19.
16 Does this mean that an agent can *provide* reasons for everything she does when the question is "Why are you A-ing?" and she *is* A-ing intentionally? Not necessarily:
"Why are you drawing those lines?"
"No reason. I'm just doodling."
There is no mystery in the exchange. But it belongs to the context in which the question arises that drawing lines is the kind of thing that one can mean to do and *therefore* that one could have a reason to do it. As Elizabeth Anscombe put it,

Now of course a possible answer to the question "Why?" is one like "I just thought I would" or "It was an impulse" or "For no particular reason" or "It was an idle action—I was just doodling." I do not call an answer of this sort a rejection of the question. The question is not refused application because it says that there is *no* reason, any more than the question how much money I have in my pocket is refused application by the answer "None." (G. E. M. Anscombe, *Intention* [Cambridge, Mass.: Harvard University Press, 2000], §17, 25)

17 Douglas Lavin, "Practical Reason and the Possibility of Error," *Ethics* 114, no. 3 (2004): 426.
18 Velleman, "Brief Introduction," 24.
19 Immanuel Kant, *The Metaphysics of Morals: Doctrine of the Elements of Ethics*, trans. Mary Gregor (Cambridge: Cambridge University Press, 1991), part 1, intro., §1, 214 (*Ak*. 6.417).
20 Kant, *Metaphysics of Morals*, §2, 214 (*Ak*. 6.417–618).
21 That is why, in the sphere of practical reason—reason in action—he held that counsels of prudence and technical precepts were not, on the face of it, *laws*, since, although these guide the actions of practically reasoning beings, not all practically reasoning beings pursue identical purposes. See Immanuel Kant, *Grundlegung zur Metaphysik der Sitten*, Abschnitt 2, *Ak*. 4.412–420.
22 On Kant's account, see Thompson, "What Is It to Wrong Someone?" §16, 379–84. The devastating objection to neo-Kantian accounts of what it is to

wrong (or, for that matter, to do right by) someone is given in §§11–12 of Thompson's essay (396–73).

23 Theists can notice that I may owe it to God to do or to avoid doing various things. My scenarios are meant to involve the trials and tribulations of those who do not have this sort of faith.

9: PILKINGTON

1. European Parliament Committee on Civil Liberties, Justice and Home Affairs, *Charter of Fundamental Rights of the European Union*, accessed December 3, 2008, http://www.europarl.europa.eu/comparl/libe/elsj/charter/art01/default_en.htm.
2. Ruth Macklin, "Dignity Is a Useless Concept," *British Medical Journal* 327 (2003): 1419–20.
3. I have argued in favor of this claim elsewhere. See Brian Pilkington, "The Problem of Human Dignity" (Ph.D. diss., University of Notre Dame, 2012).
4. Throughout this chapter, I use "dignity" and "human dignity" interchangeably, except when discussing Gilbert Meilaender's account.
5. See Macklin, "Dignity Is a Useless Concept," for these claims and her now famous claim that dignity is a useless concept. For related criticism, see Steven Pinker's "The Stupidity of Dignity," *New Republic*, May 28, 2008.
6. Martin Luther King Jr., "Letter from a Birmingham Jail," in *A Testament of Hope: The Essential Writings and Speeches of Martin Luther King, Jr.*, ed. James M. Washington (New York: Harper Collins, 1991), 289–302, at p. 296.
7. For an insightful discussion of the deep disagreement within contemporary culture that renders us unable to arrive at more than superficial agreement, see Alasdair MacIntyre's *After Virtue* (Notre Dame: University of Notre Dame Press, 2007), especially chap. 2, and his *Whose Justice? Which Rationality?* (Notre Dame: University of Notre Dame Press, 1998). We are in a very challenging position if we can only arrive at agreement on a concept, especially one that is supposed to play such a key role in our moral theorizing, if the concept is rather empty. This is agreement in name only. A concept like human dignity might play a useful role here, as it gives content to the more formal considerations of rights or the treatment of others.
8. Waldron's work on dignity can be traced back to 1995, when he published an article applying the concept to legislation. He followed this with a book devoted to the same topic in 1999 and has subsequently written a number of articles on torture and degrading treatment. See his essay "The Dignity of Legislation," *Maryland Law Review* 54 (1995): 633–65; and *The Dignity of Legislation* (Cambridge: Cambridge University Press, 1999). What he describes as shameful but necessary work was sparked by the treatment of those detained at U.S. military facilities in Guantanamo Bay, in particular the manner in which the law was employed in the justification of this treatment. See Waldron's "Torture and Positive Law: Jurisprudence for the White House," *Columbia Law Review* 105, no. 6 (2005): 1281–1750. More recently, Waldron has written about the connection between dignity and rank. I focus on this connection because it is central to both his account of dignity as a status of elevated and equalized rank and his attempt to alleviate the tension between merit and equality.

9 This constructivist account "takes its notion of dignity from actually existing systems of rank and nobility and presents human rights as a radical universalization of the status of inviolability ... traditionally associated with high rank." See Jeremy Waldron, "Dignity and Rank," *Archives Européennes de Sociologie* 48 (2007): 201–37. See pp. 235–36. He offers a similar description in "Dignity, Rank, and Rights: The 2009 Tanner Lectures at UC Berkeley" (New York University School of Law: Public Law and Legal Theory Research Paper Series, 2009), noting, "A good account of human dignity will explain it as a very general status ... comparable to a rank of nobility—only a rank assigned now to every human person, equally without discrimination. Dignity as nobility for the common man" (12). See also the 2012 publication of his Tanner Lectures, *Dignity, Rank, and Rights* (Oxford: Oxford University Press).

10 Waldron, "Dignity, Rank, and Rights," 48. I put to the side the second reason the court offers in support of its decision, that the noble has sufficient wealth to repay the debt. This may have been sufficient for the court to treat her as they did. Whether the court viewed a noble's dignity as both necessary and sufficient for her treatment is unclear, but what is clear is that Waldron's analogy to noble rank relies on nobility being (at least) sufficient.

11 See Gregory Vlastos' paper "Justice and Equality," in *Social Justice*, ed. Richard B. Brandt (Englewood Cliffs, N.J.: Prentice Hall, 1962), 31–72. Though Waldron discusses status in relation to dignity in his Tanner Lectures, his most extensive explication of status comes from his work on equality. See especially his paper "Does 'Equal Moral Status' Add Anything to Right Reason?" *New York University Public Law and Legal Theory Working Papers* (2011), http://lsr.nellco.org/nyu_plltwp/292. Originally prepared for delivery at the 2004 Annual Meeting of the American Political Science Association, Chicago, September 2–5, 2004. Waldron often equates rank and status, writing of the "rank or status" of human beings and of human dignity (e.g., see pp. 5, 6, 7, and 65 of his "Dignity, Rank, and Rights"). This lack of precision is part of the reason for turning to his work on equality. He notes, "We all have the same moral status. We have the same standing or significance for moral purposes. We are all on the same footing morally, irrespective of race, sex, birth, wealth, or national or communal membership. *We are all on the same moral footing even so far as merit and deserving are concerned, though of course we do not all have the same merits or deserts.* The idea of single moral status conveys that we all have the same basic moral rights and we labor under the same array of basic moral duties. As for our non-basic rights and duties, they vary by circumstance and by the undertakings and other relations we have entered into. But circumstances and undertakings work the same way for all of us: we have the same moral capacities (to create rights and duties) and the same moral liabilities (to find ourselves under special duties in special circumstances). In the moral world, there is no equivalent of caste or ranks of nobility: or perhaps we should say, with Gregory Vlastos, that our moral community is like a caste society but with just one caste, or like an aristocratic society but with just one rank (and a pretty high rank at that) for all of us" (Waldron, "Equal Moral Status," 2 [my emphasis]).

12 Waldron rejects the approach of giving dignity a technical definition, what he calls the "stipulative option," writing, "The meaning that 'dignity' imports into a

human rights context is a technical meaning associated stipulatively with the term" because it fails to offer the necessary perspective. To use dignity in a *purely* stipulative manner is to define it technically without reference to its ordinary meaning. Waldron offers the following example: "It is sometimes said that ... 'dignity' means something like 'The intrinsic non-negotiable non-fungible worth that inheres in every human being'" (Waldron, "Dignity and Rank," 209). We know dignity means this because that is how we define it. He posits Humpty Dumpty's attempt to define "glory" in *Alice's Adventures in Wonderland* as an example of pure stipulation. See Waldron, "Dignity and Rank," 210. Waldron also offers Ronald Dworkin's understanding of dignity as an example of pure stipulation. (Waldron discusses another kind of stipulative use, which he does not name but does define. He writes, "There is also the possibility that what began as a technical use of the term in philosophy, for example, has become so well-established that it is now part of the term's natural meaning"; Waldron, "Dignity and Rank," 209.) We might refer to these uses of dignity as *impurely* stipulative. Waldron has in mind here the Kantian notion "Würde." (Much thought has been devoted to Kant's understanding of dignity as a kind of worth beyond price that applies to humanity, but I do not devote attention to it here. Rather, I direct the reader to Waldron's paper "Dignity and Rank," especially pages 211–14.) There, Waldron argues that it is not clear that "würde" should be translated as "dignity," attributing the translation to two instances where "würde" is followed in parentheses by the Latin word "dignitas." (Both parenthetical appendages occur in Kant's *Metaphysics of Morals*.) He also mentions that *würde*, *dignitas*, worth, value, and their translations have been connected to Kant's understanding of dignity but that "none of these terms naturally means—or means independently of a technical philosophical usage—the same as 'value beyond price' or 'the intrinsic non-negotiable non-fungible worth that inheres in every human being'" (Waldron, "Dignity and Rank," 213).

On the contrary, attending to the history of dignity, what he calls the "independent option" (Waldron, "Dignity and Rank," 208–9), presents an "independent meaning of its own into its use in human rights contexts or in moral philosophy more generally. . . . We appeal to the independent natural-language sense of the term—independent of any function the philosopher might have ascribed to the term—to illuminate or elaborate some point we want to make about human rights" (Waldron, "Dignity and Rank," 208–9).

13 These are paraphrases of Waldron's categories, which can be found in Waldron, "Dignity and Rank," 227.
14 Waldron writes, "If we were to make the radical move—the reversal—and transfer this demand for respect from the nobility to every last ordinary person, what we would be transferring would not be a functional deference [deference only connected to the office], but this diffuse deference owed to the whole person" (Waldron, "Dignity and Rank," 223–24).
15 Waldron, "Dignity, Rank, and Rights," 20. He recommends "worth" or "sacred worth" as better terms for this usage because "dignity" has its own "distinctive connotations" (Waldron, "Dignity, Rank, and Rights," 19).
16 Waldron, "Dignity and Rank," 218.

17 Gilbert Meilaender, *Neither Beast nor God: The Dignity of the Human Person* (New York: Encounter Books, 2009).
18 Meilaender, *Neither Beast nor God*, 86. Unless otherwise specified, when I use the phrase "human dignity" from now on, I am referring to this notion. If I mean to draw attention to a different account of dignity or a notion of dignity that embodies what Meilaender means by human dignity *and* by personal dignity, I shall use "dignity."
19 An account that focuses on humanity is not barred from extending human dignity to other creatures—for example, an alien that lacked human DNA. This latter point may seem fanciful, but it is worth noting given the surprising number of times it is confused. If we were to come across an alien engaging in projects emblematic of Meilaender's vision of human life, then human dignity is what it would possess—not a related or analogous dignity but *human* dignity.
20 The idea of the inviolability of persons (though not necessarily described in terms of dignity) has been expressed in different ways within a number of different theories. For example, compare a libertarian, rights-based approach embodied in Robert Nozick's book *Anarchy, State, and Utopia* (New York: Basic Books, 1974) to John Crosby's claim regarding the uniqueness and incommunicability of persons in his paper "The Twofold Source of the Dignity of Persons," *Faith and Philosophy* 18, no. 3 (2001): 292–306. Nozick writes, "Individuals have rights, and there are things no person or group may do to them (without violating their rights). So strong and far-reaching are these rights that they raise the question of what, if anything, the state and its officials may do" (preface, ix). Crosby focuses on the unrepeatability of persons.
21 For a discussion of this idea, see John Rawls, "Justice as Fairness: Political Not Metaphysical," *Philosophy and Public Affairs* 14, no. 3 (1985).
22 Meilaender, *Neither Beast nor God*, preface.
23 Meilaender, *Neither Beast nor God*, 262. To anticipate some objections, I offer two points in favor of this move.

First, it is important to note that Meilaender is not simply "smuggling in" unsupported religious beliefs (see Macklin, "Dignity Is a Useless Concept"). The move is stronger and more subtle than that accusation admits. If a context in which dignity made sense is no longer the context in which we operate, we may not have the background and tools necessary to grasp it.

Second, there is a precedent for this type of explanation within moral philosophy. One notable example of this occurs in MacIntyre, *After Virtue*. Recall his point about the incommensurability of the premises of modern debates. The debate over human dignity is similar in many ways. A quick perusal of op-ed pieces, blogs, and comments in response to these depicts quite well the shrillness of this debate. Even the President's Council on Bioethics' Volume on Human Dignity, to which Meilaender contributed, includes the type of name-calling and personal attacks to which MacIntyre's thesis points. It seems plausible to say that we have lost the context in which certain arguments about morality and human life make sense, and as MacIntyre says, "We have all too many disparate and rival moral concepts.... The moral resources of the culture allow us no way of settling the issue between them rationally" (MacIntyre, *After Virtue*, 252).

See also Alasdair MacIntyre, "The Essential Contestability of Some Social Concepts," *Ethics* 84, no. 1 (1973): 1–9.

24 Meilaender, *Neither Beast nor God*, 263–64 (my emphasis). A similar way of thinking about the two elements of dignity, which may prove helpful, is as a contrast between an honor-based and an egalitarian sense of dignity. Charles Taylor writes, "As against the notion of honour, we have the modern notion of dignity, now used in a universalist and egalitarian sense, where we talk of the inherent 'dignity of human beings' or of citizen dignity. The underlying premise here is that everyone shares in this. This concept of dignity is the only one compatible with a democratic society, and it was inevitable that the old concept of honour be marginalized"; Taylor, *The Ethics of Authenticity* (Cambridge, Mass.: Harvard University Press, 1991).

25 Meilaender, *Neither Beast nor God*, 6.

26 For a true merit-only view, see Richard Taylor, "Time and Life's Meaning," *Review of Metaphysics* 40, no. 4 (1987): 675–86.

27 Meilaender, *Neither Beast nor God*, 268.

28 We might think of dolphins, gorillas, or wolves as examples. For a wonderful discussion, particularly of dolphins, see Alasdair MacIntyre, *Dependent Rational Animals: Why Human Beings Need the Virtues* (Chicago: Open Court, 1999).

29 Meilaender, *Neither Beast nor God*, 96.

10: Hain

1 A terminological note: all forms of "medically assisted death" involve the intentional killing of an innocent human being, and the central paradigm cases of medically assisted death are "voluntary euthanasia" and "physician-assisted suicide." *Voluntary euthanasia* is the intentional killing of a patient, through action or omission, by a health-care professional in response to the patient's own free and informed request. *Physician-assisted suicide* is the intentional suicide of a patient made possible by the help of a health-care professional. Although other forms of medically assisted death (such as nonvoluntary euthanasia—the intentional killing of an innocent human being unable to give or withhold consent) are of profound importance, they are not my subject here, partly because what we say about the paradigm cases will have direct implications for what we say about other forms of medically assisted death.

2 The classic form of this argument attacks those who would defend a moral distinction between killing and letting die. For a range of arguments for and against the distinction and its connection to medically assisted death, see Bonnie Steinbock and Alastair Norcross, eds., *Killing and Letting Die* (New York: Fordham University Press, 1994). James Rachels' contribution, "Active and Passive Euthanasia" (112–19; originally published in the *New England Journal of Medicine* 292 [1975]: 78–80), is an especially influential formulation of the argument against the distinction.

3 This is not an approach I have seen developed elsewhere, but it was hinted at by John Finnis in testimony before the House of Lords in 2005: "Patient autonomy pushes the doctor to accede to requests that do not meet the legal criteria of terminality or suffering. Suffering, or terminality, and medical

responsibility each push the doctor to set aside the requirement of voluntariness" (John Finnis, "Reflections and Responses," in *Reason, Morality, and Law: The Philosophy of John Finnis*, ed. John Keown and Robert P. George [Oxford: Oxford University Press, 2013], 459–584, at 534). I will argue, on the contrary, that the conflict, paradoxically enough, is the opposite of the one Finnis identifies. Autonomy turns out to involve setting aside the requirement of voluntariness whereas considerations of suffering push the doctor to grant every patient request.

4   James Rachels, *The End of Life: Euthanasia and Morality* (Oxford: Oxford University Press, 1986), 180–82; and Mary Warnock and Elisabeth Macdonald, *Easeful Death: Is There a Case for Assisted Dying?* (Oxford: Oxford University Press, 2008), 1–5.

5   Robert Young, *Medically Assisted Death* (Cambridge: Cambridge University Press, 2007), 21–22.

6   Ronald Dworkin, Thomas Nagel, Robert Nozick, John Rawls, Thomas Scanlon, and Judith Jarvis Thomson, "Assisted Suicide: The Philosophers' Brief," *New York Review of Books*, March 27, 1997, 41–47, at p. 43.

7   For examples of this approach, see David Oderberg, *Applied Ethics: A Nonconsequentialist Approach* (Oxford: Blackwell, 2000), 54–60; John Finnis, "Euthanasia and Justice," in *Collected Essays*, vol. 3, *Human Rights and Common Good* (Oxford: Oxford University Press, 2011), 211–41; Luke Gormally, ed., *Euthanasia, Clinical Practice and the Law* (London: Linacre Centre for Healthcare Ethics, 1994), 130–33; John Keown, *The Law and Ethics of Medicine: Essays on the Inviolability of Human Life* (Oxford: Oxford University Press, 2012), 17–21. For discussions of the debate over autonomy more generally, see Alexander McCall Smith, "Beyond Autonomy," *Journal of Contemporary Health Law and Policy* 14 (1997): 23–39; Onora O'Neill, *Autonomy and Trust in Bioethics* (Cambridge: Cambridge University Press, 2002); Charles Foster, *Choosing Life, Choosing Death: The Tyranny of Autonomy in Medical Ethics and Law* (Oxford: Hart, 2009).

8   Oregon Revised Statutes 2017, 127.805.

9   Termination of Life on Request and Assisted Suicide (Review Procedures) Act 2002, 2.2.1.b.

10 For vivid examples of the arbitrariness of restricting medically assisted death to those suffering from some terminal or chronic disease, see Felicia Ackerman, "Assisted Suicide, Terminal Illness, Severe Disability, and the Double Standard," in *Physician Assisted Suicide: Expanding the Debate*, ed. Margaret P. Battin, Rosamond Rhodes, and Anita Silvers (New York: Routledge, 1998), 149–61. Ackerman argues that the restriction is indeed arbitrary because the limitation to terminal illness or excruciating pain is a mistaken understanding of intolerably burdensome situations. My point is that if instead we assume that the narrow restriction is correct, this is only because we believe that terminal illness or excruciating pain justify medically assisted death and this in turn explains why we must respect the choices of patients in these circumstances.

11 Young, *Medically Assisted Death*, 22.

12 Young, *Medically Assisted Death*, 23.

13 Warnock and Macdonald, *Easeful Death*, 88.

14 Young, *Medically Assisted Death*, 147.
15 K. J. Lopez, "Euthanasia Sets Sail: An Interview with Philip Nitschke," *National Review Online*, June 5, 2001, https://www.nationalreview.com/2001/06/euthanasia-sets-sail-kathryn-jean-lopez/.
16 Lopez, "Euthanasia Sets Sail."
17 Indeed, I might respect you by *preventing* your medically assisted death. Cf. Finnis, "Euthanasia and Justice," 229–30: "If it is the case . . . that those who choose to ask to be killed are . . . 'tragically misinterpreting' their own life and its meaning . . . it must also be the case that action to prevent persons from acting on such a misinterpretation need involve no 'ultimate denial of respect for persons' but rather can manifest the most profound respect for persons, including even the persons so prevented."
18 Warnock and Macdonald, *Easeful Death*, 23.
19 An interesting example of this is J. David Velleman, "A Right of Self-Termination?" *Ethics* 109, no. 3 (1999): 606–28. After rejecting appeals to happiness or welfare but accepting that a threat to one's dignity could justify bringing about one's death, he himself translates an argument based on suffering into one based on dignity: "I think that suffering is precisely that which, as it increases, tends to make one's condition unbearable. I am therefore inclined to understand suffering . . . as a distressing perception of actual or threatened disintegration in the self. To suffer with pain is to feel oneself falling apart under it, overwhelmed by it, coming undone. So understood, suffering doesn't necessarily accompany pain, and it doesn't accompany pain exclusively. But it does necessarily touch one's dignity—the value that one has by virtue of being a person and that is jeopardized when one falls apart" (626–27).
20 See, for example, David Oderberg, *Moral Theory: A Non-consequentialist Approach* (Oxford: Blackwell, 2000), 151–74.
21 Warnock and Macdonald, *Easeful Death*, 88.
22 There is a caveat here: my arguments are formulated in terms of conscious and aware human persons. Some will argue that once a person permanently loses consciousness, his life no longer has value (or at least no longer has the same sort of value). Therefore perhaps there is an objective degree of suffering that will make a person's life lose its value—the level at which permanent unconsciousness inevitably follows. But I am setting aside these difficult cases because I believe that what we decide regarding conscious and aware persons will eventually determine what we say about unconscious persons, though I leave this argument for another day. I leave aside entirely the debate over what counts as a human person.
23 See Young, *Medically Assisted Death*, 21–24. See also Halvard Lillehammer, "Voluntary Euthanasia and the Logical Slippery Slope Argument," *Cambridge Law Journal* 61, no. 3 (2002): 545–50. Both Young and Lillehammer reverse the roles of the arguments: autonomy protects the voluntariness of the death, whereas the consideration of one's best interest protects the patient from making an irrational choice. My own presentation is more paradoxical. Yet the point is the same: each argument pulls a certain direction and needs its opposite to protect us from an undesirable implication.

11: MacIntyre

1. For a fuller account of these controversies and of Aquinas' part in them, see "Natural Law as Subversive: The Case of Aquinas" in my *Selected Essays*, vol. 2, *Ethics and Politics* (Cambridge: Cambridge University Press, 2006).
2. *Summa Theologiae* Ia-IIae 90, 3.
3. Ia-IIae 95, 2.
4. Ia-IIae 94, 2.
5. IIa-IIae 168.
6. IIa-IIae 10, 8; 10, 10; 10, 12.
7. Ia-IIae 93, 2.
8. Francisco Suarez, *On Law and God the Lawgiver*, trans. G. Williams, A. Brown, and J. Waldron (Oxford: Oxford University Press, 1966), book 1, chaps. 6 and 7.
9. Charles Taylor, *A Secular Age* (Cambridge, Mass.: Harvard University Press, 2007), 5.
10. Taylor, *Secular Age*, 8.
11. Taylor, *Secular Age*, 290.
12. Taylor, *Secular Age*, 159.
13. Taylor, *Secular Age*, 91.
14. Philip Rieff, introduction to *Outlines of the History of Dogma*, by Adolph Harnack (Boston: Beacon, 1957).
15. Philip Rieff, *Fellow Teachers* (Chicago: University of Chicago Press, 1985), 51.
16. Philip Rieff, *My Life among the Deathworks* (Charlottesville: University of Virginia Press, 2006), 16.
17. Rieff, *Fellow Teachers*, 5.
18. Rieff, *My Life among the Deathworks*, 76.
19. Rieff, *My Life among the Deathworks*, 76.
20. Rieff, *My Life among the Deathworks*, 76.
21. Arthur Danto, *Unnatural Wonders: Essays from the Gap between Art and Life* (New York: Columbia University Press, 2007), 109–10.
22. Quentin Bell, "Meeting Matisse," in *Encounters*, ed. K. Erikson (New Haven: Yale University Press, 1989), 44.
23. Rieff, *My Life among the Deathworks*, 66–68.
24. On this see Charles Rosen, *Schoenberg* (New York: Viking, 1975), 93–94.
25. *Financial Times*, March 22, 2014.
26. Published as *Secularization and Moral Change* (London: Oxford University Press, 1967).
27. Alasdair MacIntyre, "On Not Having the Last Word," in *Gadamer's Century: Essays in Honor of Hans Georg Gadamer* (Cambridge, Mass.: MIT Press, 2002).

12: Solomon

1. David Solomon, "Domestic Disarray and Imperial Ambition: Contemporary Applied Ethics and the Prospects for Global Bioethics," in *Global Bioethics and the Collapse of Consensus*, ed. H. T. Engelhardt (New York: Scrivener Press, 2006), 335–61; Solomon, "Internal Objections to Virtue Ethics," in *Ethical Theory: Character and Virtue, Midwest Studies in Philosophy, XIII*, ed. Peter French, Theodore Uehling, and Howard Wettstein (Notre Dame: University of Notre

Dame Press, 1986), 429–41; Solomon, "Keeping Virtue in Its Place: A Critique of Subordinating Strategies," in *Recovering Nature: Essays in Natural Philosophy, Ethics, and Metaphysics in Honor of Ralph McInerny* (Notre Dame: University of Notre Dame Press, 1999), 83–104; Solomon, "Early Virtue Ethics," in *The Oxford Handbook of Virtue*, ed. Nancy Snow (Oxford: Oxford University Press, 2017); Solomon, "Virtue Ethics: Radical or Routine?" in *Intellectual Virtue: Perspectives from Ethics and Epistemology*, ed. Michael DePaul and Linda Zagzebski (Oxford: Oxford University Press, 2003), 57–80.

2. She discusses this incident in the introduction to Anscombe, *Ethics, Religion and Politics* (Oxford: Basil Blackwell, 1981), vii. The pamphlet is found on pp. 72–81.
3. Mary Geach, "Introduction," in *Human Life, Action and Ethics: Essays by G. E. M. Anscombe*, ed. Mary Geach and Luke Gormally (Essex: Imprint Academic, 2005), xvii.
4. Elizabeth Anscombe, "Modern Moral Philosophy," in *Ethics, Religion and Politics*, ed. G. E. M. Anscombe (Oxford: Basil Blackwell, 1981), 40.
5. Elizabeth Anscombe, *Intention* (Oxford: Basil Blackwell, 1959), 1959.
6. Anscombe, "Modern Moral Philosophy," 33–34.
7. Anscombe, "Modern Moral Philosophy," 29.
8. Anscombe, "Modern Moral Philosophy," 30.
9. Anscombe, "Modern Moral Philosophy," 30–31.
10. Among the most important proponents of neo-Kantianism are Rawls and his students, such as Christine Korsgaard, Barbara Herman, Thomas Nagel, Thomas Hill, and others. Among the most prominent consequentialists are Derek Parfit, Samuel Scheffler, and Shelly Kagan. And among the most influential virtue theorists are Elizabeth Anscombe, Philippa Foot, Alasdair MacIntyre, Martha Nussbaum, and Rosalind Hursthouse.
11. Nor have they given up, of course, addressing the traditional metaethical questions. It is rather that it is now impossible to take up narrowly metaethical issues without recognizing their relevance to normative theory.
12. Alasdair MacIntyre, "Virtue Ethics," in *The Encyclopedia of Ethics*, vol. 3, ed. Charlotte B. Becker and Lawrence C. Becker, 1757–63 (New York: Routledge, 2001). I am not suggesting, of course, that MacIntyre is unclear about what his own commitment to the project of virtue ethics amounts to.
13. G. E. Moore, *Principia Ethica* (Cambridge: Cambridge University Press, 1903).
14. A. J. Ayer, *Language, Truth and Logic* (London: Gollancz, 1936).
15. John Rawls, *A Theory of Justice* (Cambridge, Mass.: Harvard University Press, 1972).
16. Alasdair MacIntyre, *After Virtue* (Notre Dame: University of Notre Dame Press, 1981).
17. Charles Stevenson, *Ethics and Language* (New Haven: Yale University Press, 1944), 89.
18. R. M. Hare's review of Rawls' *A Theory of Justice* appeared in two parts in 1973: "Review: Rawls' *Theory of Justice*—I," *Philosophical Quarterly* 23, no. 91 (1973): 144–55; and "Review: Rawls' *Theory of Justice*—II," *Philosophical Quarterly* 23, no. 92 (1973): 241–52.

19 The cultural involvement of Moore's ethics is, however, a complicated matter. Although he didn't talk to the prime minister, he talked as we know more than a little to many of his friends in the Bloomsbury Circle. Recall, also, his shock when he stopped by Westminster Palace to receive his knighthood and discovered that the king had never heard of Wittgenstein. Perhaps Moore thought that the king should have taken the train to Cambridge rather than the philosopher to London.

20 The crucial passage from Rawls is found here: "Definitions and analyses of meaning do not have a special place in [a theory of justice]. Once the whole framework is worked out, definitions have no distinct status and stand or fall with the theory itself. In any case, it is obviously impossible to develop a substantive theory of justice founded solely on truths of logic and definition. The analysis of moral concepts and the a priori, however traditionally understood, is too slender a basis"; Rawls, *Theory of Justice*, 44–53. Thus is revolutionary change brought about.

21 This exhaustion also probably helps explain the ripple of enthusiasm that runs through relatively popular cultural organs at the return of normative theory. Recall Stuart Hampshire's celebratory review of *A Theory of Justice* in the *New York Review of Books* and Peter Singer's equally over-the-top article in the *New York Times Magazine*, "Moral Philosophers Back on the Job," published in the fall of 1974, when the very young Peter Singer was celebrating the Rawlsian revolution; Stuart Hampshire, "Liberalism: The New Twist," review of *A Theory of Justice*, by John Rawls, *New York Review of Books*, August 12, 1993. Both are variations on the theme: ethics is back, and Harvard has got him.

22 It is important to remember that Rawls' work not only legitimates a return to the construction of large-scale normative theories but also does much to legitimate "applied ethics," which was just getting under way at the time *A Theory of Justice* appears.

23 I have said I wouldn't name (too many) names, but some others who share some radical tendencies, I think, are Martha Nussbaum, Philippa Foot, and Rosalind Hursthouse, although Hursthouse's book *On Virtue Ethics* suggests that she might not be quite as radical as she earlier appeared.

24 I am thinking especially of the view Slote develops in his book *From Morality to Virtue* (Oxford: Oxford University Press, 1992).

25 Barbara Herman, *Moral Literacy* (Cambridge, Mass.: Harvard University Press, 2008); and Shelly Kagan, *The Geometry of Desert* (Oxford: Oxford University Press, 2012).

26 I discuss these strategies in some detail in Solomon, "Keeping Virtue in Its Place."

27 On this view the big disputes among these theories will frequently turn out to be disputes about which of these items—rules, virtues, or states of affairs—can best serve these functions. So we will ask questions like, Can virtues guide actions as well as rules? And can the prospect of maximizing the good provide adequate grounds for doing our duty?

CONTRIBUTORS

MICHAEL BEATY is professor of philosophy and chair of the Department of Philosophy at Baylor University.

KEVIN L. FLANNERY, S.J., is ordinary professor of the history of ancient philosophy at the Pontifical Gregorian University in Rome and permanent research fellow at the de Nicola Center for Ethics and Culture of the University of Notre Dame.

RAYMOND HAIN is associate professor of philosophy at Providence College and associate director of the Providence College Humanities Program.

JOHN HALDANE is the J. Newton Rayzor Sr. Distinguished Professor of Philosophy at Baylor University, professor of moral philosophy at the University of St. Andrews, and chair of the Royal Institute of Philosophy in London.

THOMAS HIBBS, formerly Dean of the Honors College at Baylor University, is currently President of the University of Dallas.

IRFAN KHAWAJA is associate professor of philosophy at Felician University and director of the Felician Institute for Ethics and Public Affairs.

ALASDAIR MACINTYRE taught philosophy at the University of Notre Dame until his retirement in 2010.

JOHN O'CALLAGHAN is associate professor of philosophy, director of the Jacques Maritain Center at the University of Notre Dame, and a permanent member of the Pontifical Academy of St. Thomas Aquinas.

BRYAN C. PILKINGTON is associate professor of the School of Health and Medical Sciences, associate professor of the Hackensack Meridian School of Medicine, adjunct associate professor of the College of Nursing, and affiliate faculty of the Department of Philosophy at Seton Hall University.

W. DAVID SOLOMON was the founding William P. and Hazel B. White Director of the Notre Dame Center for Ethics and Culture and associate professor of philosophy at the University of Notre Dame until his retirement in 2016.

CHRISTOPHER TONER is associate professor of philosophy at the University of St. Thomas, Minnesota.

CANDACE VOGLER is the David B. and Clara E. Stern Professor of Philosophy at the University of Chicago.

www.ingramcontent.com/pod-product-compliance
Lightning Source LLC
LaVergne TN
LVHW041624060925
820435LV00008B/74/J